# CHARMS OF THE CYNICAL REASON:

## THE TRICKSTER'S TRANSFORMATIONS IN SOVIET AND POST-SOVIET CULTURE

# Cultural Revolutions: Russia in the Twentieth Century

Editorial Board:
Anthony Anemone (The New School)
Robert Bird (The University of Chicago)
Eliot Borenstein (New York University)
Angela Brintlinger (The Ohio State University)
Karen Evans-Romaine (Ohio University)
Jochen Hellbeck (Rutgers University)
Lilya Kaganovsky (University of Illinois, Urbana-Champaign)
Christina Kiaer (Northwestern University)
Alaina Lemon (University of Michigan)
Simon Morrison (Princeton University)
Eric Naiman (University of California, Berkeley)
Joan Neuberger (University of Texas, Austin)
Ludmila Parts (McGill University)
Ethan Pollock (Brown University)
Cathy Popkin (Columbia University)
Stephanie Sandler (Harvard University)
Boris Wolfson (Amherst College), Series Editor

# CHARMS OF THE CYNICAL REASON:

## THE TRICKSTER'S TRANSFORMATIONS IN SOVIET AND POST-SOVIET CULTURE

Mark Lipovetsky

Boston
2011

A catalog data for this book is available from the Library of Congress.

Copyright © 2011 Academic Studies Press
All rights reserved
ISBN 978-1-934843-45-1 (hardback)

Cover image and interior design by Adell Medovoy
Author photo by N. Ustinova

Published by Academic Studies Press in 2011
28 Montfern Avenue
Brighton, MA 02135, USA
press@academicstudiespress.com
www.academicstudiespress.com

To the loving and unfading memory of
Naum Lazarevich Leiderman (1939-2010),
my dear father, a prominent literary scholar,
and my ultimate professional mentor.
His entire life was a challenge to cynicism.

TABLE OF CONTENTS

| | |
|---|---|
| Acknowledgements | 9 |
| INTRODUCTION | 11 |
| 1. AT THE HEART OF SOVIET CIVILIZATION | 25 |
|     The Meaning of the Trickster Trope | 27 |
|     The Trickster's Politics | 37 |
|     The Trickster Trope and the Soviet Subjectivity | 42 |
|     Cynical or Kynical? | 48 |
| 2. KHULIO KHURENITO: THE TRICKSTER'S REVOLUTION | 61 |
|     Modernizing the Trickster | 65 |
|     The Method: Overidentification | 76 |
|     Why Did Khurenito Decide to Die? | 82 |
| 3. OSTAP BENDER: THE KING IS BORN | 89 |
|     Ostap as Trickster | 97 |
|     Social Schizophrenia | 112 |
|     A Kynical King of the Cynics | 118 |
| 4. BURATINO: THE UTOPIA OF A FREE MARIONETTE | 125 |
|     Buratino as a Mediator | 131 |
|     Buratino as an Artist | 140 |
|     Buratino as a Cynic | 145 |
| 5. VENICHKA: A TRAGIC TRICKSTER | 151 |
|     The Trickster as the Underground Author | 154 |
|     Rituals of Expenditure | 167 |
|     "I Will Not Explain to You Who Were These Four…" | 174 |
| 6. TRICKSTERS IN DISGUISE: THE TRICKSTER'S TRANSFORMATIONS IN THE SOVIET FILM OF THE 1960s–70s | 193 |
|     "Reformed" Tricksters in the Comedies of the 70s–80s | 195 |

|  |  |
|---|---|
| *Gaidai's Tricksters* | 197 |
| *Riazanov's Detochkin* | 200 |
| *Daneliia's Buzykin* | 203 |
| The Art of Alibi: Stierlitz as the Soviet Intelligent | 210 |
| *Who are you working for?* | 216 |
| *The Imperial Mediator* | 222 |
| *Stierlitz's Afterlife* | 226 |
| 7. SPLITTING THE TRICKSTER: PELEVIN'S SHAPE-SHIFTERS | 231 |
| The Society of Shape-Shifters | 233 |
| Genealogy of the Heroine | 239 |
| A Fairytale about Shape-Shifters | 244 |
| The Trickster's Magic/Politics: A Bifurcation Point | 251 |
| Cynic Versus Kynic | 257 |
| CONCLUSION | 267 |
| WORKS CITED | 277 |
| INDEX | 289 |

# ACKNOWLEDGEMENTS

This book would not be possible without generous help of my editors and co-translators Daniil Leiderman, Sean Owens, Josephine von Zitzewitz, and Math Trafton—my gratitude to these talented young colleagues is sincere, profound, and endless. I would also like to thank the Novoe Literaturnoe Obozrenie Publishing House and specifically its director Irina Prokhorova for the permission to use in chapters 5 and 7 materials previously published in my book *Paralogii: Transformatsii (post)modernistskogo diskursa v k russkoi kul'ture 1920-2000-kh godov* (Moscow: NLO, 2008). I am very grateful to Konstantin Bogdanov, Alexander Etkind, Ilya Kukulin and Maria Maiofis, who read early versions of the book's chapters and shared their excellent ideas and fruitful suggestions with me. Sergei Ushakin has organized a conference on totalitarian laughter in Princeton University, which gave me an exciting opportunity to test my tricksters against sharp minds of the conference's participants. My gratitude also goes to Marina Balina, Elena Baraban, Evgeny Dobrenko, Helena Goscilo, Caryl Emerson, Ilya Kalinin, Evgenii Kovalev, Catherine Nepomniashchy, Irina Sandomirskaya, Natalia Skradol (please forgive me if I've forgotten anybody), as well as to Laura Osterman, Artemi Romanov, and Rimgaila Salys, my colleagues at CU-Boulder, in conversations and e-mail exchanges with whom many ideas for this book were born and formulated for the first time. As usual, I enjoyed criticism most merciless from colleagues who also happen to be my family—Tatiana Mikhailova and again Daniil Leiderman. Support from the University of Colorado's GCAH, SEED and LEAP grants made possible my research trips to Russia, during which I collected materials for the book. Last but not least, I wish to thank Boris Wolfson who has encouraged me to write this book and Igor Nemirovsky, who patiently waited for its completion and was very kind about my shortcomings.

My father, Naum Leiderman, a prominent literary scholar, was teaching me this trade since I was thirteen years old. Many ideas for this book were born in conversations with him and are inspired by his works and ground-breaking ideas. Most importantly, my feel of the Soviet past and its literature is mediated by his vision and perception. He passed away when the book was in the making. I want to believe that he would like this book and dedicate it to his memory.

# INTRODUCTION

The need for this book arose once I became aware of the startling fact that, of the characters who acquired mass—today we would say cult—status in Soviet culture, the vast majority are manifestations of the ancient myth of the trickster. "Trickster" in the studies of myth and in this book as well does not simply mean "deceiver" or "rogue" (the definition of trickster according to the Oxford Encyclopedic English Dictionary), but rather "creative idiot," to use Lewis Hyde's expression (Hyde 7). This hero unites the qualities of characters who at first sight have little in common—the "selfish buffoon" and the "culture hero";[1] someone whose subversions and transgressions paradoxically amplify the culture-constructing effects of his (and most often it is a "he") tricks.

The list of mythological tricksters includes (to name just a few) Hermes, Prometheus, and Odysseus in Greek mythology; Anansi, Eshu, and Ogo-Yurugu in African folklore and myth; Coyote, Wakdjunkaga, the rabbit Manabozo, or Wiskodyak in North American Indian mythology; Loki of the Norse pantheon, and the Raven in Paleo-Asiatic folklore.[2] The image of the Devil in European folklore, as reflected in the novellas and fabliaux of the Renaissance and such works of the age of modernity as by Alain-René Lesage's *Le Diable boiteux* (1707), Nikolai Gogol's *Noch' pered Rozhdestvom* (*The Night Before Christmas*, 1829–32) or Dostoevsky's *Brat'ia Karamazovy* (*The Brothers Karamazov*, 1880), also belongs in this group.

The trickster is also a typical comic protagonist in literature—it is enough to recollect Renard the Fox from the medieval *Roman de Renard*, Panurge from François Rabelais' *The Life of Gargantua and of Pantagruel*, Cervantes's Sancho Panza, Beaumarchais's Figaro, Gogol's Khlestakov,

---

1  On the paradigmatic role of this combination of qualities for the trickster see: Carroll. See also: Meletinsky 1998: 172-176.
2  See Bascom, Basso, Boas, Brown, Gates, Hawley, Meletinsky 1973, Pelton.

Mark Twain's Tom Sawyer and Huckleberry Finn, Jaroslav Hašek's Švejk, Charlie Chaplin's Tramp, Paul Newman's and Robert Redford's grifters in *The Sting* (dir. George Roy Hill, 1977), Steve Martin's, Michael Caine's and Glenne Headly's characters in *Dirty Rotten Scoundrels* (dir. Frank Oz, 1988), Max Bialystock in Mel Brooks's *Producers*, Bart Simpson and Borat (Sacha Baron Cohen), as well as such cultural personae as Salvador Dali, Marcel Duchamp, Andy Warhol, Joseph Beuys, or Sacha Baron Cohen—to confirm this self-evident thesis.

It is telling that in *Dialectic of Enlightenment*, Max Horkheimer and Theodor Adorno use Odysseus, an archetypal image of the trickster, for their characterization of the "instrumental reason" produced by modernity. They detect the prototype of the modern reason's main principle—"the adaptation of the ratio to its contrary" (67)—in the trickster's play with numerous, mutually annihilating, identities: "…the subject Odysseus denies his own identity, which makes him a subject, and himself alive by imitating the amorphous. […] He acknowledges himself to himself by denying himself under the name of Nobody; he saves his life by losing himself." (60, 67)

A more optimistic interpretation of modern reason—yet also through reference to the trickster myth—comes from historian Yuri Slezkine. This scholar coins the term "mercurianism" after Mercury (or Hermes)—the major trickster god of the Greco-Roman pantheon—to designate certain qualities demanded by the epoch of modernity, qualities traditionally associated with internal strangers, service nomads, professional "others" (such as merchants, craftsmen, middle men, entrepreneurs, and actors, for example)—in other words, manipulators who did not sell their own goods, but only their knowledge and (frequently tricksterish) skills. Slezkine demonstrates this function through the example of Russian Jews, though, as he states, it is not less relevant to Gypsies, the Chinese (outside China), Armenians (outside Armenia), and the Parsis in India:

> The Jews became the world's strangest strangers because they practiced their vocation on a continent that went almost wholly Mercurian and reshaped much of the world accordingly. In an age of service nomadism, the Jews became the chosen people by becoming the model 'moderns.' This means that more and more Apollonians, first in Europe and

> then elsewhere, had to become more like the Jews: urban, mobile, literary, mentally nimble, occupationally flexible, and surrounded by aliens ... The new market was different from old markets in that it was anonymous and socially unembedded (relatively speaking): it was exchange among strangers, with everyone trying with varying degrees to success to play the Jew. (Slezkine, 40–41)

—or, in other words, to be a Mercurian, to be a trickster.

Therefore, the problem of the Soviet trickster directly relates to the problem of Soviet modernity and its peculiar features. In this respect, what immediately catches the eye is the immense popularity of the vast number of trickster-like characters in Soviet culture, such as Ilya Erenburg's Khulio Khurenito from the eponymous novel (1921), Ostap Bender from Il'f and Petrov's novel *Dvenadtsat' stuliev* (*The Twelve Chairs*, 1928) and *Zolotoi telenok* (*The Golden Calf*, 1931), Yurii Olesha's Ivan Babichev from *Zavist'* (*Envy*, 1927), Mikhail Bulgakov's Woland with his host of demons from *Master i Margarita* (*The Master and Margarita*, 1940/1996-7), Vasilii Terkin from the eponymous narrative poem by Aleksandr Tvardovskii (1942–45); Venichka from Venedikt Erofeev's *Moskva-Petushki* (*Moscow to the End of the Line*, 1970), Gurevich from his tragicomedy *Val'purgieva noch', ili Shagi Komandora* (*St. Valpurgis Night, or The Steps of the Commander*, 1985); and Sandro from Fazil Iskander's *Sandro iz Chegema* (*Sandro of Chegem*, 1973–89). Soviet film and television characters are no less telling in this respect: Maksim from Grigorii Kozintsev and Leonid Trauberg's film trilogy about the exemplary Bolshevik (1934–1938), and in particular, the first film *Iunost' Maksima* (*Maxim's Youth*, 1934); the famous roles played by Petr Aleinikov—Pet'ka Moliboga in Sergei Gerasimov's *Semero smelykh* (*Brave Seven*, 1936), Savka in Ivan Pyriev's *Traktoristy* (*The Tractorists*, 1939) and Vanya Kurskii in Leonid Lukov's *Bol'shaia zhizn'* (*The Big Life*, 1939–46). The sixties brought a renewal of interest in Il'f and Petrov's masterpiece, transforming Ostap Bender into a role model for the Thaw generation and preparing the ground for the emergence of new, albeit significantly transformed, portrayals of tricksters in the late 1960s–70s, such as Yurii Detochkin from El'dar Riazanov's *Beregis' avtomobilia* (*Beware of the Automobile*, 1967), Afonia (*Afonia*, 1973) and Buzykin from Georgii Danelia's *Osennii marafon* (*The Autumn Marathon*,

1979; whose initial title read *The Bitter Life of the Rogue*), Munchhausen from Grigorii Gorin and Mark Zakharov's *Tot samyi Munkhauzen* (*That Munchhausen*, 1979), and of course the Soviet spy in the Third Reich's top echelon of power—Isaev-Stierlitz from Tatiana Lioznova's television mini-series *Semnadtsat' mgnovenii vesny* (*Seventeen Moments of Spring*, 1973).

Soviet culture also adapted and/or created original versions of traditional tricksters. In chapter 4, I will closely examine Aleksei Tolstoy's *Buratino*, "adapted" from Carlo Colloddi's *Pinocchio*—but this is just one of many similar examples. Among the well-known texts which featured tricksters and enjoyed unprecedented popularity among Soviet readers, one should mention Rudolph Erich Raspe's stories about the Baron Munchhausen (1785), Alphonse Daudet's novels on Tartarin of Tarascon (1872–1896), Charles De Coster's *The Legend of Thyl Ulenspiegel and Lamme Goedzak* (1867), Jaroslav Hašek's novel *The Good Soldier Švejk* (1923, begun, incidentally, in Russia), as well as Astrid Lindgren's novels about Karlsson (1955–1968) and Pippi Longstocking (1945–79).[3] Notably, De Coster's novel alone inspired two operas, two ballets, a drama production in the Moscow Lenkom Theatre based on Grigorii Gorin's original play *Til'* (*Thyl*, 1974) and a film by Aleksandr Alov and Vladimir Naumov *Legenda o Tile* (*The Legend of Thyl*, 1976). Trickster figures were adapted not only from the Western cultural tradition, but also from traditionally Eastern archetypes, including the Hodja (Mullah) Nasreddin, popularized in the Soviet Union by Leonid Soloviev's novels *Vozmutitel' sposkoistviia* (*The Disturber of Peace*, 1946) and *Ocharovannyi prints* (*The Enchanted Prince*, 1954), which also served as the basis for Iakov Protazanov's film *Nasreddin v Bukhare* (*Nasreddiin in Buhara*, 1943). An especially large number of foreign tricksters were "naturalized" in Soviet children's culture: the old genie Khottabych (*Starik Khottabych* [1940] by Lazar Lagin)[4], Chipollino, Karlsson, and

---

3   According to the Russian State Library's data, between 1872 and 2008, 123 editions of Raspe's book the Baron Munchhausen were published; between 1888 and 2008, there were 32 editions of Daudet's *Tartarin de Tarascon*; between 1928 and 2008, there were 50 editions of Hašek's novel. Between just 1980 and 2008, 26 editions of De Coster's book were published and during the same period, 45 editions of Lindgren's Peppi-Longstocking appeared.
4   The character of Khottabych is in many ways similar to Bulgakov's Woland. See Chudakova.

Winnie the Pooh (in Boris Zakhoder's and Fedor Khitruk's versions), to name a few. Along with these characters, there coexisted originally Russian tricksters as Neznaika (from the triptych of novels by Nikolai Nosov, 1953–1966), Cheburashka and Shapokliak (Chapeau-Clack; from the animated series by Roman Kachanov, based on Eduard Uspenskii's book, 1969–1984), the cat Matroskin (from the animated series *The Village Prostokvashino* by Vladimir Popov, also based on Uspenskii's book, 1978–84), Syroezhkin as the comical double of the "culture hero" Elektronik from the late Soviet mini-series *Prikliucheniia Élektronika* (*The Adventures of Elektronik*, 1979; dir. Konstantin Bromberg, based on the book by Evgenii Veltistov), and even the post-Soviet heroine Masianya from the eponymous animated series by Oleg Kuvaev (2001–2003).[5]

Another cultural field where tricksters reigned is Soviet jokelore. Soviet-period anecdotes either amplified the tricksterish traits of film and TV characters such as Buratino, Stierlitz, Cheburashka, Winnie the Pooh, and Sherlock Holmes, or created new original tricksters such as Vovochka, Lieutenant Rzhevsky, Rabinovich, and Radio Armenia.[6]

The fantastic popularity of tricksters in Soviet and post-Soviet cultures is reflected in their expansive leadership in the sphere of public monuments to literary heroes. On the territory of the former USSR, there are presently more than a dozen monuments to Ostap Bender (in St. Petersburg, Odessa, Ekaterinburg, Khar'kov, Piatigorsk, Jeliste, Berdiansk, Starobel'sk [Lugansk region], and Zhmerinka, to name a few); a number of monuments to Buratino (in Kiev, Zelenogradsk, Kishinev [Moldova], Novosibirsk, Izhevsk, Voronezh, and Barnaul), at least four monuments to the Baron Munchhausen (in Moscow, Kaliningrad, Odessa and Kremenchug [both Ukraine]), two monuments to Vasilii Terkin (Smolensk and Karelia), the Moscow-based monuments to Koroviev and Behemoth (Ploshchad' Sovetskoi Armii), as well as the one to Venichka Erofeev (Ploshchad' Bor'by), the monument to soldier Švejk in St. Petersburg, one to Lieutenant Rzhevsky in Pavlodar (Ukraine) and the monuments to Nasreddin in Bukhara (Uzbekistan) and Moscow (Molodezhnaia Metro station). There was also a plan—

---

5   See the collection *Veselye chelovechki* (Kukulin, Lipovetsky, Maiofis) for further analyses of the trickster figure in Soviet and post-Soviet children's culture by Baraban, Kliuchkin, Kuznetsov, Kukulin, Leving, and Maiofis.
6   For studies of these cycles of jokes see: Belousov 1987, Belousov, 1996, Shmeleva and Shmelev, Graham 2008.

though apparently never executed—to erect a monument to Stierlitz, made from bulletproof glass, in his purported hometown of Gorokhvets in the Vladimir region. The vast variety of monuments to tricksters on the territory of the former USSR—and most of these sculptures were installed in the post-Soviet period, as a kind of alternative to Soviet "monumental propaganda"—testifies to the particular functions of this type of hero in Russian 20th century culture.

The strong presence of the trickster trope in Soviet times is all the more remarkable given that in Russia there has never been a recognizable tradition of the rogue novel, the most obvious vehicle for this archetype in the period of modernity. This was different in Europe, where the picaresque genre played a catalyzing role in the formation of the novel, and in America, where the rogue has assumed vast cultural importance.[7] It is certainly easy to identify a number of rogues in Russian culture— Frol Skobeev from the anonymous 17th century novella, the heroes of Mikhail Chulkov's *Prigozhaia povarikha, ili Pokhozhdenia razvratnoi zhenshchiny* (*The Comely Cook, or the Adventures of the Debauched Woman*, 1770) in the 18th century, and in the 19th century such characters as Ivan Vyzhigin from Faddei Bulgarin's eponymous novel (1829), Ivan Aleksandrovich Khlestakov from Gogol's *Revizor* (*The Inspector-General*, 1836/41), and Pyotr Ivanovich Chichikov from *Metrvye dushi* (*Dead Souls*, 1842), or more complex incarnations of the trickster archetype such as Smerdyakov from Dostoevsky's *Brat'ia Karamazovy* (*The Brothers Karamazov*, 1880) and Petrusha Verkhovenskii from *Besy* (*The Possessed*, 1871).

However, in the majority of cases these characters' popularity was rather negative and incomparable to the appeal of such heroes as Onegin, Pechorin, Andrei Bolkonskii, or Natasha Rostova. Russian literature of the classical period has few if any tricksters as loveable as Sancho Panza (Cervantes), Moll Flanders (Daniel Defoe), Truffaldino of Bergam (Goldoni), Gil Blas (Lesage), Figaro (Beaumarchais), or even Rastignac (Balzac). In Russian culture, the importance of the rogue's discourse was probably diminished by the prevalent negative view on individualism, whereas in European and American literature the ambivalent character of the rogue came to be one the most important forms for

---

7  For the cultural importance of the picaresque novel see: Benito-Vessels and Zappala, Blackburn, Guillén, Gutiérrez, Lewis, Maiorino, Monteser, Whitbourn, Wicks.

understanding the virtues and faults of the individualistic personality shaped by modernity. As Caryl Emerson notes, 19th-century Russian rogues frequently gravitate towards "a special sub-type, the *poshlyak*... designating a self-satisfied materialist, a mediocrity, the ultimate consumer mentality" (Emerson, 49). Perhaps the negative dismissal of the rogue type can also be explained by the fact that, unlike its European counterpart, classical Russian literature has a poorly developed image of "the professional roué or sexual rogue (Don Juan and Casanova for men, Milady and similar femmes fatales for women). This important type entered Russian high literary culture only during the Romantic period, and even then long retained the flavor of a European import." (Ibid., 50)

At the same time, Soviet tricksters differed from classical rogues by the unfailing love they inspired in readers and viewers. Though the two are similar, the Soviet trickster is decisively not a rogue or at least *not only* a rogue. First of all, although the Soviet trickster may possess mercantile interests, any such interests clearly pale before the self-contained artistry and theatricality of the performed trick, which sometimes yields concrete rewards, such as Ostap Bender's treasure or Buratino's theater, but nearly as often lacks any pragmatic interest. Second, and this is probably more significant, the picaro, as a rule, depends on his master, and his mobility depends on a change of masters, whereas the trickster is an absolutely independent person inclined towards cunning and betrayal (for fun, mostly).

Why is the trickster so prevalent in Soviet culture? What are his/her cultural functions? What are the needs he responds to? How does the trickster change in the course of the development and collapse of Soviet civilization and what happens to him/her in the post-Soviet period? In the first chapter, I will try to address the question of cultural functions that the trickster trope had obtained in Soviet culture. I would like to argue that the immense popularity of the trickster is mainly justified by the cultural need to provide symbolic justification to the practices of the 'shadow' economy and sociality—or, in a broader sense, to the mechanism of cynical survival and deception that existed behind the ideologically approved simulacra of the state-run economy and 'classless' society, and thus constituted the core of the Soviet "cynical reason," to use Peter Sloterdijk's concept. While I do not intend to give a complete overview of the image of the trickster in Soviet and post-Soviet culture, I will focus in the following chapters on the most distinctive tricksters (in my opinion), that is, those whose image and style became the symbol of a whole epoch and who later entered (or will enter) the cultural memory of future generations.

The crisis of modernity—which arguably resulted in World War I and the Russian Revolution—found its manifestation in the character of the Great Provocateur, Khulio Khurenito from Ilya Erenburg's eponymous novel (1921). Additionally, the spirit of NEP and the Stalinist epoch was embodied by such paradigmatic tricksters as Il'f and Petrov's Ostap Bender (1928, 1931) and Aleksei Tolstoy's Buratino (1936). Different strategies of the intelligentsia's self-identification in the late Soviet period are reflected by such transformations of the trickster myth as Venichka from Erofeev's poem *Moskva-Petushki* (1970), protagonists of popular comedies by Leonid Gaidai (Shurik from *Operatsiia Y*, 1965, and *Kavkazskaia plennitsa*, 1968), El'dar Riazanov (Detochkin from *Beregis' avtomobilia,* 1966), Georgii Danelia (Buzykin from *Osennii marafon,* 1979) and Mark Zakharov (Baron Munchhausen from *Tot samyi Miunkhauzen,* 1979), as well as Von Stierlitz/ Maxim Isaev from Tatiana Lioznova's series *Semnadtsat' mgnovenii vesny* (1973). The last chapter will trace the mutations of the trickster in the post-Soviet period through the analysis of the fox A-Huli from Viktor Pelevin's *Sviashchennaia kniga oborotnia* (*The Sacred Book of the Werewolf,* 2004).

\*\*\*

It is crucial to note that Soviet and post-Soviet tricksters are not absolutely identical to their mythological and folkloric prototypes. Certainly, there is nothing new about the mutability of the trickster myth: the folkloric model of the trickster gave birth to a number of later literary and cultural types such as the rogue, picaro, buffoon, clown, jester, thief, imposter, holy fool, etc.[8] Each of these cultural models differs from the others and from its source—the trickster as a mythological hero—and yet they are all united by a certain set of "common signifiers," that is, a collection of traits which evoke the mythological trickster to some degree. Thus, for instance, such disparate literary/cultural types as the picaro from the Spanish

---

8  See for instance: Willeford, Welsford, Panchenko, Murav, Blackburn, Otto.

novels of the 16th–17th centuries and the Russian holy fool[9] share such qualities of marginality, sometimes embellished to a degree of "cosmic homelessness" (Albert Camus), and ambivalence of their status and actions following from their liminality. Being stripped of social identity, both the picaro and the holy fool establish paradoxical relations with the "rotten" and "corrupt" world around them that include both mimicry of and alienation from the socio-cultural context through parody and transgressive performative gestures and spectacles. Furthermore, both types—albeit in different ways—manifest nothingness: while a picaro brings forward "the collapse of a personality or its submission to an experience of nothingness" (Blackburn, 22), a holy fool embodies kenoticism as the practice of "self-emptying" (Murav, 13), thus paradoxically imitating the most fallen man as well as Christ's humiliation and suffering.

Following this logic, in the first chapter I will attempt to outline these common, yet never permanent, combinations of traits derived from the trickster myth. This highly variable set is the definitive model for what I shall term *the trickster trope*. Departing from the stylistic understanding of tropes as structures of figurative language (metonymy, metaphor, synecdoche, and sometimes irony), Yurii M. Lotman interprets trope

> ... not as embellishment merely on the level of expression, a decoration on a invariant content, but as a mechanism for constructing a content which could not be constructed by one language alone. A trope is a figure born at the point of contact between two languages, and its structure is therefore identical to that of the creative consciousness itself... Moreover, if we ignore the fact that that the trope is a mechanism for producing semantic diversity, a mechanism that brings into the semiotic structure of culture a necessary degree of indeterminacy, we shall never arrive at an adequate description of this phenomenon. (44)

As for the two "languages" that the trickster trope brings together, the first is represented by an array of contemporary discourses mimicked,

---

9   This comparison follows in accordance to the observations by Blackburn (3-25) and Murav (17-29).

parodied, and deconstructed by the trickster; and the second is a discourse of the trickster myth, as well as its derivative mythoi of a jester, holy fool, rogue, etc. The trickster in modern culture thus functions as a device that drags contemporary discursive material into the field of the archaic and authoritative symbols of mockery, transgression and carnivalesque laughter, while simultaneously renovating and refurbishing these symbols in new, present-day, contexts. By its very function, the trickster trope directly retains the genre's memory—a category proposed by Mikhail Bakhtin in *Problems of Dostoevsky's Poetics*. Using this analogy, one may project Bakhtin's description of Dostoevsky's relations with the "genre memory" of the ancient menippea onto modern authors working with the trickster trope, maintaining that s/he links "with the chain" of the trickster mythological and historical discourse "at that point where it passes through his own time, although the past links in this chain, including the ancient link, were to a greater or lesser extent familiar and close to him." (Bakhtin 1984: 121)

This is why *transformations, mutations and metamorphoses of the trickster trope constitute the main focus of this study*. Some "heroes" of this book—such as the tragic drunken visionary Venichka from Venedikt Erofeev's *Moskva-Petushki*, the stern and serious Soviet spy Stierlitz from Tatiana Lioznova's miniseries *Semnadtsat' mgnovenii vesny*, set in 1945 Nazi Germany, or the idealistic Don-Quixotic car thief Yurii Detochkin from El'dar Riazanov *Beregis' avtomobilia*— all seem to be very remote from the comical trickster of myth, folklore, and classical literary texts. When analyzing these (as well as other) personages, I will first and foremost try to understand the meaning of the transformations of the trickster trope, which, as I shall demonstrate, is still detectable in the representation of these characters. The metamorphoses of the mythological motifs directly reflect the invisible shifts in the cultural logic of the given historical period, and are therefore far more valuable for such an analysis than faithfully reproduced folkloric prototypes would be.

However, the trickster is not unique in its transformation into a trope of the modern literature and culture. It is logical to ask what distinguishes the trickster from other images functioning as tropes, such as an epic hero, fool, monster, or martyr. Answering this question, I would like to argue that the specificity of the trickster trope lies in its *metasemiotic* character. Lotman's characteristics of a trope that appears "identical to the creative consciousness itself" and that "brings into the semiotic structure of culture a necessary degree of indeterminacy" are thematically—and emphatically!—represented by the modern trickster, a "signifying monkey" or "the hero with a thousand faces." The trickster performatively displays the deconstructive work of language, as s/he emerges as the living and breathing allegory of language who incessantly fuses destruction and creation (as well as the unconscious and socially-constructed), who destabilizes meanings and discovers ambivalence within established beliefs and categories, and who transgresses taboos and playfully reveals their linguistic nature. Or in William Hynes's words: "...The trickster reminds us that every construct is constructed [...]that life is endlessly narrative, prolific and open-ended [...] The logic of order and convergence, that is logos-centrism, or logocentrism, is challenged by another path, the random and divergent trail taken by that profane metaplayer, the trickster." (Hynes 1993a: 212, 216) Furthermore, as Anne Doueuhi demonstrates, even in folkloric texts, let alone literary works, the trickster discourse generates *isomorphism* between the central character/trope and the narrative:

> The features commonly ascribed to the trickster—contradictoriness, complexity, deceptiveness, trickery—are the feature of the language of the story itself. If the trickster breaks all the rules, so does the story's language ... If the trickster is a practical joker and a deceiver, is the language of the story. While the story is usually read as showing the absurdity and inappropriateness of trickster behavior, the joke is not just on trickster, but is in fact also on the reader who finds the trickster amusing. For the joke is on us if we do not realize that the trickster gives us an insight into the way language is used to construct and ultimately incomplete kind of reality. (200)

The trickster trope, according to Lewis Hyde, represents a paradigmatic example of the blurring of lines between lies, deception, manipulation—but also the truth of art, thus foreshadowing many modernist sensibilities. Hyde cites numerous programmatic statements by modern writers and artists, concluding:

> Under his [trickster's] enchantment, illusion sinks below the threshold of consciousness and appears to be truth. Many of these statements are hard to understand if we cleave to any simple sense of what is meant by 'truth' and 'lies.' They are easier to understand if such opposites collapse, whereupon we are dropped back into trickster's limbo, where boundary markers shift at night, shoes have no heel and toe, inky cloud attacks transparency, and every resting place suddenly turns into a crossroad. These artists, that is to say, claim a part of trickster's territory for their own, knowing it to be one of the breeding grounds of art and artifice. (Hyde 79–80)

Hence, the examination of the trickster trope in Russian literature of the 20$^{th}$ century appears to be inseparable from the history of the modernist discourse within Soviet culture; it also reflects the analysis of proto-postmodernist tendencies inside Soviet culture (official and non-official alike), a study that I have begun in my previous book.[10] These tendencies, in turn, testify to the complexities and contradictions of Soviet culture that remain unnoticed through the optics offered by the "totalitarian" approaches. The concealed (post)modernism of Soviet culture, obviated by the uses of the trickster trope, can also shed light on the transformations of Russian culture and society after the collapse of the Soviet ideological regime.

---

10  See Lipovetsky 2008.

1. A monument to Ostap Bender in St. Petersburg, architect V.B. Bukhlev, sculptor D.S. Charkin, photo from http://www.liveinternet.ru/users/vinokyr/post44522116/

2. A monument to Ostap Bender in Piatigorsk, architect and sculptor Georgii Miasnikov

3. A monument to Ostap Bender in Ekaterinburg, photo by M. Livopetsky

4. A monument to Ostap Bender in Kharkov, architect and sculptor Eldeniz Kurbanov, photo from Wikipedia

5. A monument to the 12th Chair in Odessa, architect M.Reva, photo by Olga Bagdasarian.

6. A monument to Ostap Bender in Zhmerinka, architect and sculptor N.Kryzhanovskii, photo from dyada.photoshare.ru

# CHAPTER 1
## AT THE HEART OF SOVIET CIVILIZATION

> "Antimodernity is possibly more modern and complex than what it rejects; in any case it is gloomier, blunter, more brutal, and more cynical."
> —Peter Sloterdijk (484)

## THE MEANING OF THE TRICKSTER TROPE

The relative stability—despite all mutations and metamorphoses—of the trickster trope is defined not only by the content of concrete images, but also by the traits we wish to see when looking at the trickster. Although the list of scholarly works on the trickster as a mythological and literary hero includes hundreds of titles, this field of research emerged only in the nineteenth century and developed exponentially in the post-war period.[1] Anthropologists of the nineteenth and the first half of the twentieth century note the ambivalence of the trickster figure in folklore and myth and try to interpret the "baser" traits of the trickster as either the outcome of the degradation of the culture hero (Daniel Brinton) or the underdevelopment of archaic cultures devoid of altruistic values (Franz Boas). The latter point of view appears in C.G. Jung's commentary to Paul Radin's famous work *The Trickster: A Study in American Indian Mythology*

---

1 See on the history of the trickster studies: Doty and Hynes, Babcock-Abrahams, and Lowie.

(1956): "[W]e can see why the myth of the trickster was preserved and developed: like many other myths, it was supposed to have a therapeutic effect. It holds the earlier low intellectual and moral level before the eyes of the more highly developed individual, so that he shall not forget how things looked yesterday." (Jung, 207)

However, in the same volume Karl Kerényi first brings up the cultural importance of the trickster's ambivalence: "Disorder belongs to the totality of life, and the spirit of this disorder is trickster. His function in an archaic society, or rather the function of his mythology, of the tales told about him, is to add disorder to order and so make a whole, to render possible within the fixed bounds of what is permitted, and experience of what is not permitted." (Kerényi, 185) This philosophical approach to the study of the trickster gained new support with the publication of Claude Lévi-Strauss's work on the structure of myth, in which the trickster was considered the mediator who guarantees communication between the binary oppositions that organize the myth. To the trickster-mediator, who unites in himself the traits of the culture hero and the buffoon, Lévi-Strauss assigned the role of the symbolic mechanism which overcomes contradictions by means of bricolage, tricks, or transgressions. A more poststructuralist understanding of the trickster emerged in the 1980s–90s on the basis of this structuralist conception, cogently summarized in the essay collection *Mythical Trickster Figure* (1993) edited by William J. Hynes and William G. Doty, as well as in the monograph *Trickster Makes the World* (1998) by Lewis Hyde. According to this conception, the very traits of the trickster that instilled the most doubt in the older generation of scholars, namely his destructive impulses, came to be understood as the founding forces of language and culture: "The trickster discovers creative fabulation, feigning, and fibbing, the playful construction of fictive worlds," he is a mediator "who works 'by means of a lie that is really a truth, a deception that is in fact a revelation.'" (Hyde 45, 72)

In Soviet culture, a similar understanding of the trickster's role was reached much earlier, namely in Mikhail Bakhtin's work on Rabelais and carnival culture (written in the 1940s, first published in 1963), as well as in his "Forms of Time and Chronotope in the Novel" (written in the late 1930s, first published in 1975), in particular in the section "The Functions of the Rogue, Clown and Fool in the Novel." The traits of these characters permit the forging of a direct link to the semantics of the trickster trope, which unite all the different personae with Bakhtin's philosophy of carnival culture and carnivalization: "These figures are laughed at by others and *themselves* as well. Their laughter bears the stamp of the public square where the folk gather. They re-establish the public nature of the human figure ... their entire function consists in externalizing things (true enough, it is not their own being they externalize, but a reflected, alien being—however, that is all they have)." (Bakhtin, 1981: 159–160)

A summary of contemporary research on the trickster reveals at least four structural and semantic aspects of the trickster trope, all of which are heavily accentuated in Soviet culture:

(1) **Ambivalence and Mediation.** These two interconnected and mutually reinforcing characteristics constitute the core of the trickster trope. All tricksters function as cultural mediators that fuse otherwise incompatible features (natural and artificial, foreign and domestic, animal and human, marginal and mainstream, ideological and non-ideological, sometimes male and female, and of course, above all, infantile and adult). This exact cultural function is responsible for the elusiveness and ambivalence immanent to any trickster:

> Anomalous, a-nomos, without normativity, the trickster appears on the edge or just beyond existing borders, classifications and categories. [...] [T]he trickster is cast as an 'out' person, and his activities are often outlawish, outlandish, outrageous, out-of-bounds, and out-of-order. No borders are sacrosanct, be they religious, cultural, linguistic, epistemological, or metaphysical. Breaking down division lines, the trickster characteristically moves swiftly and impulsively back and forth across all borders with virtual impunity. A visitor everywhere, especially to those places that are off limits, the trickster seems to dwell in no single place but to be in continual transit through all realms marginal and liminal. (Hynes 1993b: 34–35)

The ability to collapse opposites, to marry the high and the low, order and disorder, creation and destruction, is central to any trickster and is also responsible for his/her shape-shifting, the fluidity of his/her identity, and the ambivalence of his/her choices and positions. Moreover, this trait also explains why categories of morality are hardly applicable to tricksters: in Lewis Hyde's words, tricksters are "a̲moral not i̲m̲moral." (Hyde, 10)

(2) **Liminality and Transgressive Vitality.** There is a direct link between the trickster's ambivalence and his/her liminality. Barbara Babcock-Abrahams was the first researcher to connect the trickster with the concept of liminality introduced by Victor Turner in the 1960s:

> The attributes of liminality or of liminal personae ("threshold people") are necessarily ambiguous, since this condition and these persons elude or slip through the network of classifications that normally locate state states and positions in cultural space. Liminal entities are neither here nor there; they are betwixt and between the positions assigned and arrayed by law, customs, conventions, and ceremonial. (Turner, 95)

The application of this description to tricksters, Soviet tricksters notwithstanding, helps explain why the trickster so typically appears as a "gentleman of the road," even if this road is only between Moscow and Petushki (Khulio Khurenito, Ostap Bender's or even Vasilii Terkin's war itineraries are far more diverse geographically, although the principle behind them is no different from that in Erofeev's masterpiece). The Soviet trickster's origins are invariably obscure due to his/her liminality ("My father was a Turkish citizen," as Ostap Bender used to say), and his/her social position is equally elusive. Granted, Turner's description of the "threshold people" points more readily at the *homo sacer* or the neophyte undergoing initiation than the trickster: they "may be disguised as monsters, wear only a strip of clothing, or even go naked. Their behavior is normally passive or humble, they must obey their instructors implicitly, and accept arbitrary punishment without complaint." (ibid., 95) It is telling that Turner, while developing his thesis on liminal subcultures, includes Leo Tolstoy and his followers, as well as Gandhi and the hippie movement, as examples, but does not mention tricksters, making an exception only for the court jester. The reason for this "omission" is probably due to the fact that Turner ties liminality to anti-structural rituals— "rituals of status reversal and the religious beliefs and practices of movement dominated by structural inferiors." (ibid., 200) These anti-structures (exemplified by Bakhtin's carnival) do "not mean 'anomie', but simply mean a new perspective from which to observe structure," they "involve mockery and inversion, but not the destruction of structural rules and overzealous adherents to them"; they offer people "an opportunity to strip themselves of all outward tokens and inward sentiments of status distinction [...] to escape from the communitas of necessity (which are therefore inauthentic) into a pseudostructure where all behavioral extravagances are possible." (Ibid., 201–202) It is particularly important that those anti-structural rituals that immerse a subject in a liminal state are balanced out by other cultural rituals which affirm social order and stratification—"both types of rites [...] seem to be bound up with cyclical repetitive systems of multiplex social relations." (Ibid., 202)

However, unlike other liminal roles, the trickster does not require an anti-ritual to function: s/he does not generate a separate cultural sphere, instead introducing antistructural elements into the social and cultural order and exposing and creating liminal zones *within* existing hierarchies and stratifications. His principle is not inversion but deconstruction, the undermining of the system by means of revealing and subverting its logic, a dissembling that comes not from outside but from within, from a point betwixt and between. This is why in William Hynes's apt formulation, tricksterish "metaplay ruptures the shared consciousness, the societal ethos and consensual validation—in short, the very order of order itself. [...] From the advent of metaplay, all previous orders and orderings are clearly labeled contingent." (Hynes 1993b: 215)

In the culture of modernity and especially Soviet modernity, this disposition acquires the meaning of intentionally antisocial behavior inside the social space. Because of their antistructural behavior, tricksters are frequently penalized. Usually, however, the trickster's punishment is overshadowed by the pleasure and inventiveness of his/her tricks and jokes and thus the failures do not register as 'moral lessons,' but rather as the comical trips and falls of a beloved clown. The insignificance of the trickster's defeats testifies to the unfading importance of his/her social function—the transgression of the social order.

The necessary presence of transgression in the trickster's behavior can explain why there are so few female characters in the gallery of Soviet tricksters. (There are more in the post-Soviet period, especially after 2000.) Since the trickster must remain attractive despite being a transgressor, the patriarchal nature of Soviet culture makes itself known in a moral double standard: the same transgressions that guarantee the appeal of a male trickster render impossible the positive reception of a woman-trickster who, if she appears at all, acquires a negative tint—Baba Yaga, as a rule played by a man (Aleksei Milliar in Aleksandr Ptushko's cinematic fairy tales and the films of his disciple Aleksander Rou), the fox Alisa from Aleksei Tolstoy's *Zolotoi kliuchik*, or old Shapokliak from Roman Kachanov's *Cherburashka* cartoon series.[2]

### (3) The Trickster Transforms His/Her Tricks into an Art Form.

The trickster creates self-sufficient performances rather than pragmatic actions designed for a concrete purpose. The transformation of trickery and transgression into an artistic gesture—a sort of performance—is associated with the aforementioned trickster's liminality within the social order. Bakhtin was the first to reveal the artistic meaning of the trickster's liminal position: "They are life's maskers [*litsedei zhizni*]; their being coincides with their role, and outside this role they simply do not exist." (Bakhtin 1981: 159–160, 159) The trickster's position always contains an element of *ostranenie* (defamiliarization), which Victor Shklovsky defined as the fundamental effect of any artistic utterance or performance. Bakhtin, who uses a different term that is synonymous to *ostranenie*—"a form of non-comprehension"—maintains that the masks of the rogue, the clown and the fool":

> ... grant the right not to understand, the right to confuse, to tease, to hyperbolize life; the right to parody others while talking, the right to not be taken literally, not to 'be oneself'; the right to live a life in the chronotope of the entr'acte, the chronotope of theatrical space, the right to act as a comedy and to treat others as actors, the right to rip off the masks, the right to rage at others with a primeval (almost cultic) rage—and finally, the right to betray to the public a personal life, down to its most private and prudent little secrets. (ibid., 163)

---

2 The problem of the female tricksters in folklore and mythology is examined in great detail by Jurich. See also Mills, Landay, and Lock.

Symptomatically, the theatre and/or cinema, i.e., *performative arts*, are present in the majority of Soviet texts centered on the figure of the trickster. In *Master i Margarita*, not only are several important scenes set in the Variety Theatre, but also most of the novel's characters are associated with the theatre. In Aleksei Tolstoy's *Zolotoi kliuchik*, Buratino fights Karabas Barabas for control over the puppet theater. In Il'f and Petrov's *Zolotoi telenok*, Ostap Bender tries to sell his collection of compromising materials on Koreyko as a screenplay called *The Neck*. Yurii Detochkin in *Beregis' avtomobilia* plays Hamlet in an amateur production and the scene in the courtroom where his case is being tried is doubled in his triumph on stage. Gorin/Zakharov's *Tot samyi Munkhauzen* creates several levels of theatricality—Munchhausen's fun and poetic theatre for himself and his beloved, which is later replaced by the "official" theatralization of his "heroic life" after his fictitious death. At the same time, *ad hoc* performances are even more characteristic for Soviet trickster texts. Consider also Bender's numerous performances—the organization of the *Soiuz mecha i orala*, Vorobianinov's begging act or the spectacular crossing of the Romanian border; Terkin's comical productions of theatralized fables/jokes; Venichka's *simposion* in the regional train, etc.

Marilyn Jurich writes about the folkloric female tricksters (she terms this character "trickstar"): "Traditionally, women have not had access to or were denied entrance into spaces that men could easily traverse. For that reason they have had more need to 'talk their ways' into power and position. The woman's great aptitude for language, as casuist and solver of riddles, is widely demonstrated in methods used by the trickstar to change circumstances." (212) This observation certainly captures the likeness of certain female tricksters, such as A Huli from Pelevin's *Sviashchennaia kniga oborotnia*, whose artistic trickery is located in the realm of games and twists of language and discourse. However, almost the same can be said about such male tricksters as Ostap Bender or Venichka, since they are true artists of language—language occurs as the sole sphere where their freedom, manifested through tricks, can be accomplished.

(4) **Relation to the sacred** is the fourth and, in my opinion, the most important characteristic of the trickster trope concerns its necessary—direct or indirect—*relation to the sacred*. This is exactly what distinguishes a trickster from a thief or a crook, characters no less widespread in Soviet

and post-Soviet culture, as well as in modern western culture: "...most modern thieves and wanderers lack an important element of trickster's world, his sacred context. If the ritual setting is missing, the trickster is missing," writes Lewis Hyde. (13) Laura Makarius argues that the trickster is the one who best reflects upon the contradictory character of the sacred itself, in particular, the associations between the sacred and the abject (dirty, impure, etc.), establishing a connection between the sacred and taboo violations. The scholar reminds us that the trickster's "sacredness has nothing to do with virtue, intelligence or dignity: it derives from his violations, which make him a possessor of magical power—which is identified with the sacred." (Makarius, 84)

It is relatively easy to detect the "sacred context" of such paradigmatic Soviet tricksters as, for instance, Bulgakov's Woland (a.k.a. Satan). The sacred context is equally conspicuous in Stierlitz from the miniseries *Semnadtsat' mgnovenii vesny*, represented against the background of the sacred (in the late Soviet society) mythology of the Great Patriotic War and the Victory; as well as in Venichka, who spends his roundtrip between Moscow to Petushki in dialogue with angels and pursues a tragicomic quest for proof of the divine presence, culminating in and confirmed by Venichka's own murder.

The situation becomes more complex when one addresses such characters as Švejk, Khulio Khurenito, or Ostap Bender. These characters play with anything pretending to be serious, high, or important in contemporary society. Their manipulations typically include artistic hyperidentification with, and grotesque parody of, a social role, a set of values, or a discourse. As a result, even if these categories had sacred ambitions, they would be completely devalued and discredited at the trickster's magic touch, something which invariably provokes laughter. From this perspective it becomes obvious that "direct" relations with the sacred, as in the case of Woland or Venichka, are secondary to more fundamental, specifically tricksterish manifestations of the sacred. These manifestations can be explained through Foucault's concept of transgression as a method of sacred-production and George Bataille's symbolic economy according to which "a sumptuary operation of potlatch is the only way to return to the sacred world of immanence." (Surya, 384)

Transgression—i.e., the breaking of boundaries and reversal of social and cultural norms—is the most important device of the trickster.

After Foucault, transgression, especially in the culture of the twentieth century, does not undermine the sacred foundations of social and cultural norms (these foundations are already shattered) but on the contrary, paradoxically *produces the sacred*. This paradox directly emerges from "the death of God," or rather, the crisis of traditional culture which took place in the second half of the nineteenth century:

> What, indeed, is the meaning of the death of God, if not a strange solidarity between the stunning realization of his non-existence and the act that kills him? But what does it mean to kill God if he does not exist, to kill God *who has never existed?* Perhaps it means to kill God both because he does not exist and to guarantee that he will not exist—certainly a cause for laughter: to kill God to liberate life from the existence that limits it, but also to bring it back to those limits that are annulled by this limitless existence—as a sacrifice. [...] The death of God restores us not to a limited and positivistic world but to a world exposed by the experience of its limits, made and unmade by that excess which transgresses it. (Foucault, 71–2)

At the same time, the ritualistic potlatch, the unproductive squandering of goods for symbolic reasons, is treated by Bataille as a means to "intimacy with the world," which implies the release of the subject from "thinghood," from alienation and objectification:

> Once the world of things was posited, man himself became one of the things of this world, at least for the time in which he labored. It is this degradation that man has always tried to escape. In his strange myths, in his cruel rites, man is *in search of a lost intimacy from the first*. Religion is this long effort and this anguished quest: It is always a matter of detaching from the *real* order, from the poverty of *things*, and of restoring the *divine* order. (Bataille 1988: 70)

However, as Bataille shows, in modern civilization, with its cult of labor and its "principle of reality," the initial meaning of religion is either reduced or wholly lost. To compensate for this loss, archaic mechanisms of intimacy—and thus the production of the sacred—take center stage, preserved not only in religious rituals but also in cultural memory, in totalitarian spectacles and even in the functions of poetry. The most important of these mechanisms is the ritual of waste, of expenditure, to which Bataille, leaning on Marcel Mauss's interpretation of rituals of potlatch, grants the meaning of a universal, and not merely archaic, symbolic device, which guarantees sacred freedom in turn:

> The meaning of this profound freedom is given in destruction, whose essence is to consume *profitlessly* whatever might remain in the progression of useful works. Sacrifice destroys that which it consecrates. It does not have to destroy as fire does; only the tie that connected the offering to the world of profitable activity is severed, but this separation has the sense of a definitive consumption; the consecrated offering cannot be restored to the *real* order. [...] This useless consumption is *what suits me*, once my concern for the morrow is removed. [...] Everything shows through, everything is open and infinite between those who consume intensely. [...] Sacrifice is heat, in which the intimacy of those who make up the system of common works is rediscovered. (ibid., 58)

Death, devouring, eroticism, luxury, war, feasts, gifts and sacrifices, as well as all sorts of transgression, including crime—all these activities are, to Bataille, varieties of potlatch. Many of the trickster's traits, above all his vitality and greed, correspond to this conception of "consumption." The way in which the trickster combines consumption and wastefulness defines him as an extremely significant representative of *modernity's notion of the sacred*.

This meaning of expenditure and waste acquires new significance in the modern period and in Soviet culture of the 1920s–30s, especially because of the prevalent cult of efficiency and the productivity and efforts toward organizing the entire society in a near-industrial way. In this context, expenditure takes on the functions of *a private sacred ritual* that simultaneously grants freedom (illusive, perhaps, but still therapeutic) from the social machinery. Not only Ostap, Khulio Khurenito and Woland, but also Buratino and Lazar Lagin's old genie Khottabych, Petr

Aleinikov's cinema characters, along with Venichka, Yurii Detochkin from Riazanov's *Beregis' avtomobilia*, Daneliia's Afonia and Gorin / Zakharov's Munchhausen—acquired cult status in Soviet culture precisely because they possessed the ability to create a ritualistic context of potlatch-like expenditure by their every gesture, phrase, or trick. Being consistently wasteful and at the same time creative, these characters artistically generated their own sacred context which exhibited the "negative" values of non-affiliation, non-belonging, disrespect, and joyful cynicism. Their notion of the sacred is associated with both transgression and liberation from thinghood, gained by squandering anything valuable and available for the sake of performance. The Soviet trickster offers a cynical freedom from any affiliation, obligation, or idolization. (In Venichka's case, expenditure also concerns the protagonist himself, who is not only being wasteful, but also constantly wasted in the course of the narrative.)

## THE TRICKSTER'S POLITICS

The trickster's continuous expenditure of everything valuable explains not only his/her frequent failures, judged on pragmatic standards, but also transforms these very failures and all the trickster's performances into direct proofs of his/her symbolic power, since, according to Bataille, "potlatch is not reducible to the desire to lose, but what it brings to the giver is not the inevitable increase of return gifts; it is the rank which it confers on the one who had the last word." (ibid., 71) Hence, the function of the trickster as a comedic double of the authorities goes beyond a particular critique of Soviet culture, but also appears to be quite important to the culture's self-description and self-reflection. As Laura Makarius argues, "the trickster is a mythic projection of the magician who, in reality or in people's desire, accomplishes the taboo violation on behalf of his group, thereby obtaining the medicines or talismans necessary to satisfy its needs and desires. Thus he plays the role of founder of his society's ritual and ceremonial life." (Makarius, 73) This characteristic obviously resonates with the functions of the Soviet authorities, especially during the first decade of Soviet history and partially during the second.

A traditional rogue frequently substitutes himself for figures of authority (Sancho Panza as a governor, Tom Canty in Mark Twain's *The Prince and the Pauper* [1881]) but this substitution is, as a rule, justified by the carnival context and represents a *temporary* inversion of the order of things. In Soviet culture, the trickster functions differently: his/her doubling of the authorities is permanent rather than temporary; this character exposes the hidden mechanisms of official power and its core impulses. Thus the trickster can, to a certain extent, be considered the comedic representation of the *political unconscious.*

One may be sick and tired of the numerous discussions on possible parallels between Bulgakov's Woland and Stalin, and indeed, the representation of Woland as an allegory of Stalin testifies, most of all, to a lack of imagination on the part of the researchers. That aside, Woland does quote Stalin (as was first noticed by Abram Vulis[3]) while addressing Berlioz's severed head at the ball: "'Everything came true, didn't it?' continued Woland, looking into the head's eyes. 'A woman cut off your head, the meeting never took place, and I'm living in your apartment. This is a fact. And a fact is the most stubborn thing in the world.'"[4] (Bulgakov 1996: 233)

However, those who develop the "Stalinist" hypothesis fail to notice that, first, the "facts" invoked by Woland utterly contradict the materialist worldview, and second, that the context of this scene demonstrates that Woland effectively appropriates the authoritative discourse in order to demonstrate how narrow its boundaries are in comparison with his own ambivalent and liminal philosophy: "...one theory is as good as another. There is even a theory that says that to each man will be given according to his beliefs" (ibid., 233).[5] Finally, it is telling that Woland's juxtaposition of Stalin and Christ (to each—according to his beliefs) does not stop there, but immediately and parodically "defiles" the ritual of the Eucharist by replacing a chalice full of wine (symbolizing Christ's blood) with the skull of a cynic full of the blood of a murdered (sacrificed) informer and traitor, and turning the blood into wine.

A parallel that, in my view, deserves no less attention than the "Stalinist" hypothesis is the comparison of Woland to the American

---

3   Also see Burmistrov. Curiously, the English expression "Facts are stubborn" popularized by Stalin's words, entered the Russian from the English translation of Lesage's *Histoire de Gil Blas de Santillane*, one of the classical picaro novels of 18th century.
4   «Все сбылось, не правда ли? – продолжал Воланд, глядя в глаза головы, - голова отрезана женщиной, заседание не состоялось, и живу я в вашей квартире. Это – факт. А факты – самая упрямая в жизни вещь» (Bulgakov 1999: 1029).
5   «...все теории стоят одна другой. Есть среди них и такая, согласно которой каждому будет дано по его вере» (1999: 1029).

ambassador William Christian Bullitt, Jr. (1891–1967), and his 1935 reception in the Spaso-House, as justified by Aleksandr Etkind:

> In the novels and plays he wrote in the 1930s, Bulgakov offers a serious portrait, imbued with faith and hope, of the omnipotent helper, who possesses absolute social or magical powers, which he applies readily and without asking anything in return in order to save the ill and impoverished artist. At the beginning of the decade he entertained expectations that Stalin might assume a similar role. It appears that in the middle of the 1930s he re-focused his hopes and aspirations on the American ambassador in Moscow. [...] Bullitt's stay in Moscow more or less precisely coincided with Bulgakov's work on the third edit of his novel. It was there that the operatic devil acquired his more human qualities, approaching, as we can imagine, the person of the American ambassador as Bulgakov saw him— might and joviality, unpredictability and loyalty, humor and taste, a love of luxury and circus tricks... (Etkind, 283, 286)

If we take this parallel into account, Woland's power really seems to be situated betwixt and between—recalling at once the Soviet dictator and the American ambassador and overcoming both these models and Christ's authority at once. Woland's power appears as the adequate freedom from every generalizing concept, every dogma and every binary opposition.

One may interpret the trickster's mockery of the Soviet authorities as the manifestations of his/her anti-systemic character, and this will be a valid interpretation. However, it is not a complete explanation. From this standpoint, it remains unclear why the characteristics of the trickster are also detectable in *official* representations of power. For instance, a revolutionary hero in Soviet cultural mythology was initially modeled as a trickster. As Evgeny Dobrenko demonstrates in his analysis of Grigorii Kozintsev and Leonid Trauberg's film trilogy *Iunost' Maksima* (*Maxim's Youth*, 1934), *Vozvrashchenie Maksima* (*The Return of Maxim*, 1937) and *Vyborgskaia storona* (*The Vyborg Side*, 1938–9), the protagonist, an exemplary Bolshevik named Maksim, was created as a "Til Eulenspigel of Russian capitalism of the beginning of the twentieth century" (Dobrenko

2009: 333). However, as the character develops, the role of the trickster gradually transforms into a mask behind which the protagonist conceals his revolutionary activities: "Essentially, the film triptych on Maksim presents a story of the transformation of a Til Eulenspiegel into a chekist" (ibid., 337).

More frequently, in Socialist Realist literature and film the trickster played the role of sidekick to the "serious hero"—on the one hand downplaying the latter's pathos, and on the other generating empathy towards his terrifying patron. The role of the trickster-sidekick belongs to grandpa Shchukar', as a jester commenting on all the actions of the "collectivizator" Davydov in Sholokhov's *Podniataia tselina* (*Harvest on the Don*, 1932, 1960). In Aleksei Tolstoy's novel *Pyotr Pervyi* (*Peter the First*, 1930, 1934) and in the eponymous film by Vladimir Petrov (1937–38) this same function was performed by Aleksashka Men'shikov (in the film brilliantly performed by Mikhail Zharov); the same Zharov plays an analogical role in Eisenstein's *Ivan Groznyi* (*Ivan the Terrible*, 1944), there as Maliuta Skuratov. This might appear to contradict what was said above regarding the independence of the trickster as opposed to the picaro. However, this transformation is quite characteristic of the Socialist Realist adaptation of this trope: Socialist Realism tries to submit the trickster to a figure of power or to the state hierarchy. Hence, the most popular Socialist Realist trickster appears as a soldier in wartime, namely Vasilii Terkin from Aleksandr Tvardovskii's narrative poem. Yet a flipside of this process can be seen in the "tricksterization" of the sovereign—as the manifestation of the maximum amount of freedom that was permissible.

Indeed, official representations of Lenin display obvious features of the trickster, and non-official ones even more so, as Levon Abrahamian argued in his article "Lenin as a Trickster."[6] Although it is not entirely clear whether Abrahamian is discussing a historical figure or its image in the collective myths of the times, the "tricksterization" of Lenin in Soviet jokelore naturally follows from the similarity between the revolutionary power's self-presentation and the symbolic power of the trickster, who establishes a new notion of the sacred by breaking old taboos. Alexander Panchenko also remarks that in the early Soviet fakelore, "Lenin acquires the features of a cheat or a trickster: he defeats the 'exploiting classes' not

---

6   See Abrahamian.

in an open fight or even by means of a 'secret word' known to him alone, but through a trick. [...] Both fiction and memoirs about Lenin often use the topos of his 'slyness' as the main indicator of his 'folk character'"(26).

The trickster-like qualities acquire a new meaning during the period of Stalin's ascension to the role of the father of the Soviet nation. Mikhail Romm's films *Lenin v Oktiabre* (*Lenin in October*, 1937) and *Lenin v 1918—m godu* (*Lenin in 1918*, 1939) are very illuminating in this respect—there, according to Konstantin Bogdanov's astute observation:

> The preparation of the revolution is depicted in the films as a fascinating adventure that demonstrates Lenin's playful skills—that is, his ability to be sly, to hide, to disguise, to be persistent and yet cheerful, almost funny. The history of the October revolution appears not without trickery and happenstance, partly confirming the juxtaposition of existing Soviet cultural "folkloric" conceptions of Lenin-the-creator-of-the-revolution with folkloric tales of tricksters—characters who achieve success through cleverness and improvised behavior, which makes them the object of derision and astonishment. [...] Young and old viewers of Romm's film (followed by the 1939 sequel "Lenin in 1918" by the same director) could henceforth judge Lenin's role in the history of the Soviet government while looking back at his speech defect, hilarious gestures and almost clownish escapades—the slapped-on cap, the bandage worn to imitate a tooth-ache and to hide his face from the cops, Lenin's unwillingness to sleep, inability to cook porridge, and at the same time, Lenin's unfailing "love for the children." (Bogdanov, 203–204)

Furthermore, one could even argue that Soviet political culture is marked by a peculiar version of a "twin myth" in which a "culture hero" is always paired with an evil trickster-twin. The construction of the twin myth is analogous to rituals of scapegoating, since it permits the transfer of all mistakes and failures to the figure of the Other.[7] However, the trickster-twin is not entirely evil—he is creative in his own, paradoxical,

---

7   See Girard on this issue.

way. Notably, after their descent from power, personages such as Ezhov and Beriia were also "tricksterized," in the official discourse as well as in popular mythology, through an emphasis on their sexual excesses and deviations. In contemporary narratives, Beriia's trickster-like features serve as the basis for a positive re-evaluation. For instance, in Vasilii Aksenov's novels *Moskovskaia saga* (*The Moscow Saga*, 1994) and *Moskva-kva-kva* (2006) Beriia is represented as a bon-vivant and hedonist character who dreams of the radical reforming of Soviet society in the direction of liberalization.[8]

Yet even the presence of these "sidekicks" could not completely free Stalin, the perfect "culture hero," from tricksterish connotations—probably because in a mythological context the culture hero and the trickster are not just twins, but conjoined twins. In many folkloric stories about Stalin, even ones possibly told during his lifetime, he appears as a dark trickster whose jokes confirm that his power is indeed unlimited, and whose concept of excess manifests itself in the cold-blooded expenditure of human lives.

In short, it would be wrong to perceive the Soviet trickster as merely a carnivalesque alternative to Soviet values and hierarchies. As truly ambivalent and liminal personages, Soviet tricksters acquire their cultural importance exactly because they *simultaneously undermine and embody the Soviet symbolic order.*

## THE TRICKSTER TROPE AND SOVIET SUBJECTIVITY

Sheila Fitzpatrick, in her book *Tear Off the Masks! Identity and Imposture in Twentieth-Century Russia*, demonstrates that the very process of "reforging" social identities, which laid the foundation for the "Soviet project," required trickster-like qualities from ordinary people. A kind of "tricksterdom" became crucial for the invention and/or re-writing of one's past: "Many lives are double rather than binary, for self-fashioning as a Soviet citizen implies that there is a non- or anti-Soviet self that is being denied. [...] Under such circumstances, the object of the autobiographical quest is not self-discovery in the normal sense, but rather the discovery of a usable self" (Fitzpatrick 2005:152). The manipulation of class origins, family relations and biographies, as Fitzpatrick shows, did not

---

8   See also Lebedev and Beriia.

constitute an exception but was practiced on a massive scale, since every new turn in the political course demanded a new metamorphosis from the Soviet citizen. Fitzpatrick's book implies that the class approach to structuring society directly provoked impostery and trickster-like handling of ordinary identities. From this standpoint, the numerous con artists and imposters, a common occurrence in Soviet society during the 1920–30s, appear to be not delinquents but people who "laid bare" (to use Shklovsky's term) the foundational "devices" of the Soviet social (dis)order:

> Soviet conmen, as virtuosos of self-invention, had their place in the great revolutionary and Stalinist project of reforging the self and society. In a prescriptive sense, to be sure, Bender was scarcely a New Soviet Man—but in a society of Old Pre-Soviet People struggling to reinvent themselves, who was? Bored by the construction of socialism, Bender and his fellow conmen were exemplars of self-construction. This makes us look more closely at the building metaphor (*stroitel'stvo sotsializma*) that was at the heart of the prewar Stalinism. Was impersonation, the tricksters' specialty, its flip side? (ibid., 280–281)

Although this explanation is valid for the 1920–30s, it does not entirely apply to the later periods of Soviet history, not to mention the post-Soviet period, when the value of class criteria for welfare and career declined significantly. However, the popularity and presence of tricksters in social and cultural life did not fade in the 1960s–80s. Obviously some other factors continued to stimulate the need for this cultural trope and its social agenda.

One of the most important aspects of the Soviet model of modernity can be detected in the phenomena of the "shadow economy" and "blat," which—as recent scholarship demonstrates—constituted permanent elements of economic and social life in the Soviet Union, growing steadily in importance and preserving their significance in post-Soviet society, in spite of the changes in the economic system. As Alena Ledeneva argues, the phenomenon of blat as a system of social networking, comprising indirect exchanges and mutual favors, is marked by the same ambivalence and liminality as the figure of the trickster, despite its ubiquity. Blat represented an "invisible" (from the official standpoint) "compensatory mechanism against the planned economy and ideological pressure against the legitimacy of private gain. Blat articulated private interests and 'human' needs against the rigid constraints of the State order, allowed people to meet harsh conditions to maintain their social comfort and enjoy a sense of 'beating the system'" (Ledeneva 1998: 46). It served as the "intermediary between commodity exchanges and gift-giving ... [since] it involved relationships and not merely goods" (ibid. 35). While not criminal, blat was perceived as morally reprehensible, hence "the misrecognition game: it [blat] can be recognized in the case of the other, and "misrecognized in one's own case" (ibid., 60). But, most importantly, while being an obvious "transgression of social boundaries predetermined by the system" (ibid., 46), blat also functioned as its necessary component—"a reaction of ordinary people to the structural constraints of the socialist system of distribution—a series of practices, which *enabled the Soviet system to function and made it tolerable*" (ibid., 3; emphasis mine). Hence, the "self-subversive nature of the Soviet system" (ibid., 3): the anti-systemic elements are paradoxically embedded into the core of the Soviet social and economic life.[9]

It would be wrong, however, to confine the significance of blat and the informal economic and social networks to only the late Soviet era (1960s–80s). Contrary to this otherwise narrow periodization, Sheila Fitzpatrick shows that the "shadow economy" and the accompanying system of social connections were fully present as early as the Soviet 1930s: "From the very beginning, the official distribution system, based on central planning and bureaucracy, had its unofficial Doppelgänger, the blat system based on personalistic contacts and off-the-record data. [...] A web of blat networks pervaded Russian society in the Stalin period, and similar claims could also be made for patronage networks" (Fitzpatrick 2000: 167, 178). As early as 1940, a "concerned citizen" wrote to Andrei Vyshinskii, then deputy chairman of the Council of People's Commissars and former prosecutor at the infamous Moscow show-case trials: "Not to have blat, that's the same thing as having no civil rights, the same as being deprived of all rights. [...] Come with a request, and they will be all deaf, blind, and dumb" (ibid., 168). Sociality based on blat was not limited to

---

9   On the subject of informal economy and its social role in the Soviet and post-Soviet periods see also: Lovell, Ledeneva, and Rogachevskii; Ledeneva 2002; Kliamkin and Timofeev.

deficit items (consumer goods), but spread out to include job acquisition, career development, education (especially higher education), medical help, vacations, and even economic partnerships between businesses—a whole institution of procurement agents (*tolkachi*) existed to promote the informal functioning of the "official" economy by "acquiring" raw materials, machines, funding, etc. Perhaps the greatest difference between the "shadow economy" of Stalin's time and its modifications in the 1960s–80s consisted of the fact that blat in the 1930s–50s was restricted to the relatively well-off social classes ("The point that blat was only available to persons of means and substance was emphasized by many Harvard Project respondents" [ibid., 175–6]), while in late Soviet times, blat spread to virtually every social stratum.

The Soviet trickster is usually a master of blat (*blatmeister* in Soviet lingo) and extremely well aware of informal economic and social practices, but more significantly, s/he effectively exploits the vulnerabilities of ordinary citizens, who are—by default—involved with the "economy of favors." Yet ultimately it is a *symbolic* and not a pragmatic relationship that links the trickster to blat and the shadow economy. I would like to argue that the Soviet trickster serves *as the most important symbolic manifestation of the informal economy and of the blat social network insofar as they serve as the foundations of the Soviet society*. The trickster's mediation between opposites not only highlights the existence of a third path between legal and illegal practices and moral and immoral principles (though the legal and the moral in the Soviet system almost always represents opposing paradigms), but also manifests this path as the most vital course, the one carrying the most energy and artistry.

The trickster plays with double-speak and double-thought, but mostly s/he inhabits the gap between the symbolic and the real planes of Soviet society. Evgeny Dobrenko describes the separation of these two planes as follows:

> Socialism is the spectacle of socialism. It is a 'new reality' that bears witness to itself without needing a referent. [...] The total aesthetization of reality (and of economic reality above all), since it was originally included in the project of 'socialist construction' itself, in fact accounted for all the basic functions of Socialist Realism, transforming everything around it into 'art.' [...] [I]f in fascism politics

was subjected to aestheticization (with political rituals at surface level), then in socialism the process penetrated more deeply—economics was subjected to aestheticization (let us add, parenthetically, that the economics of socialism by necessity requires greater aestheticization than in capitalism, since it is far more 'ideal' economics, and its 'achievements' are far more modest). (Dobrenko 2007: 35, 38, 40)

However, this contradiction is frequently ignored in contemporary studies of Soviet subjectivity.[10] The focus *only* on the process of the internalization of Soviet modernization by Soviet subjects allows to ignore such important phenomena as guile, double-thought, mimicry, and cynicism, which, as it follows from Fitzpatrick and Ledeneva's research, were equally (if not more) crucial for the survival of Soviet subjects—and, not accidentally, were epitomized by the trickster trope. For instance, Stepan Podlubnyi, who became one of the most central figures in the studies of Soviet subjectivity, cannot be described by the means of one, even evolving, model of subjectivity. The self-modernizing subject translating the Soviet vision of modernity into everyday practice (as described by Johan Hellbeck) constitutes just one of several Podlubnyi's "personae." In a parallel course, there develops a persona of a hiding "kulak" whose exposure leads to Stepan's expulsion from the institute and who later finds himself in the prison lines seeking the information about his arrested mother. Next to these two opposite personae, Podlubnyi's diary presents the third one: a secret NKVD agent regularly meeting with his supervisor and reporting on his classmates, friends, and neighbors. Additionally, the diary documents in detail a fourth personal sub-plot, that of Podlubnyi's relationships with women, which typically take a cruel turn—it seems that he unconsciously compensates for his social humiliations through gender violence. The most amazing effect of Podlubnyi's diaries lies in the parallel coexistence of these personae, and the ease with which Stepan switches from one biographic regime to another, seemingly "forgetting" about his other "selves." This ease of inner metamorphoses and intrinsic artistism, demonstrated by an ordinary Soviet subject,

---

10  See Kotkin, Fitzpatrick 1999, Fitzpatrick 2000a, Halfin 2003, Kozlova, Kiaer and Naiman, Hellbeck.

finds a direct aesthetic manifestation in the trickster trope.

As a result, the foundations of the "shadow economy," along with the peculiarities of the Soviet subject, who—in exact correspondence with Horkheimer and Adorno's definition—"saves his life by losing himself," proves fertile ground for a "shadow ideology," or more precisely the double-faced, self-subverting politics of Soviet socialism. An astute characterization of this phenomenon was given by Slavoj Žižek in the book *Did Somebody Say Totalitarianism?*: "A whole series of markers delivered, between the lines, the injunction that such official exhortation was not to be taken too literally, that a cynical attitude towards the official ideology was what the regime really wanted—the greatest catastrophe for the regime would have been for its own ideology to be taken seriously, and realized by its subjects" (1997: 91). Further on, while illustrating this thesis, partly on the example of the double position of Dmitrii Shostakovich—who, on the one hand, remained a relatively official Soviet composer, and on the other, was perceived by the intelligentsia as profoundly critical of the regime—Žižek underscores:

> ... It is Shostakovich's very inner distance towards the 'official' Socialist reading of his symphonies that makes him a prototypical Soviet composer—this distance is constitutive of ideology, while authors who fully (over)identified with the official ideology, like Aleksandr Medvedkin [...] ran into trouble. Every Party functionary, right up to Stalin himself, was in a way a 'closet dissident', talking privately about themes prohibited in public. (ibid., 125)

The trickster trope, placed into this context, obtains its socio-cultural significance as the reflection of irresolvable contradictions and yawning gaps within the social universe, first and foremost, within the existence of ordinary citizens whose loyalty and "normalcy" are inseparable from their criminal and semi-criminal participation in the "black market" economy, sociality and politics. The Soviet trickster not only reveals the duplicity in meaning, but uses this gap as a liminal zone to stage his/her transgressive "theater," thus presenting it as artistically appealing and playful—in a word, charming. The trickster, using comedy to reveal a-systemic elements inherent in Soviet economics, sociality and even politics, paradoxically overcomes these contradictions, enacting communication between the disparate planes of Soviet society through artistic metamorphoses. This communication (mediation) is based on the transformation of everything solid into *the apotheosis of ambivalence*, and tangibly demonstrates the uncertainty and ambiguity in the whole spectrum of societal "truths" and self-definitions—ideological (*Khulio Khurenito*), socio-economic (diptych about Ostap Bender), philosophical and religious (*Master i Margarita, Moskva-Petushki*), moral (*Beregis' avtomobilia* and *Osennii marafon*). Even such fundamental oppositions as *Soviet/foreign*, sacrosanct for the Soviet cultural understanding of the war with Nazism appear blurred in *Semnadtsat' mgnovenii vesny*. The very fact that Soviet children's culture—by default intended to produce clear-cut distinctions between good and evil, the permissible and the banned, etc.—turned out to be the breeding ground for various tricksters (from Buratino to Cheburashka)—speaks volumes about the paradoxical wholeness of Soviet culture. In other words, while the Soviet trickster exposes zones of ambivalence between the various disconnected aspects of Soviet civilization, he also generates a resonance between its mutually contradictory components, thus filling the symbolic "holes" in its fabric and producing a sense of unity, albeit invariably ironic, if not openly ridiculous.

## CYNICAL OR KYNICAL?

Peter Sloterdijk in his *Critique of Cynical Reason* (1983, English translation—1987) presents "a universal diffuse cynicism" (3) as one of the crucial reasons for the failure of the Enlightenment project in the culture and ideology of the twentieth century. Sloterdijk defines cynicism as "enlightened false consciousness" (6) as opposed to Marx's classical definition of ideology as "false consciousness": "It is that modernized, unhappy consciousness, on which enlightenment has labored both successfully and in vain. It has learned its lessons in enlightenment, but it has not, and probably was not able to, put them into practice. Well-off and miserable at the same time, this consciousness no longer feels affected by any critique of ideology; its falseness is already effectively buffered" (5). According to Sloterdijk, cynical reason emerges as a product of disappointment in the practical and political effects of the Enlightenment and develops in the course of accommodating to the ever-changing repressive politics of modernity. Cynicism offers the modern subject a strategy of quasi-socialization that reconciles the unconscious and the super-ego by splitting the subject into several unstable, equally authentic and equally false social masks. As a result, the social space becomes totally theatrical, which in turn produces a culture of mistrust, where the expectation of deception, the readiness to trick and to be tricked and the admiration for tricksters become universal. For instance, Sloterdijk writes about the socio-cultural atmosphere in the Weimer Republic:

> Fraud and expectations of being defrauded became epidemic.... In those years, it proved to be an omnipresent risk of existence that from behind all solid illusions, the untenable and chaotic emerges... In such an insecure world, the impostor grew into a character type of the times par excellence.... The impostor also became an indispensable figure in the sense of collective self-assurance, a model of the times and a mythical template. With a view toward the impostor, the need to clarify this ambiguous life, in which continually everything came out differently from the way it was "intended," was accommodated in the most favorable way. (483–84)

Sloterdijk argues that fascism emerges from this cultural atmosphere, although it presents itself as an antithesis to the cynical culture. Fascism positions itself as the enemy of ambivalence, histrionics and deception, supposedly overcoming the cynical components of culture. It does so through the promotion of a radically primitive and reductionist conservative mythology, which is presented as a modern tool capable of releasing modernity from its controversial and demoralizing effects. The same can be said about the mythology of Stalinism and the Stalinist model of "archaic modernization."

However, as the philosopher demonstrates, fascism—and we can add: Stalinism, in fact, represent the highest manifestations of the cynical culture. First, totalitarian mythology originates from the same philosophical premises as cynical culture: "In their approach, they are all chaotologists. They all assume the precedence of the unordered, the hypercomplex, the meaningless, and that which demands too much of us. Cynical semantics ... can do nothing other than to charge order to the account of cultural caprice or the coercion toward a system," (399)—and coercion it is!

Second, in totalitarian culture, theatricality becomes a crucial weapon of political warfare, not only in the theatrical representation of the leader (as in Nazism) and the aesthetics of mass political spectacles (from demonstrations to show-case trials). No less important is the performance of the power's transcendental status, which is guaranteed by messianic ideology, as well as by spectacles of national unity that cover up constant, "tactical" ideological shifts, struggles within the upper echelons of power, the transformation of heroes into enemies, the appropriation of "hostile" ideological doctrines and practices etc. The fact that these cynical "tactics" hide beneath the umbrella of "monolithic ideology" explains why the model of the trickster as a figure of supreme power became so popular in Soviet culture, despite its alleged marginality/liminality.

Cynicism proves to be impenetrable to rational or emotional critique: "No critique can cope with this gelatinous realism, for critique cannot achieve any validity when it is not confronted by an ignorance ... Even a critique that itself becomes cynical in order to smash the predominating cynicism is deflected" (385). The only functional opposition to cynicism found by Sloterdijk is the category of *kynicism*: "Cynicism can only be stemmed by kynicism, not by morality. Only a joyful kynicism of ends is never tempted to forget that life has nothing to lose except itself" (194). Kynicism appears as the artistic aspect of cynicism. In the philosopher's opinion, kynicism shares two fundamental principles with cynicism: "The first is the motif of *self-preservation* in crisis-ridden times, the second a kind of shameless, 'dirty' realism that, without regard for conventional moral inhibitions, declares itself to be for how 'things really are'" (193). However, the main distinction between cynicism and kynicism lies in the fact that contemporary cynicism, as a rule, combines "a rigorous cynicism of means with an equally rigid moralism of ends" (192), while kynicism is much more radical—it undermines the concept of goals altogether:

> This means taking leave of the spirit of long-term goals, insight into the original purposelessness of life, limiting the wish for power and the power of wishing.... The essence of kynicism consist in a critical, ironical philosophy of so-called needs, in the elucidation of their fundamental excess and absurdity. [...] Kynical reason culminates in the knowledge—decried as nihilism—that

we must snub the grand goals. In this regard we cannot be nihilistic enough. (194)

The principled "cheekiness" of a kynic (and of the trickster as well) is the result of the particular integrity of the kynical position: rejecting a cynical chasm between means and ends, the kynic escapes the schizophrenic fragmentation afforded by cynical reason; instead of the manipulation of social masks, the kynic offers a *metamorphosis*, the artistic flexibility of the subject, a transformation engaging body and mind. Sloterdijk also argues that the kynic possesses a specific sort of shamelessness—which, by the way, is equally characteristic of the trickster.[11] In the given context, shamelessness implies the rejection of moral taboos surrounding bodily functions, the equation of intellectual and corporeal activities—in short, "existence in resistance, in laughter, in refusal, in the appeal to the whole of nature and a full life" (218).

The dialectics of cynicism and kynicism (as the only effective weapon against the former) can be well illustrated by Bulgakov's *Master i Margarita*. Having begun work on his "sunset novel" in the late 1920s (the first version was completed in 1928), Bulgakov, as we know, continued writing *Master i Margarita* until his death in 1940. However, the novel failed to reflect the fundamental shift in the social and political culture which, as many historians maintain, took place in the late 1920s–early 30s and signified the formation of Stalinism. Apparently, for Bulgakov the 1920s and 1930s represented a *homogenous process*, characterized by the domination of cynics and a general atmosphere of cynicism, as "announced" in the conversation between Woland, Berlioz and Ivan Besdomnyi in the first chapter of the novel. Taken together, the central characters and the seemingly marginal personages of the Moscow chapters constitute an all-embracing hierarchy of cynics and various types of cynicism.

Daniel Vyleta accurately defines the meaning of Bulgakov's cynic for the understanding of Soviet subjectivity when argues that Bulgakov depicts "a society in which everyone accepts the discrepancy between

---

11  Lewis Hyde analyzes the trickster's shamelessness through the motif of dirt associated with this character in numerous myths: "…what tricksters in general like to do, is erase or violate that line between the dirty and the clean," including "revivification through dirt" (Hyde 177). Hyde adds that in this respect the cultural function of the trickster is similar to the functions of the carnival in Bakhtin's conceptualization.

public game and private self as the 'form of life' that is theirs. Everyone is by definition, a crook, because he/she holds on to a private self, and everyone needs and cherishes a private self in order to survive.... Indeed, the [Soviet] system gains stability by having cynical subjects rather than believing ones... The cynical, liberal subject—that is the kind of subject most prevalent in Bulgakov's Moscow, and, for all the official doctrine, it may the kind of subject most conductive to political stability: a gameplayer who cannot see beyond the monopoly board" (45–6).

1. A monument to Koroviev and Behemoth in Moscow, architect and sculptor Liubov' Mirosenko. A photo from http://www.liveinternet.ru/users/novicova/post115691662/

Cynical survivors, such as the ubiquitous Annushka or the public at the black magic séance, occupy its lowest level. Then follow "those who know how to live well," in other words, exemplary family men and moralists who support their families' welfare through petty theft and bribery—the house manager Nikanor Ivanovich Bosoi, the bartender Andrei Fokich Sokov, and Maximilian Poplavsky, Berlioz's uncle from Kiev. The next level of cynicism is reserved for those who abuse the sphere of art, which in Bulgakov's book is a far worse crime than mere bribery; here the reader finds Styopa Likhodeev and Zhorzh Bengalsky, the chief of the "Acoustic commission" Arkadii Apollonovich Sempleiarov and the entire staff of the Commission of Spectacles and Entertainments (i.e. the poor souls who became the targets of Koroviev and Behemoth's tricks). Those intellectuals who "survive" in the sphere of the new Soviet ideology represent a higher level of cynicism. They include first and foremost Berlioz and initially Ivan Bezdomnyi, but also the critics who panned the Master's novel—Latunsky, Lavrovich and Ariman, the poet Riukhin ("I don't believe in anything I've ever written"[12] [Bulgakov 1996: 60]), as well as the entire MASSOLIT. All these cynics are best described in the Master's characterization of the many negative articles devoted to his novel in chapter 13: "I couldn't get rid myself of the thought—that the authors of these articles weren't saying what they wanted to say, and that that was why they were so furious." (ibid., 121)[13] Finally, the highest level of cynicism—cynical authority—is represented by the two professional provocateurs; Aloizii Mogarych and Baron Maigel (the latter sacrificed along with Berlioz at Woland's Ball), as well as by Pontius Pilate in the Jerusalem chapters.

Woland and his suite are not opposed to this cynical pyramid; rather, they represent the best and most attractive aspects of cynical reason, thus offering a comical justification (or even a subverted blessing?) to those they mock and trick. Ignoring this function of Woland's and of his associates, or interpreting them as a force of moral retribution bringing just punishment to evil-doers, leads to numerous contradictions. For instance, why does Woland openly glorify the ambivalent: "What would your good do if evil didn't exist, and what would the earth look like if all the shadows disappeared? After all, shadows are cast by things and people. [...] Do you want to strip the earth of all trees and living things just because of your fantasy of enjoying naked light? You're stupid."[14] (ibid., 305) Why do Woland's associates perform so many illogical tricks, often without the least implication of retribution? Why and for what sin is Professor Kuz'min punished when the bartender Sokov pleads that Kuz'min save him from cancer? What is the didactic value of converting Bosoi's bribe into foreign currency, or transforming the Variety's box

---

12 «... не верю я ни во что из того, что пишу!..» (1999: 894).
13 «Мне все казалось, - и я не мог от этого отделаться, - что авторы этих статей говорят не то, что они хотят сказать, и что их ярость вызывается именно этим» (1999: 944).
14 «... что бы делало твое добро, если бы не существовало зла, и как бы выглядела земля, если бы с нее исчезли тени? Ведь тени получаются от предметов и людей ... Не хочешь ли ты ободрать весь земной шар, снеся с него прочь все деревья и все живое из-за твоей фантазии наслаждаться голым светом? Ты глуп» (1999: 1088).

office earnings into scrap paper and then foreign currency in turn, provoking the arrest of innocents? Finally, why is Varenukha made into a vampire and Rimsky driven mad?

These contradictions would disappear if, instead of accepting Woland and his host as moralists (fighting injustice and punishing evil-doers), one reconsiders them as the epitome of Soviet cynicism—super-tricksters much like their victims, but different in that they free their own cynicism from the least pragmatic overtones (money = scrap paper, clothing = nakedness). Woland and his suite playfully demonstrate the relativity of all values, which is why "good" and "evil" fall victim to their tricks indiscriminately.

The excess and lack of any pragmatic motive underlying Koroviev and Behemoth's tricks are the best evidence of the artistic, self-sufficient nature of their acts: the wastefulness of these gestures denotes both the sacred and the poetic. These tricks are well characterized by Bataille's dictum on poetry: "It signifies creation by the means of loss. Its meaning is therefore close to that of sacrifice." (Bataille 1985: 120) This characteristic equally applies to all of Woland's guests at the ball (except for the repenting Frieda)—they are celebrated for acting in excess of the pragmatic, taking an almost artistic approach to evildoing, which includes terrifying transgressions (Maliuta Skuratov also appears in the crowd).

Woland's philosophy best fits Sloterdijk's definition of Mephistopheles as "a kynical enlightener" (180) who perceives "the so-called evil as an unavoidable side; that puts [him] right in the middle and above it at the same time. Evil appears to [him] as something that by its very nature cannot be anything other than what it is. The prototypes of this 'evil', which is stronger than morality are free sexuality, aggression, and unconsciousness..." (ibid.) Woland and his associates not only defamiliarize "normal" Soviet cynicism, they also manifest it in a *joyful and playful* way, thus transforming everything into a theatrical show, a ball, a cascade of jokes and puns, a clownish performance with real (real?) gunfights and fires.

Thus, from the trickster's perspective, the entire Soviet world re-emerges as united by *cynicism* if, following Sloterdijk's suggestion, we associate cynicism with the state when "the everyday ontological border between game and seriousness is blurred and the safety gap between fantasy and reality has melted away, the relation between what is respectable and what is bluff slackens." (488) Furthermore, I shall argue that the Soviet trickster's indiscriminate laughter offers *a joyful epiphany of cynicism*, thus releasing this universal Soviet modus of behavior from its sense of guilt and criminality.

Soviet tricksters provide numerous examples of kynicism. Khulio Khurenito methodically transforms all serious—and invariably cynical—rituals and discourses of power, including those of the revolutionary Russia, into self-deconstructing kynical performances (see chapter 2). Ostap Bender's lecture on the future glory of New Vasiuki as the chess capital of the world and the ensuing chess match present a kynical version of Soviet utopianism; his participation in the car race kynically devalues the spectacle of Soviet industrial progress, and his hunt for Koreyko makes a comical spectacle of both the mechanisms of the "black market" and the Soviet paranoid search for "hidden enemies" (see chapter 3.) Venichka in *Moskva-Petushki* artistically transforms alcoholism, a powerful sign of cynical alienation, into a comical spiritual practice, in which fantastic cocktails comprised of foot remedies and insect repellent are offered to God as though sacred gifts, graphs rating alcohol consumption depict the sinners' souls, and a hiccup serves as theodicy (see chapter 5.) Even the super-serious Stierlitz—as will be shown later (see chapter 6)—represented the late Soviet intelligentsia's cynical acceptance of the despised political system as an entertaining game of wits providing—as the final prize—a kynical, goal-less, alibi for collaboration with the regime.

Both cynics and kynics compensate for the "closed" character of society, creating networks of social communication outside or beyond the rigid, yet self-contradictory structure. However, if a cynic freely switches social roles and holds no beliefs while pursuing his/her pragmatic or material self-interest, a kynical trickster represents survival in a cynical, contradictory and inadequate world not as a necessity, but as an opportunity for creativity, play, and freedom.

Thus, the dichotomy of cynic/kynic provides a fitting explanation of the role of trickster trope and its functions in the Soviet culture. I would like to argue that *by creating sympathetic and profound images of tricksters, Soviet culture was uplifting its own cynicism to a kynical level.* This operation, on the one hand, provided an alibi or even an artistic justification of ubiquitous cynical practices; yet, on the other hand, it presented the sole valid alternative to cynicism.

This is why in all significant Soviet texts about tricksters, beginning with those written in the 1920s, the tricksters confront not fanatics or idealists, but rather seasoned cynics, who only pretend to have ideals and beliefs but in fact are con artists themselves, albeit far less artistic and less amenable than the protagonists. Thus, Khulio Khurenito tackles numerous political and ideological cynics, including his own 'disciples'; Ostap Bender is opposed to Kisa Vorobianinov in *Dvenadtsat' stuliev* and to Koreyko in *Zolotoi telenok*; Buratino confronts Karabas Barabas and Duremar in *Zolotoi kliuchik*; Venichka Erofeev belatedly realizes that his enemies are cynical angels; Stierlitz struggles against Müller (though their warfare ends in a truce); Baron Munchhausen in Gorin/Zakharov's film confronts an entire city of cynics; and in post-Soviet culture, the kynical werefox A-Huli is opposed to the cynical werewolf Sasha Seryi, with whom she has a dramatic love affair (see chapter 8). At the same time, these characters frequently appear as Doppelgängers of trickster-protagonists, thus highlighting the permeability of the border between the cynic and the kynic.

Artistic phenomena agree with the observations of those historians and sociologists who directly or incidentally confirm the compatibility of Sloterdijk's model to Soviet culture. Oleg Kharkhordin's research on the concept of the individual in Soviet culture of the 1930s–1960s operates partly through the concept of "dissimilation," largely synonymous with Sloterdijk's concept of cynicism. In this scholar's opinion dissimulation is, first of all, not only the product, but also the process of an individual's social adaptation, and secondly, it is the unconscious, rather than purposeful, splitting of the self into different, even opposing, social roles:

> Their double-faced life is not a painful split forced upon their heretofore unitary self; on the contrary, this split is normal for them because they originate as individuals by the means of split. [...] One of the steps in this long development was individual perfection of the mechanism for constant switching between the intimate and the official, a curious kind of unofficial self-training, a process that comes later that the initial stage of dissimilation conceived as 'closing off' (*pritvorstvo*) and one that we may more aptly call dissimulation as 'changing faces' (*litsemerie*). (Kharkhordin, 275, 278)

In Kharkhordin's book, dissimilation appears as a major vector of the socio-political "selection of the fittest" in Soviet society:

> [I]f you are not in a shell, you cannot survive. Not only because of terror that eliminates unskillful dissimulators or non-dissimulators but also because a new dynamic is now at work: dissimulators, having become the dominant type of Soviet individual, force everyone to become one. Those who did not learn to dissimulate 'naturally' will be made to learn dissimulation by force. Even the residual Bolshevik saints are forced to adopt a dissimulative posture. (ibid., 276)

Alexei Yurchak in his book on late Soviet society, *Everything Was Forever Until It Was No More: The Last Soviet Generation,* at first glance, discusses the interpretation of Soviet culture as essentially cynical, noting: "All these models share a crucial problem: although they provide an alternative to the binary division between the recognition and misrecognition of ideology, they do so by producing another problematic binary between 'truth' and 'falsity,' 'revealing,' and 'dissimulating.'" (Yurchak 2006: 17) Yurchak proposes a different approach to the study of late Soviet culture (synthesizing Derrida's, Bourdieu's, and Butler's models), focusing on the performative aspects instead and revealing those performative discourses that produced new knowledge while seemingly remaining within the ossified space of the official ideological discourse and its accompanying rituals. In this scholar's opinion:

> ... the uniqueness of the late-socialist context lay in the fact that those who ran the Komsomol and party meetings and procedures themselves understood perfectly well that the constative dimension of most ritualized acts and texts had become reinterpreted from its original meaning. [...] It became increasingly more important to participate in the reproduction of the *form* of these ritualized acts of authoritative discourse than to engage with their constative meanings. [...] The performative reproduction of the form of rituals and speech acts actually *enabled* the emergence of diverse, multiple, and unpredictable meanings in

everyday life, including those that did not correspond to the constative of authoritative discourse. (ibid., 25)

Further on, while analyzing such examples of the "performative reproduction of the form of rituals," as "Komsomol work," *stiob* and *anekdot*, black humor, the cultural activities of *Mit'ki*, conceptualist poetry and the *necrorealist* film, Yurchak indicates that the effects of these cultural practices are similar to those that we discussed above in relation to tricksters and "cynical reason." For instance, Yurchak singles out as vital certain discursive operations which, as he shows, bring about the effect of deterritorialization: "The Soviet system was undergoing an internal deterritorialization, becoming something quite different, although at the level of authoritative representation this shift remained relatively invisible. Unlike the dissident strategies of opposing, the system's dominant mode of signification, deterritorialization reproduced the mode at the same time as it shifted, built upon, and added new meaning to it." (ibid., 116) A similar semiotic mechanism was previously described in connection to the trickster, who is prone to undermining the logic and connectedness of a system while remaining at once within and beyond dominating discourses and structures.

When Yurchak discusses *stiob*, a particular type of irony formed in late Soviet culture, he describes the internal mechanism of this performative discourse as follows: "... the aesthetics of *stiob* was based on a grotesque 'overidentification' with the *form* of an authoritative symbol, to the point that it was impossible to tell whether the person supported that symbol or subverted it with a subtle ridicule. [...] In addition to the act of *overidentification* with the symbol, the *stiob* procedure involved a second act: the *decontextualization* of that symbol." (ibid., 252) This characteristic seems to correspond neatly to the peculiar artistry embodied by the trickster and Sloterdijk's kynic. It is not surprising that while determinedly contradicting the proposal that Soviet culture is cynical, Yurchak simultaneously adopts Sloterdijk's description of kynism as "humor that has ceased to struggle," finding in this formula the most fitting description of the cultural functions of all the aforementioned phenomena of late socialism. In this way, Yurchak implicitly accepts the characterization of late Soviet culture as *kynical*, though rejecting—most likely, due to the ethical aspect of the term— its characterization as cynical.

However, despite Sloterdijk's claims, it must be noted that the cynic is never absolutely opposed to the kynic. In twentieth century culture the kynic is a *super-cynic* (as the example of Woland and his retinue demonstrates), that is, a cynic who turns cynicism into an art—a self-sufficient game which is more important than any pragmatic gains. As Žižek argued, uniting in his analysis of modern ideological phantasms Sloterdijk and Lacan: a society of cynics is founded on a secret pleasure (*jouissance*), which assures agreement with the mechanisms of social repression[15]. Simply put, *jouissance* is grounded in the fact that the rigidity of the law is compensated for by laxity in its enforcement. The contemporary "slave" experiences *jouissance* from the opportunity to deceive "the master." The contemporary authority experiences *jouissance* by allowing for the opportunity to deceive it by this means on the one hand channeling opposition and resistance into harmless forms, and on the other, rendering each of its subject vulnerable, since each and everyone appears to be involved into some kind of transgression, criminal or otherwise.

But *jouissance* is always a secret, always hidden on the level of the political unconscious. The trickster turns cynicism into a performance and thus exposes this "secret," or rather *estranges* it, transferring the reception of *jouissance* to the level of aesthetic enjoyment for its very artistry, its playfulness. It is this operation that is capable of transmuting cynicism into kynicism.

The borders between the cynical and the kynical are blurred and mutable precisely because both positions are rooted in the trickster myth and discourse and appear as their manifestations. Furthermore, cynicism and kynicism offer two major—albeit interrelated—social modalities of the trickster trope in Soviet culture, and perhaps, in twentieth century culture as a whole. At the same time, the dialectic of cynical and kynical reason is directly responsible for the overtones and meanings of the trickster's function in Soviet culture.

A critical analysis of the trickster trope in literature and film offers a fertile opportunity to draw a virtual map of Soviet and post-Soviet c/kynical reason, that is, to identify its symbols, discourses, contradictions, and thus its historical development from the 1920s to the 2000s. This history begins with the perception of the revolution as the self-

---

15  See Žižek 1997: 45-60.

deconstruction of the modern methods of "hollowing out the self," which, with the help of the trickster, eagerly turn into kynical performances of their own absurdity (as in Erenburg's novel), which in its turn, leads to the realization that the cynical modernity not only survived the revolution but also assumed the role of the foundation of the new Soviet society, (as is revealed in Il'f and Petrov's dyptich and allegorically manifested in Aleksei Tolstoy's literary wondertale). If Ostap Bender and Buratino manage to overcome the restraints of the social order by their joyful kynicism while at the same time providing aesthetic justification to the former, Venedikt Erofeev transforms the trickster into a tragic character who realizes that his kynism not only places him outside of society—which he proudly accepts—but also forces him into the confrontation with the metaphysical order, no less cynical than the Soviet world. While Erofeev's Venichka becomes a paradigmatic example of the identity of the underground *intelligent*, Soviet comedies of the 60s–80s as well *Semnadtsat' mgnovenii vesny* demonstrate how the trickster trope was adopted for the justifications of the intelligentsia's strategies of survival in and adaptation to the late soviet social order. These strategies stretch from the versions of the disengagement from the universally accepted cynical reason (from Gaidai's victorious Shurik to protagonists of "sad comedies" Detochkin and Buzykin, and finally to a romantic dissident Baron Munchhausen) to the collaboration with the cynical system in the capacity of a double-agent with his own, secret, agenda (Stierlitz). The post-Soviet rearrangement of the cynical reason leads to a new conceptualization of the trickster which splits (as emblematized by Pelevin's shape-shifters) into two antagonistic, yet interconnected, positions: a violent trickster-in-power, and a postmodern "deconstructor" who resurrects the kynical impulse only to break out from another quasi-ideological self-mystification. In short, the cynical subject at first emerges as the manifestation of the revolution, then as the force—secretly undermining the regime, and eventually as the manifestation of the regime itself, yet at the same time, continuing to function as the force deconstructing the social order. Certainly, this outline does not cover the entire history of the Soviet cynical subject, yet, I believe that the trickster trope offers some important clues for its further investigation.

# CHAPTER 2

## KHULIO KHURENITO: THE TRICKSTER'S REVOLUTION[1]

---

1   This chapter is written in co-authorship with Dragan Ilic (Comparative Literature, University of Colorado-Boulder).

The trickster trope, coupled with a conceptualization of the cynic/kynic dichotomy akin to that developed by Sloterdijk (albeit much, much earlier), appears in Ilya Erenburg's famed novel *Neobychainye pokhozhdeniia Khulio Khurenito i ego uchenikov...* (*The Incredible Adventures of Julio Jurenito and His Disciples...*). Bearing the imprint of the horrible traumas of the writer's first-hand experience of World War I as well as of the Russian Revolution and Civil War, *Khulio Khurenito* paradoxically presents a vision of an alternative revolution centered on the figure of the Great Provocateur, Khulio Khurenito, or "the Teacher," as "Ilya Ehrenburg," the novelistic double of the author, calls him.[1] Erenburg not only marries the trickster trope with the revolution, but also presents a paradoxical, anti-dogmatic, intellectual model of the trickster's revolution as a response to the catastrophic turns in the history of modernity.

Written in the course of one month in 1921, just after the writer's escape from Soviet Russia (albeit with a Soviet passport in his pocket), the novel was promptly published in 1922 by the Berlin-based Russian press Gelikon and caused a literary sensation in Russia. Marietta Shaginian and Lev Lunts in their respective reviews of the novel compared it with "great satires of the ancient decadence and European satirical novels-panoramas" (Shaginian, 143) such as those by Lucian, Petronius, and especially François Rabelais' *Gargantua and Pantugruel*. (Lunts, 358) Both critics read *Khulio Khurenito* as a novel about the

---

1   Hereafter (except for critical quotations), "Ehrenburg" refers to the fictional character while the spelling "Erenburg" is reserved for the author of the novel.

crisis of modern European culture. "Khurenito knows in perfection all languages and sciences, he is familiar with customs and prejudices of all nations. He is a vehicle and an enemy of the entire world culture," wrote Lunts (359), while Shaginian added: "Ilya Erenburg rejects and destroys everything existing because it lies, and not only lies but also masks the lies as truth, i.e. represents hypocrisy. However, Ilya Erenburg does not establish any *absolute* measures and does not find any *absolute* values. He does not believe in anything, does not extract any confessions, and does not preach about anything except the destruction of lies." (146) Evgenii Zamiatin and Viktor Shklovsky also spoke highly of *Khulio Khurenito,* while Yurii Tynianov sarcastically described it in his article "Literaturnoe segodnia" ("Literary Today", 1924) as too light-weighted for a novel: "Despite the fact that Erenburg's philosophical system included Dostoevsky and Nietzsche, Claudel and Spengler, and in general whoever wasn't too lazy (*vse komu ne len'*)—or perhaps, precisely because of this—his protagonist had become lighter than a feather, he transformed into pure irony [...] Erenburg's novel is a reflected novel, a shadow of the novel." (440, 442)

The incredible success—to use Tynianov's words (440)—of *Khulio Khurenito* in Soviet Russia also had negative political repercussions. Copies of the novel were confiscated by the GPU in Petrograd in the autumn of 1922 and its publication was postponed until 1923, when after significant efforts, including Lenin's approval, the novel was published by Gosizdat with Bukharin's preface. Despite the novel's international success, it was forced into oblivion in the 1930s–50s. Joshua Rubenstein points out in his biography of Erenburg that "in 1947, during an official exhibition at the Writers' Union marking the thirtieth anniversary of Soviet literature, Erenburg noticed that *Julio Jurenito* was not included among his works. He was furious and stalked out of the auditorium [...] *Julio Jurenito* was his first, his favorite, and his most honest novel. He wanted to be remembered for it. But the novel did not appear again until 1962, when it was included in a nine-volume collection of Erenburg's works. Bukharin's preface had to be left out and the account of Jurenito's interview with Lenin was also suppressed." (81).[2] If in the Soviet Union the novel was "unmentionable" for a quarter

---

2   More on circumstances preceding the novel as well as the history of its publications and critical perception see Berar, 37-92.

of a century, in the émigré scholarship *Khulio Khurenito* was customarily accepted as Erenburg's best novel, yet more or less harsh reprimands of the novel and its author for their "corrosive, all-pervading nihilistic cynicism" (Struve, 144) became no less customary.

*Khulio Khurenito*'s incompatibility with any forms of authoritative, let alone dogmatic, discourses directly derives from the fact that Erenburg, for the first time in Russian literature, presents the trickster as a philosophical position which is also immediately inscribed into the context of recent historical events—in this case WWI, the Russian Revolution, and the ensuing Civil War and political terror. Naturally, this trickster appears here deeply embedded in the modern world, first of all intellectually and politically. The paradox of Khulio Khurenito's intellectual position lies in his expressive rejection of any coherent philosophy or system of conviction: symptomatically, in the introduction to the novel, the narrator emphasizes that the Teacher "never taught anybody anything; he had no religious canons, no ethical code, not so much as a simple tupenny-ha'penny little philosophical system [...] he was a man without conviction." (Ehrenburg 1963: 9–10)[3] This also implies that Khurenito's philosophy is performative rather than speculative. By his demonstrative contradictions, paradoxical gestures, shocking performances—in short, by his provocations—Khurenito pursues two major ends: first, to reveal "a universal diffuse cynicism" (Sloterdijk) in all the "positive" and authoritative discourses and ideologies that dominated the world from the years just before WWI up until the early 1920s; and second, to play these discourses out to their limit, transforming them into pure absurdity, into self-deconstructing spectacles or narratives—in other words, transforming authoritative discourses of modernity into material for the trickster's secular rites of waste or expenditure.

## MODERNIZING THE TRICKSTER

Khurenito displays almost the entire spectrum of features attributed to the trickster in the mythological tradition. A former gangster

---

3   «... он никогда никого не учил; у него не было ни религиозных канонов, ни этических заповедей, у него не было и простенькой, захудалой философской системы ... он был человеком без убеждений» (Erenburg, 4)

## CHAPTER TWO

and Mexican revolutionary, he noticeably enjoys *liminal* zones and conditions—the war chaos, German and Soviet concentration camps, the Cheka prison. Furthermore, he incessantly generates liminality around himself by revealing scandals, crimes and transgressions hidden underneath such institutions of peace and order as marriage, church, or politics (bourgeois or communist alike). Illuminatingly, when the novel's characters find themselves drifting in a small lifeboat in the open sea after their small ship *Hannibal* is sunk by a German submarine, the narrator is stunned by Khurenito's cheerful tranquility:

> During these solemn hours each of us was convinced of his impending death, and each expressed this in his own way. The Teacher alone maintained a perfect, I might almost say an everyday calm. He occupied himself with us, joked with Aisha and told the story of how, as a child, he had taken it into his head to cross the Atlantic in a beer barrel, but the waves—alas!—had washed him back on shore after a few minutes. I asked him whether the thought of inevitable death meant nothing to him. The Teacher shrugged his shoulders:
> 'It's a matter of habit. I don't feel secure on dry land either. My *Hannibal* was sunk long ago.' (ibid., 177)[4]

Khurenito establishes peculiar trickster's relations with the expenditure-based *sacred*, and his first appearance in café Rotonde in front of a desperate and hungry poet Ilya Ehrenburg may serve as a vivid illustration to this claim. At first, Ehrenburg thinks that a stranger drinking beer at the next table is the devil himself: "… the whole Rotonde quivered and fell silent for a moment, then broke into the murmur of astonishment and alarm… A pair of small horns rose steeply from the locks above his temples, while the coat strove vainly

---

4 «В эти торжественные часы все были убеждены в близкой смерти, и каждый это выражал на свой лад. Только Учитель был спокоен, я сказал бы, даже буднично. Он заботился о нас, шутил с Айшей и рассказывал, как ребенком вздумал переплыть в пивной бочке Атлантический океан, но был, увы! выброшен через несколько минут волнами на берег. Я спросил его неужели он совсем не воспринимает неизбежной, по-видимому, смерти? Учитель пожал плечами: "Привычка! Я и на земле не чувствую себя уверенным. Мой "Аннибал" давно потоплен…"» (ibid., 182)

to cover a pointed, pugnaciously upraised tail." (ibid., 17)[5] Having eagerly offered Khurenito his soul, Ehrenburg receives a shocking answer: "I know who you think I am. But he does not exist." (ibid., 18)[6] After Ehrenburg's exclamation, 'But *something* exists, doesn't it?' Julio smiled again... and replied politely, almost apologetically 'No.' This 'no' sounded as though I had asked him for a light or whether he had read the latest issue of *Comédia*." (ibid., 18–19)[7] Explaining to the bewildered Ehernburg his vision of the world, Khurenito adds, "'And the other thing, the one with the capital G, also doesn't exist, my dear fellow. It's all invention. They made it up for lack of anything better to do. What sort of God can there be without the devil?'" (ibid., 19)[8] Pointing out a naked prostitute entertaining a fat naked Spaniard at the nearby café table, Khurenito continues:

> 'The good' you say? Well, take a look at his girl. She hasn't any dinner today. Like yourself, you understand? She's hungry, she's got that empty feeling in her stomach, but she knows she mustn't ask. She's got to drink that sweet, sticky liqueur. It makes her sick. And the Spaniard makes her sick too; he's got cold wet hands that keep crawling about all over her body. She's got a little boy, he's with an old woman in the country, it costs her a hundred a month. Today she got a postcard, he's ill—the doctor, medicine and the rest of it. That means she's got to try and earn a bit more. And *that* means being bright and cheerful [...] In short, an everyday story, silly stuff. But it's the kind

---

5   «... вся "Ротонда" дрогнула, на минуту замолкла, а потом разразилась шепотом удивления и тревоги. Только я сразу все постиг. ... Выше висков под кудрями ясно выступали крутые рожки, а плащ тщетно старался прикрыть острый, воинственно приподнятый хвост.» (9) The discussion of parallels and juxtapositions between *Khulio Khurenito* and *Master and Margarita* is started by Nikolaev, although the analysis suggested by this author is hardly sufficient.
6   "Я знаю, за кого вы меня принимаете. Но его нет" (1922: 10)
7   "Хорошо, предположим, что его нет. Но хоть что-нибудь существует?.." Хулио снова усмехнулся [...] и вежливо, почти виновато ответил: "Нет". Это "нет" звучало так, как если бы я попросил у него спички или спросил бы его -- читал ли он последний номер газеты "Комедиа"». (ibid., 11)
8   «... и добра тоже нет. И того, другого, с большой буквы. Придумали. Со скуки нарисовали. Какой же без черта бог?» (ibid., 11)

of silly stuff to send all your saints and mystics flying head over heels. Of course, everything is classified under the headings: this is good, that's evil. The trouble is that somebody let a tiny error creep in, a misunderstanding if you like. Justice? In that case, why don't you invent a better landlord? One who'll see to it that this sort of things doesn't happen on his farm. Or perhaps you believe that evil's a 'trial,' a 'Redemption,' you say? But that's childish justifications of far from childish things. That's how he 'tries' the girl, is it? Well done, the Allmerciful! Only why doesn't he try the Spaniard as well? Scales without weights. (ibid., 19–20)[9]

After this brief lecture, Khurenito feeds the hungry poet and introduces him to "a plump little Swedish girl dressed in a transparent tunic and resembling a fresh roll" (ibid., 21), concluding: "This is real all right, not like that 'good' of yours." (ibid., 21)[10]

The paradox of this scene is twofold: on the one hand, Khurenito presents his philosophical concept of the world as deprived of absolutes and of traditional forms of ethical/metaphysical orientation— and by this means, he immediately ascribes the universal meaning to the state of liminality. On the other, this liminal world in Khurenito's depiction is filled with concrete pains, joys, and concerns—mainly associated with everyday needs of the body—which do have real, non-illusory, value. In this respect, Khurenito gloriously confronts Ehrenburg's "modernized unhappy consciousness" (Sloterdijk's

---

9 «А вот поглядите на эту девочку. Она сегодня не обедала. Вроде вас. Есть хочется, сосет под ложечкой, а попросить нельзя -- надо пить сладкий, тягучий ликер. Тошнит. И от испанца ее тоже тошнит, руки у него холодные, мокренькие, ползают, шарят. У нее мальчик - отдала бабке в деревню, надо платить сто франков в месяц. Сегодня получила открытку -- мальчишка заболел, доктор, лекарство и так далее. Прирабатывай. [...] Словом, быт, ерунда, хроника. А вот от такой ерунды все ваши святые и мистики летят вверх тормашками. Все, конечно, по графам распределено: сие добро, сие зло. А только крохотная ошибка вышла, недоразуменьице. Справедливость? Что же вы хозяина не выдумали получше, чтобы у него на ферме таких безобразий не было? Или, может, верите, зло -- "испытание", "искупление"? Так это же младенческое оправдание совсем не младенческих дел. Это он девицу-то так испытует? Ай да многолюбящий! Только почему же он испанца не испытует? Весы у него без гирек.» (ibid., 12)
10 «... познакомив меня с пухленькой шведкой, одетой в прозрачную тунику и похожей на свежую булочку ... он сказал: "Это на самом деле, это вам не добро".» (ibid., 14)

formula of cynicism), which covers indifference to others with the belief in metaphysical absolutes—with his joyful kynicism, "a subversive variant of *low theory* that pantomimically and grotesquely carries practical embodiment to the extreme" (Sloterdijk, 102). Having debunked the devil, Khurenito at the same time acts as Mephistopheles, who in Sloterdijk's words epitomizes a "kynical enlightener": "If empiricism is his program, then in the kynical, vital form: head over heels into a full life, let one's own experience be the ultimate criterion" (180, 181). Furthermore, the sad story of the prostitute entertaining the Spaniard seemingly contradicts Khurenito's final gesture—an offering of another prostitute to Ehrenburg; but this provocation just emphasizes the "devilish," or more precisely, the tricksterish, meaning of the presented philosophy.

Yet, not only the devil but Christ as well provides a necessary mythological backdrop for Khurenito's tricks. As noted by Zsuzsa Hetényi:

> Events of the Teacher's life are peppered with commonly known emblematic elements of the life story of Christ. Khurenito dies in spring, during Easter, at the age of 33. He is born 12 years before the end of the century, dies in the year 21, 12th of March... The Italian Ecole becomes his disciple in the scene that profanes and paraphrases the biblical miracle of Christ's resurrection of Lazarus: 'stand up and go.' Before his death Khurenito eats a pear and wipes his face with a kerchief—this is the Last Supper of kinds, in the company of disciples who will soon betray him... The narrator calls the circumstances of Khurenito's death 'the greatest mystery play' [*velichaishaia misteriia*] but in the end of this mystery play, the Teacher departs in the direction opposite to Christ and heaven—he is not raised to the cross but thrown into a ditch. (318)

Not only in his death, but also in his numerous other performances, Khurenito uses Christian motifs and emblems, only to subvert and problematize them, frequently filling them with meanings opposite to the canonical. For instance, during the conversation about Jews, the Teacher poses the question: "Tell me, my friends, if you were asked to keep just one word from the whole of human language, namely 'yes' or 'no'—and discard the rest—which would you choose?"[11] Ilya Ehrenburg, the Jew, appears to be the only one who chooses "no." All the other disciples are appalled by Ehrenburg's answer, but Jurenito kisses him "hard on the forehead." (1963: 116) In the context of the evangelical myth, the Teacher's kiss of the disciple should mark Judas, but, in fact, this association is misleading. Firstly, Ehrenburg turns out to be the most devoted disciple of Khurenito and even an "evangelist," since the story of Khurenito's life is supposedly written by him. Secondly, Khurenito, much like the Jews, also says 'no' to the world: as Boris Paramonov argues, "Khurenito is interpreted [in the novel] as a metaphysical type of the Jew, as his pure idea, and this interpretation, no doubt, is borrowed from Nietszche's book *Anti-Christ*." (406) [12]

Another one of Khurenito's kisses creates even a greater paradox. In chapter 27, Khurenito interviews the leader of communists—Lenin, no doubt—who in the course of the conversation directly reproduces the totalitarian ideological dictum earlier articulated by the doctrinal murderer Schmidt: "We must eliminate them [opponents of the regime], killing one man to save a thousand. ... We are driving them forward, driving them to paradise with iron whip. The Red Army deserter must be shot in order that his children should know the full sweetness of the future Commune."(1963: 252)[13] After Lenin's words, "I'm telling you it's hard. But it's got to be do you hear? There's no other way" (ibid., 253)[14], Khurenito runs up to him and kisses Lenin's "high vaulted forehead" (ibid.).[15] When Ehrenburg asks, "Teacher, why did

---

11 «Скажите, друзья мои, если бы я вам предложил из всего человеческого языка оставить одно слово, а именно 'да' или 'нет', остальное упразднив...»
12 On the similarity between Khulio Khurenito and the Jew "Ilya Ehrenburg" also see Kantor.
13 «Мы должны их устранять, убивая одного для спасения тысячи... Мы гоним их вперед, гоним в рай железными бичами. Дезертира-красноармейца надо расстрелять для того, чтобы дети его, расстрелянного, познали всю сладость грядущей коммуны!» (1922: 260) Seven chapters earlier, Schmidt was justifying the shooting of the German deserter by the exactly same rhetoric: "... for the sake of your children or, if you have none, for the children of Germany, you will have to die in ten minutes' time" (Ehrenburg 1963: 201) / «...для ваших детей, а если у вас нет детей, для детей Германии, вам придется через десять минут умереть.» (Erenburg 206)
14 «Думаете – легко? Вам легко – глядеть? Им легко – повиноваться? Здесь – тяжесть, здесь – мука!» (1922: 260)
15 «... его высокий крутой лоб» (ibid.)

you kiss? Was it reverence or pity?" (ibid.)[16] Khurenito responds: "No. I always respect the traditions of the country I'm in [...] As I listened to him, I remembered similar precedents in your Dostoevsky's works, and maintaining the rules of etiquette, I bestowed on him that ritual kiss on behalf of many." (ibid., 253)[17]

The reference to Dostoevsky, and more particularly, to "The Legend of the Grand Inquisitor" once again places Khurenito in the shoes of Christ and simultaneously qualifies Lenin as a new Grand Inquisitor, although Khurenito is in no way silent and victimized during the conversation with "the Grand Inquisitor outside the legend" (this is the title of the chapter); rather he enthusiastically supports the opponent (and provokes him by his enthusiasm). As Mikhail Odesskii sensibly noted, "The symbolic imitation of Christ by such a character as Khurenito in relation to such a character as Lenin—permits one to qualify the behavior of the Mexican Teacher as Anti-Christ-like (which, naturally, in Erenburg's system does not imply a negative assessment)" (7). In this, as well as in previously mentioned cases, connections established between Khurenito and Christ are tinted by the trickster's ambivalent irony. On the one hand, Khurenito adopts the "mythical" position, on the other, he invariably splits an authoritative religious symbol into a bunch of self-contradictory paradoxes, thus performatively transforming the *doxa* into the field of *freeplay*, to use Derrida's terminology.

Furthermore, the inevitable intra-textual parallel between the two kisses from Khurenito establish the direct connection between the Jewish "no" to the world leading to the inevitable victimization of Jews, and Lenin's (or Schmidt's for that matter) merciless utopianism, which promotes the creation of future happiness by means of present firing squads. Despite the fact that during Khurenito's conversation with Lenin, Ehrenburg, scared to death, hides behind the Kremlin pillar, these characters—the ideologue of modern, scientifically justified, violence and its victim—turn out to be alike, which is made obvious by Khurenito's quasi-Christ-like gesture.

---

16  «— Учитель, зачем вы его поцеловали, от благоговения или из жалости?» (ibid., 261)
17  « — Нет. Я всегда уважаю традиции страны. ... Выслушав его, я вспомнил однородные прецеденты в сочинениях вашего Достоевского и, соблюдая этикет, отдал за многих и многих этот обрядный поцелуй.» (ibid., 261)

In all these scenes, Khurenito displays important features of the trickster, such as *mediation*: the Teacher performatively connects and places next to each other seemingly opposite forces and phenomena. The performative interpretation of these phenomena, provided by Khurenito, reveals their connections to the Great Provocateur and his own version of the revolution: all those characters that attract Khurenito's attention, gain his approval, or cause his enthusiasm, are despite their dissimilarities and mutual confrontations united by one common denominator: being legitimate products of modernity, they all, intentionally or inadvertently, mock, question, and directly undermine modernity's cultural and ideological foundations. Yet, their unity would not be seen without Khurenito's acts of mediation and his presence as the paradoxical center that connects opposites by creating such situations in which unlike characters would act the same way.

1. Illustrations by Adolf Hoffmeister to *Kulio Khurenito* (1961), from Erenburg's *Collected Works* (1990)

This mediation effect is implicit to Khurenito's trickery and can be best exemplified by the Teacher's collection of his "disciples," which can of course also be perceived as an obviously subverted (seven instead of twelve) reference to Christ's apostles. The circle of "disciples" that Khurenito collects around him plays a dual role in the logic of the novel. On the one hand, it presents an "external" reflection of Khurenito as the center of this circle. On the other, it exemplifies modern humanity as seen through Khurenito's eyes. All his disciples embody different aspects of what Sloterdijk calls "modern strategies of quasi-socialization"—the very source of cynicism. At first glance, the system of the novel's characters is based on a set of oppositions. The poster-boy American pragmatist/missionary Mr. Cool is opposed to the French bourgeois Monsieur Delet, an indulgent hedonist who Khurenito compares to the Buddha. The anarchic and idle Ercole is counterweighted by the fanatic of discipline and order, Karl Schmidt. Aisha, a Senegalese immigrant who creates Gods for himself out of mundane objects, is in contrast to the Russian émigré Alexey Spiridonovich, who is constantly and insatiably "God-seeking." Always indecisive, hysterical and weeping, Ilya Ehrenburg, the Khurenito's sole true disciple, appears as the psychological opposite to the Teacher himself, who always knows what to do and is never afraid of anything.

However, in the course of the novel, it becomes clear how easily these characters change their positions for the opposite ones. Schmidt metamorphoses from the proponent of German imperial order to the Russian Red commissar and the designer of the communist utopia, yet in both cases he eagerly sends his friends to the concentration camps. Both the "savage" Aisha and the "champion of civilization" Schmidt joyfully glorify the war when it begins, and both Aisha and Alexey Spiridonovich—an optimistic god-maker and a melancholic god-seeker—become murderers when they are recruited to the front. An epitome of capitalism, Mr. Cool, flourishes in the communist concentration camp, and a former hedonist, Monsieur Delet, enthusiastically seeks and persecutes spies and later propagates heroic self-sacrifice. Only the position of negation exemplified by Ehrenburg and Khurenito alike appears to be quite stable despite all the odds and through all the historical turmoil—which paradoxically testifies to the unshakeable character of universal cynicism.

Obviously, Khurenito's collection of "disciples" displays variations of human stupidity and absurdity. Married with national stereotypes, these human exhibits provide an impression of the micro-model of the entire humanity. Yet by selecting these characters as his disciples Khurenito displays a strategy different from Ehrenburg's "total negation." The Teacher enjoys the company and genuinely loves all of his disciples because they represent human, all-too-human, amplification of grand narratives, which involuntary produce effects similar to Khurenito's own provocations/tricks. In fact, the position of each disciple magnifies and exaggerates one of the values laying the foundation of modernity—order for Schmidt, profit for Cool, hedonism for Delet, freedom for Ercole, faith for Aisha, god-seeking for Alexey Spiridonovich, skepticism for Ehrenburg, etc.—but taken together all these "grand narratives" comically annihilate one another. In this respect, all of the disciples reflect certain facets of Khulio Khurenito's personality, thus modeling him as a fluid set of the *irreducible multiplicity* of positions; at the same time, through these mutually annihilating reflections he appears as the "empty center" of modern civilization. The oxymoronic combination of universality and emptiness in Khurenito's representation affirms destabilization of any absolute values and one-sided "truths" as the main driving force of his personal permanent revolution.

It is this "emptiness"—for which many critics had blamed Erenburg—that makes Khurenito a fully accomplished kynic. His motto is truly kynical: "Defile the sanctum, break the commandments, laugh, laugh, laugh loudly when laughing is forbidden, and with your laughter your torment, your fire, clear a place for him who is to come so that there should be emptiness to receive that which is empty." (1963: 49)[18] Khurenito's emptiness as the tool for the kynical repudiation of grand narratives, absolutes, and abstraction can be also seen in the following description:

> Later the Teacher came back repeatedly to questions of faith, creeds and religion. He spoke of them—as he did of other so-called important questions—in a jocular,

---

18  "Оскорбляй святыни, преступай заповеди, смейся, громче смейся, когда нельзя смеяться, смехом, мукой, огнем расчищай место для него, грядущего, чтобы было для пустого - пустое" (ibid., 44).

flippant manner. The Teacher maintained that the only subjects on which you can talk seriously—academically, with a catch in your throat or with a bibliography, from the bottom of your heart or with quotations from German authors—were methods of breaking in a new pipe, various kinds of spitting (with or without a whistling sound), and the structure of the inimitable Charlie Chaplin's legs. In all other cases he preferred a smile to a prayer and a jolly newspaper article to a work in many volumes. (ibid., 39–40)[19]

Sloterdijk argues that kynicism produces "the dialectics of disinhibition": "Those who take the liberty of confronting prevailing lies provoke a climate of satirical loosening up in which the powerful, together with their ideologists of domination, let go affectively precisely under the onslaught of the critical affront by kynics." (103) Khurenito develops the same idea when he discusses with Ehrenburg one of his disciples—lazy kynic Ercole who "prefers to spit because [he] has a strong and passionate loathing to all sense and all organization. He does everything the wrong way round. Clowning, you say? Perhaps, but isn't the clown haloed with the dying gleams of freedom?... Ercole will be with us, like the chaotic form of freedom, like the jar of dynamite packed in the suitcase next to the bottle of brilliantine and Coty perfume" (1963: 83–4)[20].

For Khurenito, being a trickster means being a kynic, and vice versa. His playful "emptiness" is inseparable from his ambivalence, which qualifies him as an accomplished trickster. Khulio overcomes

---

19  «Впоследствии Учитель неоднократно возвращался к вопросам веры, верований и религии. Он говорил об этом, как, впрочем, и о других так называемых "важных проблемах", шутя и балагуря. Учитель утверждал, что серьезно, академически, проникновенным голосом или приводя библиографию, можно говорить лишь о способах обкуривания трубок, о различных манерах плеваться, со свистом или без свиста, о построении ног неповторимого Чаплина. Во всех других случаях он предпочитал молитве усмешку, многотомному исследованию веселый фельетон.» (ibid., 33)

20 «...предпочитает плеваться, потому что ненавидит крепко и страстно всякий смысл и всякую организацию. Он все делает наоборот. Скажешь, клоунада? Может быть, но не на рыжем ли горят последние отсветы свободы? [...] Эрколе будет с нами, как хаотическая любовь к свободе, как баночка с взрывчатым веществом в саквояже, рядом с брильянтином и духами Коти!» (ibid., 81)

the fragmentariness of cynical conformity, of multiple mutually contradictory positions through a typical kynic's/trickster's gesture—the exposure of his shamelessness: "Have you only just noticed that I'm a scoundrel, traitor, *agent provocateur*, renegade, etc., etc.?" (ibid., 259)[21] This shamelessness also stems from the trickster's trope: Khulio's provocations are his *art*, akin to the actions and performances of the avant-garde and especially Dada artists.

## THE METHOD: OVERIDENTIFICATION

Erenburg wrote about his protagonist: "Khurenito is dear to me because nobody (even myself) knows where his smile ends, and his pathos begins [...] In him I am more truthful than anywhere else without obligations toward any kind of totality."[22] (2004: 150) The ambivalence of the author's attitude resonates with the main method employed by Khurenito for the trickster's critique of modernity, which can be after Alexei Yurchak defined as *overidentification*. The key strategy of overidentification is to take the ideological grand narrative more seriously/literally than it takes itself—simply put, to *over*-identify with it. Slavoj Žižek describes the whole mechanism in terms of an element which *out-embodies* or *over-fulfills* itself. According to Žižek, the formula at work is something like: an element which does not belong to the genus X is more X than X itself. Žižek invites us to consider, for instance, the popular catchphrase: somebody is "more Catholic than the Pope," which most aptly captures the mechanism at stake. Overidentification may be metaphorically described in terms of burdening something fragile—most likely the ruling ideology—with additional weight. As a consequence, the ideological structure simply collapses under the augmented pressure. Thus, overidentification actually *makes visible* a series of hidden points of contact that the particular ideology has to keep concealed in order to preserve its power. There is always an excessive component that can both frustrate and paralyze the system if uncovered or over-stressed, so

---

21  «Неужели ты только что заметил, что я негодяй, предатель, провокатор, и прочее, прочее?» (ibid., 267)
22  «Хуренито мне дорог потому, что никто (даже я сам) не знает, где кончается его улыбка и начинается пафос. (...) В нем я более чем где-либо правдив, без обязательств хоть к<акой>-н<ибудь>, хоть иллюзорной цельности»

to speak (Žižek 1991, 92–93). Therefore, as Alexei Monroe shrewdly observes, the process of overidentification is always entwined with the very opposite process, that of *disidentification* (47) or in Yurchak's terminology, *decontextualization*. In other words, the process of overidentification presupposes its antithetical side: "creating distance by approaching too closely." (Monroe, 48)[23] By bringing to light the obscene super-ego of the system, over-identification undermines its most solid—and, at the same time, most perverse—foundations (ibid., 79). No wonder that deconstruction by overidentification—pioneered by Khurenito—becomes quite popular among twentieth-century tricksters: in this respect, among Khurenito's followers one may list such diverse fictional and real-life characters as Ostap Bender, Andy Warhol, Dmitrii Prigov, late-Soviet Mit'ki and other practitioners of *stiob*, Laibach and NSK group, and Stephen Colbert.

Khurenito's overidentifications can be illustrated by his numerous provocations, such as: his Circle of Prostitutes in Aid of Society Ladies and his suggestion that prostitution be placed "amongst our most respectable institutions, on equal footing with the Senate, the stock exchange and the Academy of Arts" (1963: 75);[24] his creation of the fictitious state Labardan whose policy represents a sarcastic parody of the "humanist" and "just" wartime demands of the European states; and his collaboration with the Bolsheviks, including his decrees "exorcising... the phantom of personal freedom" (he placed sexual relationships under the control of the state and forbade the issuing of philosophical and theological books by the libraries in order "to avoid putting the brains of Soviet workers under unnecessary strain" [ibid., 232]).[25] In addition to this, Khurenito's overidentifications with the grand narratives of modernity can be detected in: his demands to have all forms of art banned, except for those that have pragmatic value; his

---

23 Monroe quotes Žižek's article "Why are Laibach and NSK Not Fascists?," *M'ARS* (1993): 4-5.
24 «Проституция является одним из наиболее ярких выражений нашей культуры, и я предлагаю не только не бороться с ней, но поставить ее под охрану международных законов, отнести ее к числу самых чтимых учреждений наравне с сенатом, биржей и Академией искусств.» (Erenburg, 72)
25 "До выработки центральными советскими органами единого плана рождений на 1919 г, запрещается с 15-м с. м. гражданам г. Кинешмы и уезда производить зачатья [...] В целях экономии мозгов работников, из общественной библиотеки временно прекращается выдача книг философских и теологических.» (ibid., 238)

defense of war as the vehicle of progress; his praise for revolutionary terror and "the new society" charted by Schmidt, the fanatic of order; and his invention of super-weapons using "certain radiation effects of electric waves and radium" (ibid., 148), among other things. All of these and many others of Khurenito's performances have one purpose only, namely to reveal through comical overidentification the absurdity of modernity's goals and values, including such sanctimonious ones as Freedom, Civilization, Culture and most of all, Progress.

In fact, Khurenito even overidentifies with the very idea of modernity. If we take the myth of modernity as signifying that whatever is new is by default "better," "more" progressive, "more" desirable, or "more" justifiable, then Khurenito overidentifies with the very project of modernity because he does not just embrace the future, he goes so far as to detest the present, doing his best to destroy it literally: Khurenito "taught us to hate the present and, in order that our hatred should be strong and hot, he opened before our thrice astonished eyes a chink of the door leading to the great and inescapable tomorrow," (ibid., 10)[26] says Ehrenburg. In other words, modernity's *tomorrow*, as justified by the idea of progress, brings death to everything that is dear and vital today. The image of the future derived from this vision is apocalyptic indeed, and the apocalypse appears as the inevitable result of the modern concept of history. When picking up Mr. Cool, just because the latter is utterly vile, Khurenito further justifies the logic of his choice by explicitly pointing out: "Remember, we want to destroy everything. Cool is first-class heavy artillery." (ibid., 34) In the same vein, Khurenito enthusiastically praises the Cheka terror in a way reminiscent of Dostoevsky's Grand Inquisitor for lifting the yoke of freedom:

> You are the greatest liberators of mankind, for the yoke you bring is a most excellent one, not of gilt but of iron, sturdy and well-made. [...]If you don't shoot me I'll collaborate with you to the full: that is, I shall destroy beauty and freedom of thought, feeling and

---

26 «...учил ненавидеть настоящее, и, чтобы эта ненависть была крепка и горяча, он приоткрыл пред нами, трижды изумленными, дверь, ведущую в великое и неминуемое завтра.» (ibid., 4)

## CHAPTER TWO

> A short time ago, the leader of the English punk group, The Stranglers, celebrated the neutron bomb in a frivolous interview because it is what can set a nuclear war into action. 'Miss Neutron, I love you.' Here he had found the point where the cynicism of protesters coincides with the brazen-faced master cynicism of the strategists. What did he want to say? Look how wicked I can be? His smile was coquettish, nauseated, and ironically egoistic; he could not look the reporter in the face. As in a dream, he spoke past the camera for those who will understand him, the little, beautifully wicked punk devil who causes the world to rattle with unthinkable words. That is the language of a consciousness that earlier perhaps did not mean to be so wicked. But now, since the show demands it, not only is it unhappy, it also wants to be unhappy. In this way misery can be outdone. The last act of freedom is used to will what is terrifying. (Sloterdijk, 127)

Even though Sloterdijk does not explicitly mention the concept of overidentification, he actually provides a brilliant example of it. If the last act of resistance is to will what is terrifying, then Khurenito's *modus operandi* seems to be quite along *The Strangler*'s line: "Miss Neutron, I love you." His variation on the same theme might be something like: "the war [is] not merely a step, [but] a leap into the future." (1963: 193) Indeed, the ultimate kynical trickster's act of liberty is to identify with what is most terrifying and dismantle it by doing so.

Khurenito's overidentifications foreshadow postmodernism since they are based on the deconstruction of binary oppositions, be they the opposition of good and evil, progress and regress, civilization and barbarism, sacred and profane, family and prostitution, war and peace, the revolutionary utopia of universal happiness and the concentration camp, discipline and chaos, etc. The deconstructive effect of the overidentification directly derives from the cynical character of modern ideologies as defined by Žižek: in the 20$^{th}$-century phase of modernity dominated by the cynical reason, ideology no longer can be defined (after Adorno) as:

action wherever I can in the name of a unified, lawful and correct organization of mankind [...] I beg of you do not trim your cudgel with violets! Your mission is a great and complicated one: to accustom men to their fetters until they come to regard them as a mother's tender caress." (ibid., 237–9)[27]

Thus, Khurenito—through the trickster's ambivalent and artistic overidentifications—arrives at the same understanding of modern history, which was dramatically if not tragically epitomized by Walter Benjamin's famous interpretation of Paul Klee's *Angle Novus* as the modern angel of history:

> A Klee painting named 'Angelus Novus' shows an angel looking as though he is about to move away from something he is fixedly contemplating. His eyes are staring, his mouth is open, his wings are spread. This is how one pictures the angel of history. His face is turned toward the past. Where we perceive a chain of events, he sees one single catastrophe which keeps piling wreckage upon wreckage and hurls it in front of his feet. The angel would like to stay, awaken the dead, and make whole what has been smashed. But a storm is blowing from Paradise; it has got caught in his wings with such violence that the angel can no longer close them. The storm irresistibly propels him into the future to which his back is turned, while the pile of debris before him grows skyward. This storm is what we call progress. (Benjamin, 257–8)

Khurenito is himself such "Angelus Novus"—albeit in the trickster's rather than messianic attire. Quite fitting in this respect is an amazing anecdote recounted by Sloterdijk in his *Critique of Cynical Reason* about the famous English punk group, *The Stranglers*:

---

27 "Вы уничтожаете свободу, поэтому я приветствую вас. Вы величайшие освободители человечества, ибо несете ему прекрасное иго, не золоченое, но железное, солидное и организованное <...> Умоляю вас, не украшайте палки фиалочками! Велика и сложна ваша миссия – приучить человека настолько к колодкам, чтобы они казались ему нежными объятиями матери." (ibid., 244–5)

a system which makes a claim to the truth—that is, which is not simply a lie but a lie experienced as truth, a lie which pretends to be taken seriously. Totalitarian ideology no longer has this pretension. It is no longer meant, even by its authors, to be taken seriously—its status is just that of a means of manipulation, purely external and instrumental; its rule is secured not by its truth-value but by simple extra-ideological violence and promise of gain. (1991: 30)

Therefore, the overidentification breaks the backbone of the cynical "social contract" and forces the ideology to expose its lies through absurdist comical spectacles. Furthermore, although Erenburg had written his novel before the emergence of the full-fledged totalitarian regimes, Khulio Khurenito's trickery directed against various ideological constructs—political and moral, capitalist and communist—vividly proves that cynical reason lies in the core of any modern ideology, not only totalitarian ones.

This vision is deeply embedded in the novel's intellectual plot-line. The catastrophic events experienced by the novel's characters—as well as by the entire European civilization—seem to "follow" Khurenito's method: modernity deconstructs itself while trying to overidentify with its ideological discourses. The war, the concentration camps, the revolution and the "Red terror"—all of these episodes demonstrate the effects of these overidentifications.

Thus, the celebrations accompanying WWI clearly illustrate the illusory nature of the borderline between culture and barbarity: in the former case, a necklace made of human teeth—a gift from Aisha, who gathered them from fallen soldiers—decorates the monument to the "Champion of the Civilization." Aisha's necklace as a sarcastic symbol of civilization will reappear in the scene that takes place in the German concentration camp, only to further problematize the distinction between barbarity and civilization: there, in the camp, a naïve Aisha tells the Germans about his trophy. As a result, they "gave Aisha a merciless beating, breaking his pride and joy, the Ultima [prosthetic] arm—and were going to shoot him but changed their minds and set about photographing him instead, and exhibiting him to various Swedes and Dutchman as an example of cruelty and barbarism." (1963: 204–205)[28]

Analogically, during the scenes of the Russian revolution, one slogan is immediately replaced by another, opposite in meaning, the call to brotherhood leads to a massive melee, and the "kingdom of freedom" is glorified in a Cheka prison by a Cheka officer, while Mr. Cool's capitalist projects appear to be most successful in a Soviet concentration camp.

The similarity between Khurenito's method of provocations and the "deconstructive" effects that historical catastrophes produce on cynical societies testifies, on the one hand, to the adequacy of his strategy to the historical condition captured by the novel, but on the other hand, it also demonstrates the radical chasm that separates the kynic and the cynical world. The main difference between Khurenito's intellectual revolution and the effects war and revolution have on cynical societies lies in the direction of further transformations: Khurenito *multiplies* viewpoints, discursive possibilities, and scenarios, etc., while the cynical societies, tired of chaos and catastrophes, tend to mask their chaotic tendencies under a simulacrum of order and unified progress. Much like Sloterdijk's *Critique of Cynical Reason*, Erenburg's *Khulio Khurenito* strikingly demonstrates how this masking generates what can retrospectively be defined as fascism or totalitarianism.

## WHY DID KHURENITO DECIDE TO DIE?

It is the resonance between the trickster's overidentifications and the self-deconstructing "logic of history" that allows Erenburg to bring forward a proto-fascist potential hidden in humane and civilized modern discourses, and in so doing, the author—together with his protagonist—plays a trick not only on the novel's heroes but also on the novel's readers. Perhaps the most illuminating example of this effect can be detected in Khurenito's announcement in chapter 11, inviting the public to attend "Solemn Performances of

---

28   «Айшу нещадно избили, сломав его гордость и радость – руку "Ультима", потом хотели расстрелять и не расстреляли лишь потому, что начали фотографировать и показывать различным голландцам или шведам как образец варварства.» (ibid., 211).

the Destruction of the Tribe of Judas which will take place shortly in Budapest, Kiev, Jaffa, Algiers and many other places," the program of which will include "apart from the traditional pogroms—a public favorite—a series of historical reconstructions in the spirit of the age, e.g., burning of Jews, burying same alive, sprinkling of fields with Jewish blood, as well as modern methods of 'evacuation,' 'removal of suspicious elements,' etc., etc.... Time and place will be announced later. Entrance free." (ibid., 111)[29] Although these ghastly visions were suggested to Erenburg by actual pogroms he lived through in 1918-19 while in Kiev, they also, with shocking precision, predict the Holocaust. The flamboyantly theatrical character of Khurenito's announcement is indicative of the overidentification: the concealed anti-Semitism ingrained in cynical modernity is presented by him through shameless provocation, thus revealing the medieval underpinnings of modernity's humanism.

Certainly, Erenburg could not know about the prophetic effect of this provocation, but he made sure to demonstrate how Khurenito's "invitation" comes to life in the chapters to follow, especially while depicting the Russian Revolution and the "revolutionary masses," like those portrayed in chapter 28:

> According to them, God did not exist, having been invented by the priests for the purpose of funerals, weddings and other ceremonies requiring paying the clergy, but the churches should be left standing, for what sort of village was it that had no church? It would be better still to kill all the Jews. As for those who were against the communists ... not enough of them had been killed yet, and there would have to be more done in that way. But it wouldn't do any harm to knock a few

---

29   «В недалеком будущем состоятся торжественные сеансы уничтожения еврейского племени в Будапеште, Киеве, Яффе, Алжире и во многих иных местах. В программу войдут, кроме излюбленных уважаемой публикой традиционных погромов, реставрированные в духе эпохи сожжение евреев, закапывание их живьем в землю, опрыскивание полей еврейской кровью, а также новые приемы "эвакуации", "очистки от подозрительных элементов" и пр., пр. ... О месте и времени будет объявлено особо. Вход бесплатный.» (ibid., 110)

communists either." (ibid., 258)[30]

If Khurenito's provocation in chapter 11 is met by his audience indignantly, later in the novel much more real, and no less terrifying, manifestations of anti-Semitism do not incite any protests whatsoever. Even Ehrenburg learns to react to the constant danger of being killed as a Jew in a mundane—and kynical! —manner: "One night some officers stopped me in the street, 'Halt! Are you a Yid?' In reply I swore, juicily and going into great detail, just like a shoemaker in Dorogomilovo might swear when he's been paid for an order and had a bit to drink. This seemed convincing, and they let me go." (ibid., 283)[31]

Equally symptomatic are repetitions invariably associated with acts of violence, which pepper the adventures of the Teacher and his disciples: two times they are placed into a concentration camp—the first time in a German one, the second time a Soviet one—and both times Karl Schmidt appears to be in charge of their incarceration (which does not relieve their destiny). Khurenito and Ehrenburg are arrested by the Cheka twice, and even put into the same prison both times. The illuminating description of Yelizavetgrad appears in the novel's final chapter (31): it is a town in which political regimes alter with an annoying regularity during the Civil War; however, no matter who controls the town, the Bolsheviks, the Whites, "just Ukrainians, Ukrainian Socialists, just Socialists, Anarchists, Poles, and not less than three dozen major atamans" (ibid., 279), the routine of violence remains the same:

> The townspeople, liberated every week from one yoke or another, did not even notice it, for the actions of the tyrants and the liberators were surprisingly alike. ... Besides, the tradition of places proved stronger than

---

30   «Господа бога, по их словам, не имелось, и выдуман он попами для треб, но церкви оставить нужно, какое же это село без храма божьего? Еще лучше перерезать жидов. Которые против большевиков... их мало еще резали, снова придется. Но коммунистов тоже вырезать не мешает.» (ibid., 266)

31   « Как-то ночью меня на улице остановили военные. "Стой! Ты жид?" В ответ я выругался; сочно и обстоятельно, как ругаются в Дорогомилове сдавшие заказ сапожники. Это показалось убедительным, и меня отпустили.» (ibid., 291)

human change: the furnished rooms which had housed the Cheka were later used by the 'counter-intelligence' and all ten subsequent institutions of the same kind. The prison went on being the prison, though people who put others in it were always being put in it themselves: it did not become a musical academy or kinder-garden for all that. Even the shootings were carried out on the same traditional waste ground behind the prison. Each successive regime, as it came in, issued laws on the freedom and inviolability of the individual and the death penalty for the slightest expression of dissatisfaction with that freedom. Then, for the duration of their short existence, they would hasten to 'establish normal living,' i.e., rob the greatest possible number of Jewish watchmakers and shoot all persons with unprepossessing faces or ill-sounding surnames. (ibid., 280)[32]

The *routinization of violence,* the transformation of brutality into the everyday norm, was predicted by Khurenito much earlier in the novel, as the main outcome of the war experience: "It isn't that people have adjusted themselves to war, but the war had adjusted itself for people. From a hurricane it has become merely a disagreeable draught ... As for putting the end to this adjusted, established war, you can't do it... The war will change its forms, like a stream that sometimes runs underground ... The war'll cease to be war, it will install itself cleverly in men's hearts, so that the town boundary, the bedroom threshold,

---

32  «Освобождаемые еженедельно от ига обыватели даже не замечали этого, так как действия "тиранов" и "освободителей" были до удивительного сходны между собой, притом одеты все были одинаково, донашивая серые шинели царской армии. Кроме того, сказывались традиции мест: в меблированных комнатах, где помещалась Чека, разместилась контрразведка и все десять последующих учреждений однородного характера. Тюрьма оставалась тюрьмой, хотя в нее приводили тех, кто вчера еще сам приводил в нее смутьянов,- ни консерваторией, ни детским садом она не становилась. Даже расстреливали на том же традиционном пустыре, позади острога. Все, приходя, издавали законы о свободе и неприкосновенности личности, вводили осадное положение и смертную казнь за малейшее выражение недовольства дарованной свободой. Засим, в течение краткой мотыльковой жизни, спешили "наладить нормальную жизнь", то есть ограбить как можно больше еврейских часовщиков и успеть расстрелять всех лиц с несимпатичными физиономиями или с неблагозвучными фамилиями.» (ibid., 287)

will become the fronts." (ibid., 163)[33] Contemporary historians agree with Khurenito: this very routinization of violence he speaks about proves to be the most fertile soil for Nazism and Soviet communism alike.[34]

All these and other similar examples of normalized violence in the novel may be identified as the stabilization of the liminal state—something that Khurenito tried to achieve by his provocation. The modern history following his "prompts" had performed this total "liminalization" in a global context, yet despite Khurenito's expectations, this process did not lead intellectual liberation from stale dogmas and absurd beliefs: the dogmas and beliefs changed and multiplied, but new ideologies born from the state of liminality methodically reproduce the same repressions which the revolutions tried to eliminate. As a result, both in Nazism and Soviet communism, the modern cynicism acquired more brutal and bloody forms; now, after the catastrophic war and consequent revolutions, modernity already knows about chaos hidden underneath its grand narratives and tries to smother it once and forever.

The story of Khurenito's performances and provocations, death included, amidst progressively normalizing violence refutes rather than supports Sloterdijk's assumption that "cynicism can only be stemmed by cynicism…" (194). As Erenburg's novel demonstrates, this effect can be achieved only *temporarily and locally*; yet even the most skillful of tricksters—even the Great Provocateur!—cannot stop the logical evolution of cynical reason towards different forms of fascism; the tendency, not invariably but frequently, stemming from the routinization of violence and the stabilization of the

---

33   «Не люди приспособились к войне, война приспособилась к людям. Из урагана она превратилась в сквозняк. ... Зато уничтожить эту приспособившуюся войну нельзя. [...] Она будет менять свои формы, как ручей, порой скрываться под землей и напоминать до отвратительности трогательный мир. ... Война не будет войной, она умело рассосется по сердцам; ограда города, забор дома, порог комнаты станут фронтами.» (ibid., 167)

34   For instance, the similarity between Nazi and Soviet politics of violence is defined as the following: "Mass violence is not simply a matter of police or other repressive state organs. ... It would seem that 'initiatives from below' and public participation or support were important as well, such as what could be called a given polity's 'overall acclimation to violence,' a factor related to that polity's recent experience of war, revolution, and counterrevolution" (Gerlach and Werth, 172).

liminal condition in society. This is why the normalization of violent liminality fails to erase the "universal diffuse cynicism" against which Khulio's personal revolution was intended. Rather, it produces a new, much more terrifying type of cynic: a clerk-murderer, the flexible cog of modernity based on the utopia of homogeneity and its flipside—hatred towards multiplicity of truths: "In my last hours," says Khurenito right before his death, "I should like to see something else, the next stage, the thing still shrouded in mist. Here comes a man with a pile of papers. On his hip, in a special pocket, he carries a Browning. Don't be afraid, he isn't a bandit, he's an honest official. This morning having typed something under a serial number, he has shot a man who has disagreed with him on some issue or another. Now he has dined and is briskly walking to a meeting" (1963: 300).[35] The similarity of this apparition with the socio-psychological type epitomized by Hannah Arendt in *Eichmann in Jerusalem: A Report on the Banality of Evil* (1963), is just stunning. When foreseeing *this* outcome of the modernity's catastrophes, Khurenito refuses to live and decides to allow himself be killed. The logic behind this seemingly irrational decision is quite obvious: if the cynical subject who is mundanely performing the role of a murderer for the sake of social homogeneity, is indeed a "new man," then the trickster's kynical revolution had failed.

At the same time, Khurenito's death for the pair of boots defies any "great ideals" for which a person should sacrifice his or her life, thus challenging any myth-making, including the Christian, and raising the Great Provocateur's final trick as the fully embodied kynical act of freedom from the "logic of history" driven by cynical adaptations to the increasing violence of modernity. In confrontation with new/old cynical grand narratives generated by the routinization of violence, Khurenito does not want to die for any purpose, truth, or symbol, thus elevating his *la raison de Déat*, or even himself as a sacrificial victim, to the "absolute" level. In this he foreshadows the self-destructive freedom epitomized by another tragic trickster—Venichka in *Moskva-*

---

35 «... Мне хочется в последние мои часы прозреть иное, следующее, туманное. Вот идет человек с папкой бумаг. У него сзади в кармане браунинг. Не бойтесь, это не бандит, но честный чиновник. Утром он отстучал нечто на машинке за номером и расстрелял человека, с ним несогласного. Сейчас он пообедал и бодро идет на заседание.» (ibid., 207)

*Petushki* (see chapter 5) and by this connects to the future history of Russian postmodernism, in which *Moskva-Petushki* had become one of the "foundational" texts. Apparently, the foundations of Russian postmodernism were already laid by the Great Provocateur.

# CHAPTER 3

## OSTAP BENDER: THE KING IS BORN

*Dvenadtsat' stuliev (The Twelve Chairs*, 1928) and *Zolotoi telenok (The Golden Calf,* 1931, Soviet book edition 1933), by Ilya Il'f and Evgenii Petrov, hold a unique place in Soviet culture. Although incorporated into the official canon of Socialist Realist satire (a phenomenon whose very existence was constantly put into question), the books "became a pool of quotes for several generations of Soviet intellectuals, who found the diptych to be a nearly overt travesty of propagandistic formulae, newspaper slogans, and the dictums of the founders of 'Marxism-Leninism.' Paradoxically, this 'Soviet literary classic' was read as anti-Soviet literature." (Odesskii and Feldman, 6)

As Mikhail Odesskii and David Feldman (12–25) have shown, *Dvenadtsat' stuliev* was commissioned to Valentin Kataev and his "brigade" in 1927 by Vladimir Narbut, editor-in-chief of the journal *30 days*, which serialized the novel throughout the first half of 1928. Narbut also was a director of a major publishing house, "Zemlia i Fabrika" ("Land and Factory"), which released the novel in book form after the journal publication. Kataev, already a recognized writer, invited two young journalists into his "brigade," his brother Petrov and Il'f—an old acquaintance from Odessa and a colleague at the newspaper *Gudok (Train Whistle)* where Kataev had also worked in the past—letting them develop his story of a treasure hidden inside one chair of a dining room set. However, once Kataev had ascertained that the co-authors were managing fine without a "master's oversight," the older brother left the group and the agreement with the journal and publisher was passed on to Il'f and Petrov. As Odesskii and Feldman suggest, Kataev purposefully acted as the project's "locomotive" by securing a contract for the unfinished novel in his name and then passing it on to his co-authors. These researchers also show that the novel was commissioned as part of the campaign against Trotskyism, waged by the "Stalin wing" throughout 1927. The pretense of attacking Trotskyism gave Il'f and Petrov free reign to mock NEP (which Trotsky actively defended) and left-wing ideology. Later the authors excised a number of chapters which related to Trotskyism too directly, as the subject lost its relevance with the onset of the attack on Bukharin, Stalin's past ally, and the "right opposition" in 1928. Generally speaking, these events benefited the novel as they involuntarily broadened the scope and focus of the satire from mere Trotskyism to include "real socialism" and Soviet ideological language. Of course, even the first novel went far beyond the boundaries of the politically motivated commission, mostly thanks to the figure of Ostap Bender. It was Bender who filled Il'f and Petrov's novels with his own, alternative and unorthodox, ideology: himself embodying the discourse of *total irony* and *kynical trickery* as a form of social resistance and even a type of romantic pose, which was later inherited by several generations of Soviet readers.

The novel's first critics sensed this. It is no accident that Soviet criticism of the 1920s and 30s at first accused Il'f and Petrov's novels of "thematic pettiness" (*melkotem'e*) and "insufficiently profound hatred for the class enemy." For instance, *Dvenadtsat' stuliev* provoked criticism along the lines of: "… By laughing at the nincompoopery of daily life and speaking ironically of the representatives of philistinism, the novel does not rise to the height of satire… the authors passed real life by—it is not reflected in their observations, their artistic lens only caught the types who are leaving the stage of life: the doomed, 'former people.'" (Sitkov, 38) Even after favorable publications in *Literaturnaia gazeta*, such as an article by Anatolii Tarasenkov that took *Dvenadtsat' stuliev* beyond the dangerous discussion on the necessity of satire in a perfect Soviet society (Tarasenkov), Il'f and Petrov's novel instilled unease in the Soviet official organs.[1] It is a small wonder, then, that *Zolotoi telenok*, after the initial (abridged) publication in serial form in 1931, was released as a novel in Germany, Austria, the U.S. and England two years prior to the first book edition in the USSR. The publication

---

1  See: Zorich, Selivanovskii, Troshchenko.

would not have occurred at all if Gorky had not pressed A.S. Bubnov, the then People's Commissar of Enlightenment.² Anatolii Lunacharsky (a former Commissar of Enlightenment) supplied a foreword to the American edition in which he described Ostap Bender in the following words: "This unusually dexterous, daring, ingenious, and, in his own way, great-hearted rogue, Bender, who showers derisions, aphorisms, paradoxes around him, seems the only real person in the midst of these microscopic vipers [the novel's characters—ordinary Soviet 'philistines']... This Bender is more attractive and more human than those who surround him. His band is lost in the rays of light shed by its talented leader who is almost a genius." (Lunacharsky, xvii) Having said that, Lunacharsky carefully disclaimed: "… Further sympathy for such a type [Ostap Bender] assumes the natures of anarchism." (ibid., xviii)

1. Ostap Bender and Koreyko by Kukryniksy

The response of the critics of the 1960s–70s to the renewed interest in Il'f and Petrov's diptych and the new popularity of its protagonist, who was to become a real hero for the new generation, did not add much to Lunacharsky's duality. Thus, Abram Vulis, in the first book written about Il'f and Petrov, argues that the authors "underestimated

---

2   See about this in Munblit and Raskin, 209.

the attractiveness of this, essentially negative character who was armed with their fabulous irony" (Vulis, 270), while Ostap's "negative" characteristics derive from the fact that "rejecting both Soviet power and its enemies, Bender finds a place between two warring forces." (idem., 278) Vladimir Sappak formulated a similar idea in "Manichean" terms: Bender is "a negative character who fulfils a positive function. [...] His ability to see the real value of things [...] his talent for ridicule, mockery and parody towards everything that deserves to be ridiculed, constitutes the immense positive charge carried by Ostap Bender..." (Sappak, 123)[3]

2. Ostap Bender by Kukryniksy

Yurii Shcheglov and Alexander Zholkovsky were the first critics to dispense with this awkward interpretational construct. In Shcheglov's view, the character Bender is formed at the intersection of two

---

3   Somewhat similar interpretation of Ostap is presented in Ianovskaia, 94–107.

archetypal models: the rogue and the "demonic hero." Bender's roguish genealogy is self-evident—the scholar indicates numerous parallels with the characters of Mark Twain, O. Henry's "noble conmen," some of Chaplin's heroes, Babel's Benya Krik, Bulgakov's Ametistov (also see Likhachev), as well as older examples of rogues from Lazarillo de Tormes and Gil Blas de Santillane, to Gogol's Chichikov and Dickens's Mr. Alfred Jingle, and Sam Weller from *The Pickwick Papers*.[4]

All the same, Ostap's intellectual brilliance, the virtuosity of his parodic aphoristic formulae, his masterful manipulation of linguistic stereotypes, his aptitude at momentarily recognizing people's weaknesses and exploiting them for his own benefit, multiplied by his charm, all bring him into the "scattered family of intellectually sophisticated heroes, rising above the 'crowd' and lonely atop their Olympus... Such a hero habitually gives himself the right to dispose of 'little people' and their lives as cheap material for his titanic experiments... In less appealing variations he exhibits such traits as emptiness, cynicism, a mockery of everything and all, and the Devil's famous lack of a stable character, his endless multiplicity of masks and guises." (Shcheglov, 31) A few years before Shcheglov, Maya Kaganskaia, and Zeev Bar-Sella demonstrated parallels between Ostap and Bulgakov's Woland (see Kaganskaia and Bar-Sella). Shcheglov and Lurie point at a resemblance between Ostap and Erenburg's Khulio Khurenito ("the great provocateur"—"the great combinator") and even Sherlock Holmes (death and resurrection; the likeness in plot between "Six Napoleons" and *Dvenadtsat' stuliev* was noticed as early as in 1929 [Kashintsev]).

Though presented ironically, Bender's romanticism and sometimes "demonism" is apparent in several of his features and particularly evident in *Zolotoi telenok*; examples include Ostap's resurrection after the finale of *Dvenadtsat' stuliev*, his agency's specialization in "horns and hooves," his debate with the catholic priests over Kozlevich's soul (analogous to his tormenting Father Fyodor in the first novel), and his tragic defeat during the crossing of the Dniestr—the mythological boundary between this world and the other—completing the realization of Bender's own maxim that "the ice is moving"; this scene

---

4   Viktor Shklovsky was one of the first to detect the genealogy of Ostap in rogue novels. See Shklovsky, 1934.

is comparable to the "infernal" depiction of the Crimean earthquake which accompanies the loss of hope for the recovery of the 11<sup>th</sup> chair in the second-to-last chapter of *Dvenadtsat' stuliev*.

However, both as the rogue and as the "demonic" hero, embodying a philosophical superiority over the "crowd," Ostap appears as the sole *free* character in the whole Soviet world. Shcheglov suggests that in Il'f and Petrov's novels the characters' involvement in the utopian project of building the communist future serves as the main criterion for their aesthetic evaluation by the authors (22–24). This principle of aesthetic evaluation, however, does not appear to extend to Ostap (at least until the finale of *Zolotoi telenok*). His virtuoso juggling of masks, his glorious disdain for all things Soviet ("Building socialism bores me"[5] [2009: 58]), his principled refusal to engage with the collective utopia and focus on his personal quest instead does not undermine Ostap's charm in the least, but rather testifies to his artistry and intellectual superiority.

Furthermore, as Shcheglov shows, Ostap mocks the old pre-revolutionary and the new Soviet symbols, discourses and ideas *in equal measure*: "Bureaucracy, slogans, ideological campaigns, the domestic chaos of contemporary Russia are, for Ostap, merely the various forms and faces of universal stupidity on par with monarchist plots, the squabbles of communal life and personal eccentricities, such as Ellochka's competition with fashionable foreign lionesses… Perhaps for socialism it is this failure to distinguish the Soviet from the rest that constitutes the most hurtful aspect of Bender's ridicule" (45).

Alexander Zholkovsky also proposes interpreting Ostap as a paradoxical poet of individual freedom:

> The official view on individual rights (the collective is all, the individual—nothing, morally suspect, and most likely criminal) is inseparably intertwined with the Western view, furthermore both are extolled and mocked, perhaps even with a certain spiritual advantage in the West's favor. Ostap walks through the Soviet world like a certain knight of the bourgeois image, deriving his values, Don Quixote-like, from an idealized historical past, but

---

5  «Мне скучно строить социализм» (Il'f and Petrov 1995b: 25).

appearing a head above his surroundings. It is not only, as is sometimes written, that Ostap is a charming criminal, but that he is a charming individualist, at his limit—a charming anti-Soviet, though this charm is offered with a heavy pro-Soviet flavor. (49-50)

This last paradox points at Ostap's ability to create or call into life certain anti-structural elements within the very system, in other words, to perform one of the most significant functions of the trickster.[6]

## OSTAP AS TRICKSTER

Just like the other characters discussed in this study, Bender represents only certain aspects of the trickster archetype, reducing or altogether effacing other components. The traits that are most defining of Il'f and Petrov's hero are: ambivalence in union with liminality, artistry and vitality that are inseparable from a very specific sense of the sacred.

**Ambivalence/liminality.** Even the brief history of Ostap Bender's reception and interpretation cited above, illustrates the ambivalence of his image. This ambivalence is also validated by Ostap's position within the system of characters in both novels. The diptych presents Ostap in the company of tricksters who belong to a lower order than he does. On the one hand, the others double some of Ostap's isolated features; on the other hand, they accentuate his superiority. Bender's intellectual power and multifacetedness, as well as his animal vitality and artistic flexibility, stand out when he is contrasted with Vorobianinov, while his resemblance to this character affords Ostap a certain aristocratism. By the novel's end, Vorobianinov comes to resemble Ostap, although he acquires only "the traits of determination and cruelty." (1992: 386)[7]. By killing Ostap, Kisa loses the remnants of his own humanity: "It was an insane, impassioned wild cry—the cry of a she-wolf shot through the

---

6   For a detailed analysis of Soviet and post-Soviet critical responses to the character of Ostap Bender from the 1920s to the 2000s see in Fisher, 142–220.

7   «В характере появились не свойственные ему раньше черты решительности и жестокости» (1995a: 402).

body..."⁸ (1992: 394) At the same time Bender, although sacrificed, not only secures the reader's compassion, but even resurrects himself in the next novel, as though a god defying death. Ostap's three partners in *Zolotoi telenok*, clearly below him with respect to wit and talent, only highlight Bender's superiority through their adoration and failures alike. At the same time they really do become his "milk brothers": Shura Balaganov accentuates Ostap's strength and youthfulness, Kozlevich brings out Ostap's "angelic" side, and Panikovsky, the "demonic." It is also possible to detect in Ostap's "milk brothers" representation of three cultural/religious traditions—Russian/Orthodox (Balaganov), Jewish (Panikovsky), and Polish/Catholic (Kozlevich)—which, on the one hand, adds a sense of universalism to the representation of Ostap, and on the other, emphasizes his position as a liminal mediator situated "betwixt and between."

Ostap acts as a **mediator** between various—social, cultural, and geographical—spheres of the Soviet world, and this function of his becomes the axis of both novels. As a mediator, Ostap Bender is himself inevitably liminal. His liminality is accentuated by his unclear social status and education; certainly he is a "gentleman of the road" in the proper sense. Curiously, in a world where one's class origins are decisive, Ostap turns this, seemingly predetermined, identity into a game: my father, he would say, "was a Turkish citizen," (1992: 340, 2009: 58)⁹ his mother "a countess who lived off labor-less profits,"¹⁰ and he is repeatedly—albeit ironically—called by authors a "descendant of the janissaries" (*potomok ianycharov*). The sum of these pseudo-romantic quotations transfers the very question of "social origins" to a literary or fantastic dimension.¹¹

At the same time, while functioning beyond the bounds of the

---

8   «Крик его, бешеный, страстный и дикий, - крик простреленной навылет волчицы...» (ibid., 408).
9   «Отец... был турецко-поданный» (1995а: 366)ь, «Был у меня папа, турецкий поданный...» (1995b: 25).
10   «Мать... была графиней и жила нетрудовыми доходами» (1995а: 366).
11   Mikhail Odesskii and David Feldman decipher "the Turkish origin" as a non-ambiguous indication of Bender being a Jew, since Jews from Odessa frequently accepted the Turkish citizenship in order to save their children from Russian discrimination and, most importantly, from the recruitment to the Russian army (see their commentary in Il'f and Petrov 1997: 467).

text, as a personage belonging to both the official and the unofficial subcultures, Ostap mediates between the symbolic planes of the Soviet ideological discourses and the concrete social experience of Soviet people. Bender's quasi-legitimate presence in the Socialist Realist canon points at certain voids, certain liminal zones of indeterminacy within the Soviet discourse. We will return to the contents of these uncertain zones, noting for the moment that in the diptych, Bender frequently creates artificial, although clearly liminal, situations—something that naturally follows from his function as a trickster-mediator.

A particularly telling example of a liminal situation is found in the "Alliance of the Sword and the Plowshare" chapter in *Dvenadtsat' stuliev*, formed by Ostap for the sole purpose of extracting money from the circle of Stargorod's old elites, in order to pay for his wedding with M-me Gritsatsueva. At the meeting, Bender inundates those gathered with monarchist and "conspiratorial" formulae—for example: "You support Kirillov, I hope" (1992: 126); "Russia will not forget you" (ibid., 127);" Which regiment were you in?" (ibid., 130); "The West will help us! Stand firm" (ibid., 130); "As a representative of private capital you cannot remain deaf to the pleas of the motherland" (ibid., 130–131); "…I warn you, we have a long reach." (ibid., 131)[12] At the same time, Ostap declares the meeting's stated goal to be a charity collection for homeless children. This goal cannot be interpreted as "conspiratorial," though it is packaged in the clichés of a pre-revolutionary and not at all Soviet liberal discourse: "It is only the young children, the waifs and strays, who are not looked after. These flowers of the street, or, as the white-collar proletarians call them, 'flowers in asphalt,' deserve a better lot. We must help them, gentlemen of the jury and, gentlemen of the jury, we will do so." (ibid.,131–32)[13] The meaning of the speech is deeply ambiguous; it may equally be read as a call for anti-Soviet activity and as proof of Bender's and the entire "Alliance's" political

---

12   «Вы, надеюсь, кирилловец?», «Россия вас не забудет!», Вы в каком полку служили?» «Вы дворянин?... Вы, надеюсь, остались им и сейчас? Крепитесь», «Запад нам поможет. Крепитесь», «Вы как представитель частного капитал не можете остаться глухим к стонам родины», «... у нас, предупреждаю, длинные руки» (1995а: 206, 208-209).

13   «Одни лишь маленькие дети, беспризорные дети, находятся без призора. Эти цветы улицы, или, как выражаются пролетарии умственного труда, цветы на асфальте заслуживают лучшей участи. Мы, господа присяжные заседатели, должны им помочь» (ibid., 210).

loyalty. By creating such an internally contradictory discourse, Ostap exploits two strong feelings yoking the Stargorod "aristocracy"—hatred for the Soviet regime—and terror at being drawn into a risky political situation: "'Two years of solitary confinement at best,' thought Kisliarskii, beginning to tremble. 'Why did I have to come here?'" (ibid., 131)[14]

At first sight, in this scene Bender overcomes a fundamental opposition between permitted and anti-Soviet public activity. However, his game is much more complicated. He sets up a situation where political taboos are broken and draws the gathered party into this transgression. In other words, Bender creates a liminal situation in which he feels thoroughly at home ("Ostap was carried away. Things seemed to be going well" [ibid., 130][15]), while regular citizens feel a very understandable horror at the disintegrating order of things around them ("Kisliarskii became [pale] like marble. That day he had had such a good, quiet dinner of chicken gizzards, soup with nuts, and knew nothing of the terrible 'Alliance of the Sword and the Plowshare.'" [ibid., 131][16]) At the same time, Bender offers his "co-conspirators" a way out of this unbearable (for them) situation, in the form of help for vagrant children. Briefly put, he creates a particular sort of ritual transgression, a temporary chaos, a limited liminal situation—akin to those that traditionally involve the trickster in mythology and folklore. In order to end the ritual transgression and the accompanying feeling of perilous freedom, a sacrifice is necessary. Ostap activates this exact symbolic logic by collecting money from the "assembly."

The organization formed by Ostap is suspiciously reminiscent of the infamous government operations "Sindikat-2" (1921–1924) and "Trest" (1921–1927).[17] In both cases the OGPU created a fictitious anti-Soviet underground organization (in operation "Trest" the organization was called the "Monarchist Union of Central Russia,"

---

14 «В лучшем случае, два года со строгой изоляцией, - подумал Кислярский, начиная дрожать.—Зачем я сюда пришел?» (ibid., 210).
15 «Остапа несло. Дело как будто налаживалось» (ibid., 209).
16 «Кислярский сделался мраморным. Еще сегодня он так вкусно и спокойно обедал, ел куриные пупочки, бульон с орешками и нечего не знал о страшном «союзе меча и орала» (ibid., 210).
17 See Brook-Shepherd; Andrew and Mitrokhin; Costello and Tsarev; Spence.

which cannot help but recall Ostap's "monarchism") which served to attract not only such famous opponents of Bolshevism as Boris Savinkov and Sidney Reilly (in the course of these operations both were lured to the USSR and executed), but also dissidents living in the USSR who were willing to fight the Soviet regime. At the time *Dvendatsat' stuliev* was written the details of both operations were widely known, which is why Ostap's "conspiracy" could not help but evoke the corresponding associations.

Analogously, in *Zolotoi telenok,* Ostap performs a "mock" internal police investigation of Koreyko's machinations, discovering along the way that "Hercules" acts as a façade for the "underground millionaire." It is no accident that Ostap's investigation takes place against the backdrop of an official "purge," to say nothing of the fact that Bender effectively exploits his victims' fear of the arrest by the OGPU. Consider this scene:

> The commissioner of hooves appeared in the corridor. Swinging his enormous hands like a member of the Royal Guard, Balaganov walked up to Berlaga and handed him a summon:

> > TO: COMREDE BERLEGE.
> > UPON RECEIPT YOUR ERE
> > DIRECTED TO REPORT
> > IMMIDIATELEY FOR THE EXPLICETION
> > OF CERTEIN CIRCUMSTENCES.

> The paper bore the seal of the Chernomorsk Division of the Arbatov Bureau of Horn and Hoof Procurement and a round stamp, the text of which was rather difficult to decipher, even if such a thing had entered Berlaga's head. But the fugitive accountant was so dispirited by all his troubles that he just asked, "Can I call home?"

CHAPTER THREE

"There won't be any calling home," said the commissioner of hooves glowering. (2009: 220)[18]

Obviously imitating and thus mocking the ritual of the arrest, Ostap, however, does not take his provocation to the level of "full exposure"—which is something, by the way, that Soviet critics berated him for.[19] Unlike the OGPU, and even unlike Bulgakov's Woland, Ostap does not ruin his victims, but leaves them in a suspended state—already exposed, they expect the inevitable (or so they believe) repressions. The transformation undergone by Ostap's "clients" after his interrogation is stupendous:

> Yegor Skumbriyevich had undergone an amazing transformation. No more than half an hour before, the waves had welcomed to its bosom the most active of public servants, the kind of person about whom no less a figure than comrade Niderlandyuk, the chairman of the local union committee, used to say "Other people might let us down, but not Skumbrievich." Except that Skumbrievich had let them down. And how!
> What the little summer wave deposited on shore was

---

18 «В коридоре показался уполномоченный по копытам. Гвардейски размахивая ручищами, Балаганов подступил к Берлаге и вручил ему повестку:
—«Тов. Бэрлагэ. С получэниэм сэго прэдлагаэтся нэмэдлэнно явиться для выяснэния нэкоторых обстоятэльств».
—Бумажка была снабжена штампом Черноморского отделения Арбатовской конторы по заготовке рогов и копыт и круглой печатью, содержание которой разобрать было бы трудновато, даже если бы Берлаге это пришло в голову. Но беглый бухгалтер был так подавлен свалившимися на него бедами, что только спросил:
—Домой позвонить можно? —Чего там звонить,—хмуро сказал заведующий копытами.» (1995b: 161–162).

19   Iakov El'sberg notorious by his collaboration with the NKVD, in his book *Voprosy teorii satiry* (1957) criticized the writers for not bringing Bender's provocation with "The Alliance" to the "logical" conclusion: "Those who depict [Bender's] cons as a prankish parody of the real conspiracy, are too one-sided. [...] The reflection of the anti-Soviet activity in such an innocent way, testifies to the fact that the satirical principle is not accomplished in this work with sufficient consistency" (334–5). Yurii Borev in his *Vvedenie v estetiku* (1964) commented this interpretation with a sarcastic remark: "It is a pity that I. Il'f and E. Petrov were not mentored in a professional way by Ia. El'sberg. He could have taught them wonderfully how to make a large-scale conspirator and organizer of the anti-Soviet activities from such a nice swindler (милый ловкач) as Ostap Bender" (Borev 1964: 100).

not a wondrous woman's body with the head of a shaving Englishman, but a sort of shapeless sack full of mustard and horseradish.[20] (2009: 244–5)

He [Ostap] gave Chamois Mikhailovna a sleepy look and walked off, swinging a yellow file folder tied with bootlaces. Polykhaev sprang out after him, emerging from the life-giving shade of the palms and sycamore figs. Chamois took one look at her tall friend and fell back speechlessly onto the little square matt that alleviated the rigidity of her chair. How fortunate that the other employees had already gone home and couldn't see their boss right now! A diamond tear sat on his mustache like a little bird on a branch. Polykhaev blinked his eyes with astonishing rapidity and rubbed his hands together so energetically that it looked as if he wanted start a fire with friction, in the manner of the savages of Oceania. He ran after Ostap, arching his back and smiling embarrassingly.[21] (ibid., 252–3)

These descriptions cannot help but remind us of the reactions produced by Soviet state terror. Bender robs people of their social masks and armor—leaving behind a formless ("a sort of shapeless sack full of mustard and horseradish") or radically primitivized existence ("rubbed his hands together so energetically that it looked as if he wanted start

---

20 «Удивительное превращение произошло с Егором Скумбриевичем. Еще полчаса назад волна приняла на себя активнейшего общественника, такого человека, о котором даже председатель месткома товарищ Нидерландюк говорил: «Кто-кто, а Скумбриевич не подкачает.» А ведь подкачал Скумбриевич. И как подкачал! Мелкая летняя волна доставила на берег уже не дивное женское тело с головой бреющегося англичанина, а какой-то бесформенный бурдюк, наполненный горчицей и хреном» (1995b: 183).

21 «[Остап] сонно посмотрел на Серну Михайловну и пошел прочь, размахивая желтой папкой с ботиночными тесемками. Вслед за ним из-под живительной тени пальм и сикомор вынырнул Полыхаев. Серна взглянула на своего высокого друга и без звука опустилась на квадратный матрасик, смягчавший жесткость ее стула. Как хорошо, что сотрудники уже разошлись и в эту минуту не могли видеть своего начальника! В усах у него, как птичка в ветвях, сидела алмазная слеза. Полыхаев удивительно быстро моргал глазами и так энергично потирал руки, будто бы хотел трением добыть огонь по способу, принятому среди дикарей Океании. Он побежал за Остапом, позорно улыбаясь и выгибая стан» (ibid., 189).

a fire with friction, in the manner of the savages of Oceania"). Ostap drags his victims into a liminal situation and leaves them there. But the irony of the shift is that Bender resides in the same state permanently! Here we see the most important effect of Bender's trickery—he does not so much create liminal situations as reveal liminalities with which the novels' characters *already live* in close proximity (if unknowingly). By his very existence, Bender proves that liminality grants a certain freedom from predestined (or concealed and substituted) identity and social dependency. But his "clients" are so afraid of this freedom that they prefer—like all the inductees of "The Alliance of the Sword and the Plowshare" in *Dvenadtsat' stuliev*—to go running to the OGPU to eagerly vindicate themselves and their "comrades in arms."

**Artistry:** Shcheglov proposes that if in the first novel Bender "is still, in part, described as a lowlife (*bosiak*)," then from the first pages of the second novel he "appears as a being of a higher order ... his roguishness emerges here intellectualized, seems like art for art's sake; Bender is a mere conman no more, but the "great combinator"/"smooth operator." (Shcheglov 38–9). (Incidentally, this was the working title of *Zolotoi telenok*.[22]) Bender's artistry is most evident in his manipulation of language, or rather the many languages of Soviet culture. Pre-revolutionary quotations and clichés of Soviet bureaucratic lingo mostly occur side-by-side in Bender's speech; more often he creates "eccentric and mocking hybrids," which knock the "last remnants of sense from pre-packaged formulae." (ibid., 43)

The irresolvable contradiction between incompatible components, between appearance and essence, between old cliché and Soviet newspeak, is resolved in the majority of Bender's witticisms through a joyful and ironic game that does not remove the contradictions, but makes them laughable and therefore insignificant. The artistic estrangement of colliding clichés simultaneously devalues the various grand narratives and authoritative discourses that stand behind them. Among all the Soviet tricksters, Ostap is perhaps the one who most clearly illustrates the essentially *linguistic* nature of the Soviet world. The majority of his triumphs are based on virtuoso language games: the manipulation of discourses, linguistic gestures, and masks—which

---

22  "Now we writing a novel under the title *The Great Combinator* [*The smooth operator*]," states "Dvoinaia biografiia" ("The Double Autobiography," 1929) (Il'f and Petrov 1961: 24).

in turn yield a tangible material profit. At the same time, Ostap makes it evident that the "new" Soviet world is built on analogous language games. All of Bender's formulae are parodic reproductions of the *unintentional* and often serious hybrids of incompatible discourses and symbols that feature in the diptych. Consider, for instance, "The Odessa bakery 'Moscow bagels'" (1995a: 394), the movie theatre "*Kapitalii*" (1995b: 142); numerous Soviet posters "written mainly in Church Slavonic script" (2009: 99); or the grumbling of a "simple peasant" (ibid., 181) Mitrich, "who was once His Imperial Highness's court chamberlain" (ibid., 179), about his neighbor the famed pilot Sevriugov, who was allegedly lost during a polar expedition: "'Icebergs!' Mitrich said mockingly. 'Now that's something we can understand. Ten years after the last Romanov, ten years later we're even worse off. We got our Eisbersg, our Weissbergs, our Eisenbergs, and all those Rabinoviches.'" (ibid., 181)[23]

In much the same way, Bender's brilliant "Complete Celebrator's Kit, and Irreplaceable Aid for the Composition of Jubilee Articles and Timekeepers' Fuilletons, As Well As Ceremonial Poems, Odes, and Troparia" (ibid., 345)[24]—the "universal generative model of Soviet art" in Zholkovsky's words (48)—not only exposes the explosive mixture, which makes up the Soviet official and semi-official discourse, but also parodically relates to the "universal stamp," (2009: 250)[25] quite seriously utilized by Polykhaev, the director of "Hercules."

**Vitality/ sacredness:** As was said, Ostap is not the only trickster in the diptych. It must be noted that all other tricksters in the novels meet ultimate defeat: Vorobianinov goes insane; Panikovsky dies; Balaganov is caught committing a minor, impulsive theft while having 50,000 rubles in his pocket; finally Koreyko is forced to hand over a million rubles to Ostap. The mythological trickster also constantly meets defeat, which only spurs him on to new adventures. This logic applies to Ostap as well. Ostap appears in a laughable (or sad) state more than

---

23 «—Айсберги! - говорил Митрич насмешливо. - Это мы понять можем. Десять лет как жизни нет. Все Айсберги, Вайсберги, Айзенберги, всякие там Рабиновичи» (1995b: 128).

24 «Торжественный комплект незаменимое пособие для сочинения юбилейных статей, табельных фельетонов, а также парадных стихотворений, од и топарей» (ibid., 264).

25 «Универсальный штемпель» (ibid., 184).

once: there is the scene of the auction, when he loses the whole set of chairs due to his lack of money; the demonstration of his hand-made billboard while serving as an artist on the boat *Skriabin*; his shameful loss to the Vasiuki chess-enthusiasts; the unreasonable spending of the 500 rubles gained from Kisliarskii on a drinking binge with Kisa, and thus wasting time that ultimately results in the loss of the last chair. In the end, only Ostap's naivety can explain his lack of caution at the finale of *Dvenadtsat' stuliev*, for which he pays with his life (albeit temporarily). Equally telling are: the heroes' exposure during the car race in *Zolotoi telenok*; Ostap's and Koreyko's duels—when Ostap visits Aleksand Ivanovich, trying to return the stolen ten thousand rubles, and also when Koreyko escapes from Bender using a mock gas attack to his benefit—both of which end with the smooth operator's sound defeat; the fire at "Crow's Nest" that destroys Ostap's "magic bag"; the impossibility for Bender, and Koreyko alike, to enjoy the beautiful life of a millionaire; Bender's unsuccessful attempt at acting as the benefactor to Balaganov and Kozlevich; the fiasco when he tries to win Zosia's heart; and of course, the final scene of *Zolotoi telenok*, where the "smooth operator" is robbed and beaten by Romanian border patrol on the Dniestr ice.

All of these are examples of wastefulness that prompt the reader, as was pointed out above, to pose questions about the specific relationship between the trickster and the sacred. Bender is associated with representatives of the sacred throughout the plot of the diptych. Significantly, he opposes Father Fyodor in *Dvenadtsat' stuliev*, engages in an anti-religious debate with the Catholic priests in *Zolotoi telenok*; his speech (as was noted by Shcheglov in his commentary to the novels) is interspersed with numerous evangelical and biblical intertexts. But the trickster's notion of the sacred is still of a different order than religiosity (even subverted religiosity).

Perhaps the finales of both novels are the most illuminating instances with respect to Bender's relation to the sacred. In *Dvenadtsat' stuliev*, Bender, on finding the last chair, is murdered by his partner; he will never know that the treasures hidden in the chair have long been found and spent to build the Palace of Culture, where the last—empty—chair is kept. In *Zolotoi telenok*, Ostap, having converted the million into luxury goods, is robbed by Romanian border guards while trying to leave the USSR. Critics have often written about the "forced" character of

Bender's defeats at each novel's conclusion. If in *Dvenadtsat' stuliev* one is startled by the unrealistic speed with which the treasures hidden in the chair are converted into the Palace of Culture (the chair is auctioned off in January, the Palace is built by October of the same year), in *Zolotoi telenok* the situation is much more complicated.

The "ideal plan" (see Shcheglov, 12-14) of socialism, with which the new millionaire must clash in the authors' conception, is far from ideal. The grandiose celebration of the railway junction is suspiciously reminiscent of the public launch of the tram in *Dvenadtsat' stuliev* (chapter 13 "Breathe Deeper: You're Excited!"). It is significant that the completed railroad does not actually work: Ostap and Koreyko ride away on camels, but it is entirely unclear how the other builders of Turkmenistan-Siberian railroad leave the desert. The town, transformed by socialism, "delights" with "alabaster dust" (2009: 375), and pearly soup from the factory-kitchen, "surrounded by tiled walls and long ribbons of flypaper hanging from the ceiling"(ibid., 376), while "tambourines and cymbals" are replaced by "The Bebel and Paganini Grand Symphonic Quartet." (ibid., 377)

However, Ostap's mishaps—intended to undermine his faith that "the dear little golden calf still has a certain power in our country" (ibid., 378)[26]—seem quite artificial against the backdrop of the preceding plot. After all, Koreyko's capitalist success and the secret activities of "Hercules" testify to the social cynicism that has overtaken the economy in the USSR: behind a socialist façade, a "black market," true to the principles of capitalism, blooms and bears rich fruit. Did Ostap, having recently exposed the affairs of Koreyko and "Hercules," really forget all about the shadow economy, thus trying, with idiotic persistence, to utilize his million legitimately?

Furthermore, in *Dvenadtsat' stuliev* and *Zolotoi telenok* alike, all of Ostap's defeats are situated within the large mythological cycle of temporary death, inevitably followed by the resurrection of the immortal trickster. In *Dvenadtsat' stuliev* this includes not only Ostap's murder, but the scene of the Crimean earthquake where, having realized that the eleventh chair contains nothing, "the smooth operator fainted" (1992: 384) and then spoke "like a patient recovering from typhus." (ibid., 384) Already in the next chapter Ostap's "energy and

---

26 «Золотой телёночек в нашей стране еще имеет кое-какую власть» (ibid., 291).

good spirits were inexhaustible." (ibid., 386) In *Zolotoi telenok*, Ostap directly mentions his resurrection ("The surgeons were barely able to save my young life, for which I am deeply obliged." [2009: 365][27])

Another instance of temporary death is Ostap's "poisoning" during the mock gas attack—the point of this scene is, of course, the escape of the seemingly demoralized and defeated Koreyko's from the "smooth operator." After this death resurrection follows as it should—during the scene where Ostap *laughs* at his partners, who sawed through Koreyko's exercise weights. Bender's laughter in this scene is clearly hyperbolical:

> The smooth operator fell back on his chair without saying a word. He started to shake, grasping the air with his hands. Then volcanic peals erupted from his throat and tears ran down his face, and laughter rang out in the bomb shelter, a terrible laughter expressing all the exhaustion of the previous night and all his disappointments in the battle with Koreyko, a battle the milk brothers had parodied so pitifully. [...] Laughter was still bubbling up in Ostap, prickling him with a thousand little Narzan needles, but now he felt refreshed and rejuvenated, like a person who's gone through all the barbershop's formal procedures: friendship with the razor, acquaintance with the scissor, the light shower of eau-de-cologne, and even the grooming of the eyebrows with a special little brush. (ibid., 286)[28]

(The motif of resurrection is enhanced here by the reference to "friendship with the razor," which resonates with the finale of *Dvenadtsat' stuliev*.)

---

27 «Хирурги еле-еле спасли мою молодую жизнь, за что я им глубоко признателен» (ibid., 280).
28 «Не говоря ни слова, великий комбинатор свалился на стул. Он затрясся, ловя руками воздух. Потом из его горла вырвались вулканические раскаты, из глаз выбежали слезы, и смех, в котором сказалось все утомление ночи, все разочарование в борьбе с Корейко, так жалко спародированное молочными братьями .... Смех еще покалывал Остапа тысячью нарзанных иголочек, а он уже чувствовал себя освеженным и помолодевшим, как человек, прошедший все парикмахерские инстанции....» (ibid., 216).

Finally, an extended state of temporary death is played out in the last chapters of *Zolotoi telenok*, after Ostap acquires his million. It is no wonder that he states, again before his victory: "The carnival is over!" (ibid., 305)[29] and even more definitively: "Now our acting career is finished." (ibid., 311)[30] No less tellingly, Ostap and Koreyko's journey through the desert takes them to the "ashen city of the dead" (*pepel'nyi gorod mertvykh*, 1995b: 287), the black sea pigeons coo "*umru, umru*" (will die, will die) (1995b: 313), and Ostap adds "I don't want to live a life everlasting. I want to die." (2009: 407)[31] Another sign of temporary death is Ostap's loss of his sense of triumph and his strange desire to be accepted by the young crowd of students, uninteresting except for their youth, who nonetheless perceive Ostap's tricks with "the superiority of the viewer over the master of ceremonies." (ibid., 400)[32]. At the same time, we witness the culmination of this liminal state, namely Bender's crushing defeat during his attempt to leave the USSR, which returns the hero back to life and to himself. If, in Ostap's words "going abroad is the myth of life after death" (ibid., 384)[33], then the fiasco at the Romanian border acquires an ambivalent meaning: it is another *resurrection* of the invulnerable trickster.

All these transformations indicate a link to the mythological trickster's mediation between life and death (which elucidates Ostap's light-hearted approach to death, conveyed, for instance, in his self-written epitaph in *Dvenadtsat' stuliev* [1992: 339-40]). Ostap's recurring resurrections relate to the trickster's boundless vitality. Simultaneously, there is a sense of a greater underlying logic: on gaining that which he seeks—the twelfth chair; Koreyko's million—Bender inevitably loses something—his life in the first novel; his wealth in the second. The constancy of this logic presupposes its reversal: by losing everything Bender gains something greater—but what?

First and foremost, Bender gains the experience of *passage through death*: be it a "playful" death, as in the scene of the "gas attack"; a symbolic one, as on the Dniestr ice; or a real one at the finale of *Dvenadtsat' stuliev*. This experience clearly singles out Bender from the

---

29  «Карнавал окончился!» (ibid., 232).
30  «Теперь наша артистическая карьера окончилась» (ibid., 237).
31  «... я не хочу жить вечно. Я хочу умереть» (ibid., 315).
32  «... превосходство зрителя перед конферансье» (ibid., 310).
33  «... заграница—это миф о загробной жизни» (ibid., 296).

other characters, defining an alternate structure of his personality: instead of living through a variety of faces/masks, Bender lives out numerous *lives*, united by moments of nonbeing—the experience of the Real (in Lacan's terminology). Illuminatingly, when the German journalist Heinrich tells the story of Adam and Eve, in which he tries to refute modernization with the logic of "eternal return" ("What's the big idea, sticking your iron in my face? It's the spirit of things that counts! Everything will be repeated! There'll be a Thirty Years' War, and a Hundred years' War, and once again they'll start burning people who dare to say that the earth is round. [...] Everything will be repeated, everything. Even the Eternal Yid will wander the earth, just like before..." [ibid., 337-8])[34], Bender responds to the journalist with the story of the Wandering (in Russian—Eternal) Jew killed *finally and irreversibly* by the nationalist peasant army of the warlord Petliura. With this sad myth, as well as with his existential style, Ostap affirms the *end of all eternities* and the same time *the endlessness of everything final:* each catastrophe breeds new life; each achievement leads to catastrophe.

This logic resembles the carnival as described by Bakhtin, but differs from it as well. Bakhtin, in his work on Rabelais, extols the "joyful relativity of being," which transforms falls and degradations (and at the limit—death) into the birth and renewal of the world. The trickster is seemingly at the center of the carnival world, but the very centrality of this position belies his engagement in the chaotic whirlpool of the carnival. The trickster maintains "the right to be 'other' in this world" (Bakhtin, 159), which Bakhtin ascribes to the jester, rogue, and fool. Ostap, though in the center of the Soviet social carnival and seemingly possessing the necessary autonomy and distance from the other characters, is nonetheless drawn into the "whirlpool" and even sacrificed regularly. In other words, Il'f and Petrov radically modernize the trickster's position. Ostap not only embodies the ambivalent vitality, but also the sacrifice as the tragic price of the social carnival. Through his temporary deaths he provides the fuel without which there would

---

34 «Что вы мне тычете в глаза свое железо? Важен дух! Все повторится! Будет и тридцатилетняя война, и столетняя война, и опять будут сжигать людей, которые посмеют сказать, что земля круглая [...] Все, все повторится! И Вечный Жид по-прежнему будет скитаться по земле...» (ibid., 258).

be no eternal turmoil; he supplies the finality that guarantees infinity.

As mentioned, after their return from the writers' trip to the White Sea Canal in 1933, Il'f and Petrov publicly promised to write a third novel—about Ostap's interment in the White Sea Canal concentration camp (see Il'f and Petrov, 1933). However, this promise was never fulfilled. The writers were not able (or did not want) to write a novel where, one imagines, a complete unfolding of Ostap's "being in nonbeing" would be presented. Perhaps this is because their ambivalent hero simply did not fit the given frame of the "despicable scoundrel" (*Podlets*—the proposed novel's working title). Conceivably, this is because a complete "reforging" is, in principle, impossible for the trickster—he is unchanging in his multiplicity. Finally, one might propose that Ostap, according to the logic of these rather pro-Soviet novelists did not deserve imprisonment—being as he was, the living and joyful "soul" of the Soviet world. Furthermore, as Anne O. Fisher suggests, I'lf and Petrov, in a way, imitated Ostap's trickery by their 'solemn promise':

> The Bender novels prove that Ilf and Petrov were masters of ambiguity, but "Our Third Novel" [the article in which Il'f and Petrov promised to depict Ostap Bender as a prisoner of the concentration camp at the White Sea Canal] was arguably the most important feat of ambiguity they would ever perform. It was published on a special tribute page to the White Sea Canal project, yet it talks about their (never-to-be-written) third Bender novel, not the Canal. In fact, the coauthors somehow managed to turn the *absence* of their continuation of the Bender saga into the *presence* of their "support" for the White Sea Canal book. With this one article, they neither contribute to the White Sea Canal book, nor show Ostap Bender becoming a good, useful Soviet citizen[35]. They escape their slippery situation as

---

[35] In fact, the transformation of a Jewish rogue, Abram Rottenberg, into a useful Soviet citizen was demonstrated by Mikhail Zoshchenko's contribution to the infamous volume. See Zoshchenko. However, the trickster's artistic flexibility leaves open the question whether the transformation of Rottenberg into a Stakhanovite is genuine or just another trickster's metamorphosis.

smoothly as Ostap bender himself. (Ilf and Petrov 2009, 30–31)

## SOCIAL SCHIZOPHRENIA

It is usually suggested that social mimicry in the novels signifies what is "almost the greatest sickness of the time." (Shcheglov' 44) However, this observation is only partially just. Thus in *Dvenadtsat' stuliev,* only Vorobianinov, Korobeinikov, the members of the Alliance of the Sword and the Plowshare and, to a degree, Nikifor Lyapis, author of the *Gavriliada,* may be said to mimic their way into the new social order. Mimicry is more prominent in *Zolotoi telenok:* here we find Koreyko and all the depicted staff of "Hercules" (Berlaga, Skumbrievich, Polykhaev, Bomze), as well as "the children of Lieutenant Schmidt." However, the category of mimicry fails to explain the comical paradoxes associated with Ellochka the Cannibal or, the closet monarchist Khvorobiev (who suffers from hideously pro-Soviet dreams) as well as Madame Gritsatsueva, the humorist Avessalom Iznurenkov, numerous journalists depicted in *Zolotoi telenok,* Ostap's "milk brothers," or Vasisualii Lokhankin and, even more importantly, Aleksandr Koreyko.

I would argue that social mimicry appears in the novels as an isolated trait, although it is related to those qualities that unite the members of the vast rogues' gallery in the diptych. A far more general unifying quality can be defined as *inadequacy*: a comical disjunction between the personae and their social self, the interpersonal and the intrapersonal, the face and the mask. This quality is exhibited by the priest who, longing for a small candle factory, shaves his beard and launches himself headlong into the world; by the spouse of the unassuming engineer, whose speech consists of seventeen linguistic units (including suffixes and prepositions) but who nevertheless competes with Western millionaires and socialites (it is hard not to perceive this as a parody of the Soviet economic "competition" with the West); by the brilliant, witty man who is always in a hurry and scared of everyone; by the loving and romantic "poet's dream," who furiously haggles over the price of information about her elusive "husband," all the while insisting that her informant "take everything"; by the penniless vegetarian who dreams of meat but persuades himself and his wife that "a pork chop takes away a week of a man's life" (1992: 153); by the provincial chess enthusiasts, drunk on the thought of their town becoming the chess capital of the world; and by many others. All these characters are distinguished by the radical contradiction between the way they wish to be seen (or who they imagine themselves to be) and their *real selves*. This contradiction, between social role and actual identity, is often not recognized by the characters themselves, but it betrays the co-existence of *two social orders*—the official "spectacle of socialism" and the unofficial life dependent on semi-legal mechanisms of blat, social networking, doublespeak, etc. (At times, this contradiction is evoked by extraordinary circumstances, as in the case of the engineer Shchukin, who finds himself in a "terrible state"—covered in foam, naked and locked out of his apartment.)

The characters who *consciously* present themselves as other than they really are, are a wholly different story. This category includes not only all the aforementioned "mimics," but also such characters as Al'khen, who hides his thievery behind a mask of shyness, or Polesov, who disguises utter passivity behind a front of furious activity, or Lokhankin, who effaces his incomplete school education by posing as a keeper of cultural values and selfless seeker of the "the great homespun truth" (2009: 185, *sermiazhnaia pravda*); or even the Catholic priests, who invoke God in Kozlevich's soul while their sight is set on his automobile. This category also includes: the actors and musicians of the Columbus theater from *Dvenadtsat' stuliev;* the artist Feofan Mukhin from *Zolotoi telenok,* whose primary medium consists of various oats and grains; and the literary opportunist Khuntov, who shamelessly "harmonizes with the epoch" (from an early edition of *Dvenadtsat' stuliev*)—each presenting cheap trickery and half-baked work as though it were art. Of course, a place of honor in this rogues' gallery belongs to Aleksandr Ivanovich Koreyko, a con artist of national proportions and an underground millionaire masking as a "timid Soviet mouse." In all of these cases the contradiction between the social mask and the secret social identity is immediately apparent.

A special, though perhaps particularly vivid case, is presented by those characters who suddenly, and to their own great surprise and dissatisfaction, discover a disjunction between their conscious self and their unconscious reflexes. This group includes: Treukhov, who, mechanically and in spite of his own best intentions, delivers the same routine speech about the state of the capitalist world at the meeting in honor of the launch of the city tram; Khvorobiev, who despite his hatred for the Soviet regime, is forced to dream Soviet dreams each night; or Balaganov who, with 50,000 rubles securely in his pocket, still "mechanically" pickpockets a wallet. To this group, we might also add the aforementioned journalists who are unable to resist the unconscious lure of stereotypes.

The latter group is particularly significant, not only because it recalls the motifs of the romantic grotesque (the split personality, the transformation of men into automaton, the loss of sovereign control over the self), but also because in the world of the diptych all of the characters—with the exception of Ostap Bender—are inseparable from their societal environment and lack any individual features, conscious or unconscious. Khvorobiev's dreams, which fail to become his sphere of independence from the social environment, or Berlaga's inability to feign an "asocial" madness in *Zolotoi telenok,* are the clearest examples of this paradox. But if the "authentic" individual selves are radically erased, then the novels' characters possess only masks, roles, and given, inalterable identities.

Thus, almost all of the diptych's characters suffer from a peculiar sort of *social schizophrenia*, and if in *Dvenadtsat' stuliev* individual cases predominate (with the exception of the newspaper staff, the Columbus theater actors and the Vasiuki chess club, which all exhibit true group madness), in *Zolotoi telenok* collectives unified by a "split personality" take center stage. This is apparent in "Lieutenant Shmidt's children," the artists from the "Dialectic traditionalist [*dialekticheskii stankovist*]" group, the employees of "Hercules," the workers of the Chernomorsk film studio, and the journalists.

This social schizophrenia certainly represents a symptom of the social cynicism described by Sloterdijk. The fracturing of the self, which is often uncontrolled but always social, testifies to the disintegration of the desired Soviet subjectivity into autonomous and equally inadequate social masks—in other words, into cynical consciousness. The application of Sloterdijk's categories to Il'f and Petrov's diptych reveals the principle which, according to this philosopher, constitutes the foundation of cynical consciousness: modernity and modernization transform into their opposites. The transformation is apparent in a number of scenes that portray the "new life" of the Soviet world: the paper-thin walls of the hostel named after the monk Bertold Schwartz (the inventor of gunpowder); Ellochka the Cannibal's modernized lifestyle driven by a "competition" with Miss Vanderbilt, the famous American billionaire's daughter; the "social care" in the old folks' home supervised by the kleptomaniacal Al'khen; the construction of the tram line (*Dvendtsat' stul'iev*) and the railroad (*Zolotoi telenok*), which both finish with the inventor being driven home in a horse-drawn carriage, despite his insistence that others "take the tram," and in the latter case, as we have seen, with Ostap and Koreyko's inability to leave the site of the rail link except by camel; and finally in such examples of "Soviet efficiency" and pragmatism as the car race with a roguish gang in the lead and the "universal stamp" in *Zolotoi telenok*. At the same time, it is not surprising that the diptych's cast includes such a prominent assembly of journalists, film makers, and writers, both Soviet and foreign: each of them, as Il'f and Petrov tirelessly demonstrate, seek to inscribe the events around themselves into the discourse of modernization, positively or negatively, by either presenting themselves as connoisseurs when, in fact, their knowledge is faint at best, or by masking a contradictory set of experiences beneath an irrelevant mode of description (in particular the clichés and stereotypes of Soviet journalism, collected by Bender in his "Complete Celebrator's Kit").

The greatest effect of the cynical self-denial of modernity becomes apparent in Il'f and Petrov's depiction of the new Soviet—modernized society that was built in the post-revolutionary decade. It inevitably reveals the *principal lack of distinction* between basic categories of social order, such as the permissible and the criminal, the laudable and the abominable, the normal and the pathological, the genuine and the false. In other words, what is revealed is the gaping *absence* of social structure emerging from the mutual annihilation of the (presumably liquidated) traditional principles and the (presumably triumphant) new Soviet principles. This constant (and constantly obfuscated) zone of uncertainty is the strategic foundation of Bender's victories.

Ostap intuitively detects the uncertainty that gives birth to his targets' social schizophrenia, seizes it, and plays it like a virtuoso. In this sense, Bender acts as a trickster who is particularly sensitive to liminal zones and able immediately to make himself at home in them. Bender diagnoses the type of social schizophrenia before him with astounding quickness and precision—for instance, on meeting

Ellochka "Ostap went into a room which could only have been furnished by a being with the imagination of a woodpecker...Ostap knew at once how he should behave in such high society." (1992: 212)[36] To achieve the required effect, Bender artistically imitates the style of speech and behavior, which will have the greatest effect on the "client" (in this sense he really is a "super-chameleon", to use Zholkovsky's words [48]).

For instance, at his first meeting with Vorobianinov, Bender suppresses the will of this past Marshal of provincial nobility by demonstrating that despite his best efforts, Ippolit Matveevich will never be able to prove that he *did not arrive* in Stargorod on a secret assignment from Paris, but rather from the city of N: the boundary between the external and internal émigré is manipulated far too easily. With Ellochka, Bender plays on the lack of distinction between genuine and questionable value: in her "world of fashion," a tea strainer, said to have been brought from Vienna by a diplomat, outweighs a chair "from the palace." When Ostap draws the propagandist billboard on the *Skriabin,* he obviously parodies the activities of the Columbus Theater (as well as the extortion of money from the population by the government during the floating propaganda campaign). It is not surprising that the creation of Bender's "magnum opus" is accompanied by an argument between a classical orchestra and experimental musicians playing enema pipes: Ostap's artistic boldness grows from the clear lack of boundaries between genuine "avant-gardeness" and charlatanry. For the Vasiuki chess club, Bender creates a parodic utopia, thus revealing the uncertain borderline between a utopian ideology presented as political "program" and dissolute, flimflamming nonsense. While charging admission to the "Drop" in Piatigorsk, Bender exploits the ill-defined limits of government greed: "'What a remarkable thing,' mused Ostap, 'that the town has never thought of charging ten kopeks to see the drop. It seems to be the only place where the people of Piatigorsk allow the sightseers in free." (1992: 347)[37] In this instance, Bender appropriates the functions of government while artistically (and for added realism) imitating the bureaucratic rhetoric of dubious

---

36 «Остап прошел в комнату, которая могла быть обставлена только существом с воображением дятла ... Остап сразу понял, как вести себя в светском обществе» (1995a: 272).
37 «Как город не догадался до сих пор брать гривенники за вход в Провал. Это, кажется, единственное место, куда пятигорцы пускают туристов без денег» (ibid., 372).

discounts: "Children and Red army servicemen free! Students, five kopeks! Non-union members, thirty kopeks!" (ibid., 348)[38]

This principle of Ostap's activities is preserved in *Zolotoi telenok*, in fact increased in scope. Thus, while touring as Lieutenant Schmidt's son, or leading the car race, Ostap exploits the lack of distinction between symbolic and material values. By forming "Horns and Hooves," Bender parodies a genuine governmental organization ("Hercules") with a blurred boundary between an outward flurry of activity and secret schemes that are enabled by a universal imitation of work. It is no wonder that later, Ostap's mock organization is adopted by the state (chapter 35) and transformed into The State Horn and Hoof Association. (2009: 411)

It would be wrong to assume that the discussed uncertainty is only distinctive to the period of transition from the NEP to Stalinism. The figure of the "sitz-chairman" (2009: 206), who was imprisoned during the reign of several Russian tsars, or the prototype of Koreyko—a famous con-man, Konstantin Korovko, who in 1912 created the first Russian financial pyramid, permit to correlate this state with the pre-revolutionary epoch as well, and in a broader sense with the condition of modernity.[39] The historical studies demonstrate that the uncertainty of criteria separating the legal from criminal, as well as the instability of a borderline between an enemy and a loyal citizen, was intentionally cultivated in the years of the Stalinist terror. This ambivalence, as Sheila Fitzpatrick explains, was inherent to the Soviet regime:

> The Soviet state with which citizens' lives were so entangled, was a peculiar phenomenon. On the one hand, it remained revolutionary committed to changing the world and shaking up the lives of its citizens, and retaining all the violence, intolerance, and suspicion that pertain to those aims. On the other hand, it was moving towards the

---

38  «Дети и красноармейцы бесплатно! Студентам—пять копеек! Не членам профсоюза—тридцать копеек!» (1995b: 372).
39  Lev Lur'e devoted a TV program to this conman, "Koreyko's Predecessor" as a part of his documentary series, *Crimes in Modern Style* (Prestupleniia v stile modern) at the Russian NTV channel (2003). Later, the scripts for this series were published as a book (see Lur'e, Lev).

welfare-state paternalism that would characterize Soviet-type systems in the postwar period... These two facets of the state seem very different, but they had important elements in common. First, both the revolutionary and the paternalist states disdained law and bureaucratic legalism preferring voluntarist solutions in the first case and personalistic ones in the second. (1999: 225–6)

Through all these means, Ostap artistically exploits social cynicism, simultaneously diagnosing the inner contradictions in the Soviet social and symbolic orders. It is characteristic that Bender's defeats are connected to precisely those characters who either are not yet (Zosia, the students) or no longer (Vorobianinov at the conclusion of *Dvenadtsat' stuliev*) socially schizophrenic. But, Bender himself does not resemble the majority of his clients because he is free of dichotomies; in spite of his numerous shapes and masks, Bender is remarkably whole.

## A KYNICAL KING OF THE CYNICS

"In one respect, one might agree with Ostap's opponents on the right and left alike: his behavior, his existential plans, and his philosophy radiate a cynical chill ("I ask you for the last time—will you serve?"; "Rio de Janeiro—the crystal dream of my youth, don't touch it with your dirty paws"; "I no longer need you. The government, on the other hand, will probably take an interest in you soon enough")," notes Zholkovsky (50). The observation is absolutely just, but Ostap is more than a cynic—he is a kynic.

Ostap overcomes social cynicism by openly playing out and *multiplying* its manifestations. If the majority of Il'f and Petrov's characters hide beneath a mask or perform an inadequate role (but never more than one or two), Ostap *turns inadequacy into a carnival,* juggles *a multiplicity* of masks, and launches an incalculable parade of social roles and ideolects. From this perspective, it is clear why the acquisition of a million rubles causes Ostap's temporary death: for the very first time, he acquires a fixed identity—the secret millionaire. Bender's lighthearted and joyful game of social tongues and roles liberates him from the weight of social definitiveness—a luxury quite inaccessible to other characters—and he loses this when he gets his million.

Ostap's "non-involvement" is acted out through a paradox: he is artistically "absorbed" into any given social role, submitting it to his will while never submitting himself. In this lies Ostap's radical difference from the other characters. Ostap's freedom is at once an example, a temptation, and a provocation aimed at undermining the unwritten conventions of the Soviet world.

The juxtaposition of Ostap and Koreyko is probably the most illuminating example of the fundamental conflict between cynics (Koreyko) and kynics (Ostap). Koreyko appears as Ostap's double. Significantly, in the novel's finale Aleksandr Ivanovich and Ostap Ibragimovich are traveling together "as two wandering sheiks." Koreyko is no less skilled at trickery than Ostap: the competition between the two tricksters in the scene of Ostap's first visit to Koreyko proves this. Most importantly, both of them are victorious in imitating *spectacles of socialism*, which, in Guy Debord's formulation, are based on the circular reproduction of ideological—i.e., discursive—entities: "Eventually both ideology and the goal sought dissolved in a totalitarian ideology proclaiming that whatever it said was *all there was*." (75) Bender's utopian rage at the Vasiuki chess club, his version of "purges" among the "Hercules" staff, and his Celebrator's Kit all artistically exploit the magic power of the ideologically charged discourse that is perceived as reality, and thus belong to the same genre of spectacle.

Debord, however, argued that Stalinism operated by the "concentrated spectacle," with the totalitarian dictator in the center and the greater part of surrounding society escaping it. The panorama of cynical society presented by Il'f and Petrov, in fact, testify to the presence in the Soviet society of the 1920s–30s of a higher and more complex form of a social spectacle, defined by Debord as "integrated spectacle":

> The integrated spectacle shows itself to be simultaneously concentrated and diffuse...For the final sense of the integrated spectacle is this—that it has integrated itself into reality to the same extent as it was describing it, and that it was reconstructing as it was describing it. As a result, this reality no longer confronts the integrated spectacle as something alien ... The spectacle has spread itself to the point where

it now permeates all reality. [...] The spectacle proves its arguments simply by going round in circles: by coming back to the start, by repetition, by constant reaffirmation in the only space left where anything can be publicly affirmed, and believed, precisely because that is the only thing to which everyone is witness. (1990: 9, 19)

All of Koreyko's numerous cons use the power of the "integrated spectacles," and the best of them are confused with the state's productions. The most illuminating example of such imitation can be found in his activities in a remote Soviet republic, where in order to raise funds for the construction of an electric power station, he had been producing and selling photo cards with view of the construction site. For the sake of this "revenue-yielding subsidiary," the construction is moved to a more picturesque location. In pursuing this end, Koreyko eventually squanders the entire budget allocated for the project: "Work on the power station shut down completely. The construction was deserted. The only thing to be seen were the bustling photographers and the flickering of their black hoods. The venture was flourishing, and Aleksandr Ivanovich, the honest Soviet smile never leaving his face, set about printing postcards with movie stars' portraits on them." (2009: 89–90)[40] The image of "socialist construction" emerges here as the source of the capitalist profit, obviously distributed through the channels of the *blat*-based economy between Koreyko and the construction administration. Thus, the spectacle of socialism appears as the source of the "shadow economy."

This is why Koreyko embodies the epitome of Soviet cynicism—characteristically, at first glance Ostap does not even recognize the underground millionaire among the staff of "Hercules" and then loses him in a crowd of people in gas masks (chapter 23). Unlike Ostap, who can play any social role with equal artistry—and at the

---

40  «Работа на электространции прекратилась. Строительство обезлюдело. Возились там одни лишь фотографы и мелькали черные шали. Дело расцвело, и Александр Иванович, с лица которого не сходила честная советская улыбка, приступил к печатанию открыток с портретами киноартистов» (1995b:52)

same time remain distanced from it—Koreyko "could only act two parts, the office worker and the underground millionaire. He didn't know a third." (2009: 137)[41] It is no less important that Koreyko postpones his true life for the future, like a monk or ascetic. It is not only that he "was saving himself for capitalism," but also that he lived for a distant, almost transcendental goal ("the moralism of goals," in Sloterdijk's words). As for Bender, his "transcendental goal"—Rio-de-Janeiro—is a self-parody; hence, the absurdist notes in his description of this paradise: "One-and-a-half million people, each and every one in white pants." (ibid., 58)[42] The self-deconstructive irony of his own "distant goal" is quite natural for a kynic such as Ostap—first and foremost, he is a hedonist (as any trickster should be), and an expert at enjoying the present moment and not taking his victories and defeats seriously. Symptomatically, at a certain point he even attempts to send his major trophy—one million rubles—to the minister of finance (something Koreyko would and could never think of). No less telling is the fact that Ostap appears in the first novel dressed in an old wool scarf, shoes but no socks, and with an astrolabe in his hand. And on the last pages of the second novel, we see him without a hat and wearing only one boot, but with the Golden Fleece medal on his chest.

It is due to his kynical freedom that Ostap often acts as a parodic double to rulers and spiritual authorities: lacking stable social dependency, he holds a unique place—a liminal zone, *within but also without* the Soviet social sphere. This quality is evident even when Bender is not masquerading as an undefeatable grand master or Indian guru. "I will command the parade!" ("*Komandovat' paradom budu ia*")—as any other of Ostap's joking formulae, this phrase adequately reflects the situation: Bender truly commands the parade of Soviet cynics, while at the same time deconstructing cynicism by the means of his kynical tricks and exaggerations.

Ostap's commanding, kingly role is especially apparent in *Zolotoi telenok*. Ostap's "medal-like profile," his "cap with a white top"—first described as "artistic" (*artisticheskaia*, 1995b: 9) then as a "captain's"

---

[41] «...знал только две роли: служащего и подпольного миллионера. Третьей он не знал» (1995b: 93).
[42] «... полтора миллиона человек, и все поголовно в белых штанах» (ibid., 25).

(2009: 313); a tattoo of Napoleon on his chest; and his declaration of his "very serious differences of opinion with Soviet power" (ibid., 58)[43]—all mark Ostap as an alternative leader, the "shadow king" of the Soviet world. Bender's authority is recalled by authorial remarks like the following: "To your knees!—cried Ostap with the voice of Nikolai the First, as soon as he saw the accountant" (ibid., 231), or even "Ostap was roaring as the king of the deep." (ibid., 243)[44]

Commentators on the novel have noted other parallels between Ostap and authority. Thus, Kaganskaia and Bar-Sella remark that the famous typewriter with a "Turkish accent" (missing the letter "E" and so forcing the use of "é" [э] instead) is described differently in Il'f's notebooks: namely, it "produces business papers with a *Caucasus* accent." (Kaganskaia and Bar-Sella, 28). Shcheglov argues that Bender's eulogy for Panikovsky imitates the characteristic style of Stalin's speeches (Il'f and Petrov 1995b: 565-6): "...was the dearly departed a morally upstanding person? No, he was not a morally upstanding person. He was a former blind man, a pretender to the throne, and a goose-thief. He devoted all his strength to living at society's expense. But society didn't want him to live at its expense. And Mikhail Samuelevich couldn't bear this difference of opinion, because he was irascible by nature." (ibid., 313-4)[45]

Twice Ostap directly compares himself to the "King of Judea," another sort of alternative ruler. The first time he speaks jokingly: "I've worked wonders myself. As recently as four years ago I had to spend several days being Jesus Christ in a certain small town. And everything turned out fine. I even fed several thousand faithful with five loaves. I got them fed, all right, but the crows were something wild. (ibid., 226)[46]

---

43  «У меня с советской властью возникли за последний год серьезнейшие разногласия» (ibid., 25).
44  «Остап кричал, как морской царь» (ibid., 182).
45  «Но был ли покойный нравственным человеком? Нет, он не был нравственным человеком. Это был бывший слепой, самозванец и гусекрад. Все свои силы он положил на то, чтобы жить за счет общества. Но общество не хотело, чтобы он жил за его счет. А вынести этого противоречия во взглядах Михаил Самуэлевич не мог, потому что имел вспыльчивый характер» (ibid., 239).
46  «Я сам творил чудеса. Не далее, как четыре года назад мне пришлось в одном городишке несколько дней пробыть Иисусом Христом. И все было в порядке. Я даже накормил пятью хлебами несколько тысяч верующих. Накормить-то я их накормил, но какая была давка» (ibid., 167-168).

It is interesting that this story has a miraculous effect on Kozlevich: "Ostap's unconvincing, comic exerted a lively effect on Kozlevich. A rosy glow started playing over chauffer's cheeks and his mustache gradually lifted." (ibid., 227)[47]

The second comparison to Christ sounds mournful: "'I am thirty-three, the age of Jesus Christ,' Ostap said quickly, 'But what have I accomplished up to now? I haven't created any teachings, I frittered away my disciples, I didn't resurrect Panikovsky...'"(ibid., 412)[48] While trying to call up Zosia's pity, Ostap is clearly unfair to himself: while he failed to resurrect Panikovsky, he certainly resurrected himself more than once, and he also created a doctrine—essentially unserious, but all the more innovative for that—and has disciples too (and although though these do not justify his trust one could say the same of Christ).

Certainly, all these parallels have an ironic tint. However, the fact that at the diptych's finale Ostap, having lost everything, nevertheless miraculously keeps the Order of the Golden Fleece —"only a few people in the world had such an order, and of these, most were crowned personages" (ibid., 419)[49]—suggests that this hero really posesses a *power* within the Soviet world of fictitious values (other kinds of values seem absent from Il'f and Petrov's novels). Perhaps this is why Ostap cannot cross the Soviet border. Without his kingdom the king loses meaning and greatness: the center does not belong to the system, but it is still inseparable from it. The decision to "to get re-trained as an apartment building supervisor" (ibid., 423)[50] does not signify Ostap's defeat, but shows him remaining true to his "royal" calling.

Unwittingly, Il'f and Petrov made a grandiose discovery. Behind the façade of the revolutionary utopianism of official ideology, they revealed the formation of something not at all idealistic, but rather of a *thoroughly—top-to-bottom—*cynical civilization, perhaps the only one of its kind. Here the role of the real, not the fictive, center belongs

---

47   «Неубедительные, но веселые доводы Остапа влияли на Козлевича самым живительным образом. На щеках шофера забрезжил румянец, и усы его постепенно стали подниматься кверху.» (ibid., 168)
48   «Мне тридцать три года, - поспешно сказал Остап,—возраст Иисуса Христа. А что я сделал до сих? Учения я не создал, учеников разбазарил, мертвого Паниковского не воскресил...» (ibid., 319).
49   «... такой орден есть только у нескольких человек в мире, да и то большей частью коронованных особ» (ibid., 324).
50   «Придется переквалифицироваться в управдомы» (ibid., 328).

not to the ruler or the bureaucrat, but to the trickster—the artist and the philosopher of manipulation. It is this very discovery that explains the long sustained readership of the diptych, the diffusion of the novel into popular aphorisms, and certainly Ostap Bender's cult status as a genuine superstar of the Soviet civilization, undimmed even after the end of the epoch.[51]

---

[51] The proof of unfading popularity of Il'f and Petrov's dyptich can be found in numerous film, TV, and theatre productions based on the novels: in such films as *Zolotoi telenok* (1968) by Mikhail Shveitser, *Dvenadtsat' stuliev* (1971) by Leonid Gaidai, and *Mechty idiota* (*The idiot's dreams*, 1993) by Vasilii Pichul; TV mini-series *Dvenadtsat' stuliev* (1977) by Mark Zakharov and *Zolotoi telenok* (2006) by Uliana Shilkova; as well as two musicals based on *Dvenadtsat' stuliev*—by Tigran Keosaian and Aleksandr Tsekalo, composer I. Zybkov (2003) and by Maksim Papernik, composer Maksim Dunaevskii (2004). See also Anne Fisher's analysis of various "sequels" to Il'f and Petrov's diptych created from the 1930s to the 1990s (see pp. 67–93).

# CHAPTER 4

## BURATINO: THE UTOPIA OF A FREE MARIONETTE

Aleksei Tolstoy was perhaps the first Russian writer to initiate what is today called a "project." Miron Petrovskii indicates (169) that as early as 1933 Tolstoy signed a contract with Detgiz to rework the retelling of Carlo Collodi's *The Adventures of Pinocchio* (1880) he had co-authored with Nina Petrovskaia, which had been released by the Berlin-based press Nakanune in 1924. The fairy-tale novel *Zolotoi kliuchik, ili Prikliucheniia Buratino* (*The Golden Key, or the Adventures of Buratino,* 1935) was but the first stage of this project. It was followed by the eponymous play for the Central Children's Theater (1936), which was soon staged across the whole country, and a movie script (1937) was soon after filmed by Aleksandr Ptushko (1939).

As such, "project Buratino" unfolded between 1933 and 1937, although Tolstoy began to write the fairy tale only in early 1935, while recovering from a heart attack he had suffered in December 1934. During this period, Tolstoy's life was rather eventful: in the summer of 1933, he took part in the writers' trip to the White Sea-Baltic Sea Canal—an infamous Soviet concentration camp glorified in the volume *Belomoro-Baltiiskii kanal imeni I.V.Stalina: Istoriia stroitel'stva* (1934), which has an entry by Tolstoy. In 1933, he first became a deputy of the Soviet in Detskoe selo and then in Leningrad. In 1934, he also co-presented a keynote address on dramaturgy at the First Congress of the Union of Soviet writers, denouncing, among others, the Symbolists and Acmeists,[1] and was elected to the Board of the Union (*postoiannyi*

---

1 "This 'magic' of the Symbolists' and mystics' heritage, this school of Andrei Bely are responsible for a lot of trouble. The shaman-like attitude to word is not eliminated yet until now.... Equally false was the "acmeist" attempt of Gumilev, Gorodetsky, and Osip Mandel'shtam to implant ice flowers of the French Parnace into the Russian wilderness. By complex epithets and overlap of one image over another, the Acmeists substituted the fire of the poetic emotion..." (Tolstoy 1960:10: 258)

CHAPTER FOUR

*presidium*). In the spring of 1934, Tolstoy finished the second book of *Pyotr Pervyi* (*Peter the First*) and immediately afterwards wrote the script to the eponymous film (the first part in 1937, the second in 1939, director Vladimir Petrov). By October 1937, Tolstoy completed the first Soviet literary work on Stalin: the novella *Khleb* (*Bread*), formally part of the then-unfinished trilogy *Khozhdenie po mukam* (*The Road to Calvary*), the second volume of which had been completed in 1928. Put plainly, between 1933 and 1937 Tolstoy underwent the total and irreversible transformation from an émigré writer, a suspect "fellow-traveler," into a cornerstone and classic of Soviet literature.

1. Illustration by A.Kanevsky (edition of 1950)

*Zolotoi kliuchik* is solidly inscribed into this historical-biographical plot. On March 8th, 1935, Tolstoy wrote to his wife (then still Natalia Krandievskaia) in Moscow: "Today at Gorky's read the opera [Yurii A. Shaporin's *Dekabristy*, whose libretto was written by Tolstoy] to Voroshilov. Also read Pinocchio there on the 6th. Very well received. Maria Ignat'evna [Budberg] was there... She is going to take Pinocchio to England..." (Grekov, 303). Elena D. Tolstaia adds a significant detail to this famous episode: "It was then that he [Tolstoy] decided on a brilliant move: asking Voroshilov for his advice on how to complete *Khozhdenie po mukam*. The latter explained that Tolstoy had made an extremely vital omission by failing to show the central importance of the defense of Tsaritsyn (in which Stalin participated). Tolstoy quickly rectified his error and wrote *Khleb*..." (Tolstaia, 38). Thus project "Buratino" unfolded parallel to his work on the servile *Khleb*. Perhaps it was after this conversation that Tolstoy decided to change his hero's name (and the book's title) from "Pinocchio," the given name of Collodi's protagonist (from Italian for "cedar nut") to the noun "un burattino," Buratino, which means simply "marionette"—a puppet in a marionette theater— the very nature that Collodi's hero overcomes.[2] In any case, before spring 1935 (as Petrovskii notes) Tolstoy used the name "Pinocchio," and "Buratino" only appears in the final draft of the fairy tale. This circumstance seems to have a direct influence on the conception and inner logic of *Zolotoi kliuchik*.

The success of project "Buratino" far exceeded the author's expectations. The vast subculture around Tolstoy's fairy tale will be remembered by anyone who has lived in Soviet times. There were numerous theatrical versions, films (in addition to Ptushko's classic film, Dmitrii Babichenko and Ivan Ivanov-Vano produced an animated film in 1959 and Leonid Nechaev transformed *Buratino* into a TV musical in 1979[3]), songs (including those Bulat Okudzhava wrote for the musical), candy, waffles, lemonade, toys, masks, table-top and floor-top games, and many, many more incarnations, including a wide repertoire of jokes and ditties, which were, as a rule, adult. Finally, the expression "Land of Fools" [*Strana durakov*], borrowed from Tolstoy's fairy-tale novel, became a universally accepted synonym for "sovok" (a derogatory term for all things Soviet) in Perestroika times, as is confirmed further by the title of the hyper-popular game show "Field of Miracles" [*Pole chudes*]. In Tolstoy's text, this Field constitutes the magic (or rather quasi-magic) center of the Land of Fools.

---

2  "Pinocchio wants to get rid of his persona and become a boy: to leave behind the wicked circle and start growing up. 'Burattino' is this persona, a wooden doll, a dummy..." (Tolstaia, 30).
3  For a detailed analysis of films based on Tolstoy's fairy tale, from Aleksandr Ptushko to Leonid Nechaev's musical, see Prokhorov, 2008.

It would seem that this plethora of forms was generated, in one way or another, by Soviet sponsorship, leading one to expect that in post-Soviet times, Buratino would disappear into the domain of cultural memory (along with Arkadii Gaidar's Timur and his gang and the pioneer-heroes), giving way to Barbie and Pokemon, if not Pinocchio.

Nothing could be further from the truth. Looking for "Buratino" in a Russian search engine turns up thousands of hits. One does not merely find stores and companies named after Tolstoy's hero; Buratino remains an inexhaustible source of *creative fantasy*. Alongside numerous new jokes about Buratino and Mal'vina (where Buratino often appears in the guise of the "New Russian") and fan-fiction, like "The Tale of How Buratino killed Mal'vina," the internet offers us several sequels to Buratino's adventures (L. Vladimirskii, "Buratino Searches for Treasure," and "Buratino in the Emerald City"); the 1997 film *The Newest Adventures of Buratino*, featuring all the stars of post-Soviet pop; a song by the popular rock group "Neschastnyi Sluchai," with the refrain "Buratino Is a Sex Machine" (*Buratino-seks mashina*); the Moscow-based "interactive museum of Buratino-Pinocchio"; a new theatrical version of *Buratino* written by Adol'f Shapiro for the Moscow Theatre of the Young Spectator and directed by Genrietta Ianovskaia; and even a rocket launcher widely used in Chechnya combat operations ("Buratino—enough for anybody" [*"Buratino – malo ne pokazhetsia"*])

One could provide far more examples; however, it is obvious that Buratino's impact extends beyond the bounds of the Soviet epoch, and that Iurii Stepanov was right to call Buratino a "constant in Russian culture" (see Stepanov). It is interesting to look at Tolstoy's fairy tale from this perspective and with the intent of understanding the surprising *depth*s that turned this wooden puppet into a trope embodying some vital elements of the cultural unconscious, open to numerous creative interpretations, while retaining its own unique and recognizable traits, on a par with Ostap Bender and Stierlitz.

Buratino represents one of the brightest examples of the adaptation of the trickster model to Soviet culture. From the very first scenes of Tolstoy's fairy-tale novel, Buratino is presented precisely as a trickster. He beats up Giuseppe while still a log, his long nose is an obvious sign that he is a liar, he constantly engages in tomfoolery, he escapes from Karlo almost as soon as he is created, immediately gets himself into trouble (thereby foreshadowing the plot of the fairy tale), and refuses to obey the talking cricket's warning.

Buratino differs from Khulio Khurenito, Woland, and even Bender by his *ontologically pure tricksterdom*—he is an absolute miscreant, prankster, breaker of conventions, and hooligan, enjoying the game itself far more than its profits. Buratino is the most *non-ideological* character in Soviet culture—utterly disconnected from all social and political models. Incidentally, this is why Soviet and post-Soviet folklore is so fixated on Buratino's sexual escapades: they demand no socially motivated settings. Buratino is perhaps the first character in Russian culture to manifest a focus on what Americans call "fun." Buratino tries to *have fun* at any price and under any circumstances, never giving a thought to pragmatic issues. His vitality in post-Soviet times is guaranteed by his status as the most potent embodiment of this sort of joyous hedonism.[4]

As a trickster, Buratino brings to the forefront the traits of the mediator and the artist. The qualities of the mediator are implicitly linked to the conception of freedom he embodies. As for this trickster's relationship to the sacred, it is conveyed through a particular conception of art, largely inherited from Symbolism (art as a sacred game), yet transformed in a peculiar way.

## BURATINO AS A MEDIATOR

How could one define the central structural model of a fairy-tale text, Collodi's "prototype" notwithstanding? Is its structure binary? It seems so. But in Tolstoy's fairy-tale novel, the binary structure is grounded less in oppositions than in doubling, in a duality bordering on tautology and the duplicity of meaning.

Thus, for instance, Symbolist and other modernist intertexts cheerfully coexist in *Zolotoi kliuchik* with markedly Soviet overtones. Indeed, interest in the traces of the Silver Age in *Zolotoi kliuchik* arose to counterbalance the more traditional interpretations that placed the emphasis on the Soviet aspects of the fairy tale. The depiction of Karabas, in Petrovskii's apt characterization: "united into an indivisible whole the poster-image of the bourgeois and the evil fairy-tale wizard"

---

4   This interpretation was suggested to me by Elena Baraban, to whom I am happy to extend my gratitude.

(207). Duremar is not simply despicable, but despicable as an exploiter of the "poor man": "For four soldi a day I hired this poor man—he would strip down, enter a pond up to the neck and stand there until leeches covered his naked body" (Tolstoy 1960: 8: 223).[5] The Land of Fools is depicted in accordance with the canon of Soviet caricatures on the "world of capitalism": here thin dogs in rags yawn from hunger, scrawny cows suffer, and emaciated chickens stumble about, while "fierce bulldogs stand at attention," guarding the peace for "sated tomcats in golden glasses walking arm in arm with cats in frilly hats" (ibid., 214).[6] The rulers of the Land (or city) of Fools, as of another, unnamed town, inevitably defend "the richy-rich and the self-important" and abuse the poor and the weak. Let us also not forget Buratino's class superiority over Mal'vina and Pierro. Just like Bulgakov's Sharikov (*Sobach'e serdtse* [*Heart of the Dog*], 1925), he simply cannot understand why one does not eat jam with one's fingers or drink cocoa straight from the pot. In accordance with the "class" expectations, Buratino shines in crisis situations:

> Buratino said:
> Mal'vina, fly out, and get some branches for the bonfire.
> Mal'vina gave Buratino a disapproving look, shrugged her little shoulder, and brought back a few dry stems...
> Buratino said:
> All the trouble with these well-bred types!
> Then he went and got some water, and some branches and pine cones, and lit a fire by the cave entrance that roared so loudly that the branches stirred on the tall pine... and boiled the cocoa himself. (ibid., 235)[7]

---

5  «За четыре сольдо в день я нанимал одного бедного человека, -- он раздевался, заходил в пруд по шею и стоял там, покуда к его голому телу не присасывались пиявки» (Tolstoy, 223)

6  «покой сытых котов в золотых очках, под руку с кошками в чепчиках» (Tolstoy, 214)

7  "Буратино сказал: – Мальвина, слетай-ка, набери веток для костра. Мальвина с укоризной взглянула на Буратино, пожала плечиком – и принесла несколько сухих стебельков. Буратино сказал: – Вот наказание с этими, хорошо воспитанными... —Сам принес воды, сам набрал веток и сосновых шишек, сам развел у входа в пещеру костер, такой шумный, что закачались ветви на высокой сосне... Сам сварил какао на воде.» (Tolstoy, 235)

Finally, there is the plot itself, in which the pauper, Buratino, and his disenfranchised friends defeat the rich man, the "doctor of puppet science," Karabas, which reveals a clear-cut logic of class-conflict. This is not the only example of binary opposition in Tolstoy's fairy tale. There are many more, and they create a wholly different fairy-tale logic, far more fanciful than the contrasts of Soviet propaganda.

First of all, the spaces of *Zolotoi kliuchik* appear in doubles. There are two theaters—Karabas' puppet theater and Buratino's new theater, named "Lightning" (*Molniia*); two cities—the nameless city where most of the action takes place (ruled by the Tarabar king) and the City/Land of Fools (ruled by governor Fox); two ponds—Tortilla's home and the swan lake; two underground tunnels—the "rat's route" from Mal'vina's cellar and the subterranean path behind the magic door; two fireplaces—the painted one in Karlo's hovel and the real one, where Karabas threatens to burn Buratino; and Mal'vina's isolated homestead, doubled by the cave, which is immediately transformed into a comfortable and beautiful home through the efforts of "helpful" beasts and insects. Even "singular" spaces such as Karlo's hovel and the tavern of the "Three Little Fish" (*Tri peskaria*) are each featured each twice.

Secondly, many plot motifs occur twice in *Zolotoi kliuchik*. Twice Buratino plays dead—at the very beginning when he runs away from Karlo (ibid., 186) and much later, while fleeing from the "bandits": the tomcat Basilio and the vixen Alisa (ibid., 205). Twice he tries to slip away between his opponents legs—the policeman's at the beginning (ibid., 185) and the tavern keeper's in the middle (ibid., 200). Twice he meets the wise Cricket (ibid., 187, 254) and the rat Shushara (ibid., 189, 254). Twice Buratino uses a bird for transportation—first a swan (ibid., 204), then a rooster (ibid. 239–240). Twice he travels to the Land of Fools; twice he is warned by birds of Basilio and Alisa's deception (the "elderly crow" cries, "They lie! They lie!" [ibid., 199], and the sleepy owl seconds, "do not trust, do not trust, do not trust" [ibid., 202]). Twice Mal'vina makes the effort to teach Buratino to write properly; twice the cocoa gets spilled (209, 228); twice appear the Doberman-detectives (ibid., 215, 244), the police bulldogs of the City of Fools (ibid., 219, 231–2) and even the governor Fox (ibid., 214, 243-44). Buratino changes his costume twice—first he is dressed by his father Karlo, then Mal'vina gives him a new outfit. Pierro is beaten twice: first in the theater, where he cries helplessly, and the second time when the detectives seize Mal'vina and he "fights like a lion" (ibid., 245). Twice Buratino acquires and then loses something valuable—his alphabet book the first time and the money given to him by Karabas the second. There are two chases—Pierro flees pursuit riding a rabbit and Buratino escapes on a rooster. There are two scenes of eavesdropping—first Pierro overhears Karabas' conversation with Duremar, then Buratino does the same. There are two battle-like confrontations—the chapter "The Terrible Battle at the Forest Clearing" and the chapter "For the First Time in His Life Buratino Feels Despair, but Everything Ends Well." Twice Buratino ends up in water—the first time he falls into the swan lake while fleeing the "bandits" and the second time he is tossed into Tortilla's pond. (It is characteristic that Tolstoy demonstratively prevents Buratino from a third fall into the water: "He fell crookedly through the air, and would have landed into the pond and under aunt Tortilla's protection, if not for a strong gust of wind. The wind lifted Buratino's light wooden frame ... and falling, he smacked right into the cart, straight onto the head of governor Fox" [ibid., 244].[8]) Some situations recur in perfect reversal of the original situation. As a rule, these reversals are connected to the motif of wood: thus Karabas wants to burn Buratino (ibid., 195), while the policemen try to drown him (ibid., 216), and it is his "woodenness" that makes the first threat so terrible and the second so futile. Twice Buratino ends up atop a tree—the first time upside down, hung by the cat and fox (ibid., 205) and then under his own power sits on an Italian pine jeering at Karabas (ibid., 230–231). Significant formulae occur twice as well: thus the narrator's words about Buratino's "tiny little thoughts" ("We shouldn't forget that Buratino was but a day old. His thoughts were tiny little things, trivial as can be" [ibid., 186],[9]) and a repetition of the same characterization uttered by Tortilla ("brainless trusting little fool with tiny little thoughts" [218][10].) Karabas is twice compared to a crocodile: in the narrator's words: "his huge mouth clashed its teeth as though he

---

8   «Он описал в воздухе кривую и, конечно, угодил бы в пруд под защиту тетки Тортилы, если бы не сильный порыв ветра. Ветер подхватил легонького деревянного Буратино, закружил, завертело "двойным штопором", швырнул в сторону, и он, падая, шлепнулся прямо в тележку, на голову губернатора Лиса.» (Tolstoy, 244)

9   «Не нужно забывать, что Буратино шел всего первый день от рождения. Мысли у него были маленькие-маленькие, коротенькие-коротенькие, пустяковые-пустяковые.» (Tolstoy, 186)

10  «безмозглый доверчивый дурачок с коротенькими мыслями» (Tolstoy, 218)

were not a man, but a crocodile" (194)[11] and in Karlo's speech "You are worse than any crocodile" (ibid., 248).[12] The phrase "enough smooching" (*dovol'no lizat'sia*)[13] sounds twice—the first time spoken by Karabas (ibid., 194), the second by Buratino ("enough, enough smooching— grumbled Buratino." [ibid., 245][14].)

Third, the reader has a distinct impression that practically every character, with the exception of Buratino, appears as one half of a pair. Next to Karlo we find Guiseppe, next to Karabas there is Duremar, at Mal'vina's side there is either the poodle Artemon or Pierro, and Pierro in turn appears next to either Arlekino (Harlequin) or Mal'vina. The wise advisors and the Talking Cricket and Tortilla are also paired, while the partner of the evil rat Shushara is the Bat "who resembles an imp" and leads Buratino via the *rat's route* straight into the paws of the cat Basilio and the fox Alisa. There are two rulers (the Tarabar king and governor Fox) and two pairs of dogs, namely the two police bulldogs, and two Doberman detectives.

Tolstoy openly emphasizes this device in his depiction of the tomcat Basilio and the fox Alisa. These not only appear as a pair but have a contrasting set of twins: the governor Fox and the "fat cat with puffed-up cheeks and golden glasses—who served the governor's ear as a secret-whisperer."[15] (ibid., 243) Furthermore, *Zolotoi kliuchik* has two Basilios: at the very beginning Buratino struggles with the temptation to pull the tail of the "striped tomcat Basilio" (ibid., 191), and then when the "real" Basilio makes an appearance, he is introduced as such: "This was not the tomcat Buratino had met last night on the street, but another—also named Basilio and also striped"[16] (ibid., 198). Alisa has a double as well—the governor of the City of Fools walks along with a "haughty vixen, who held a night violet in her paw"[17] (ibid., 214).

---

11  «огромный рот лязгял зубами, будто это не человек, а крокодил» (194)
12  «А ты -- хуже всякого крокодила» (248)
13  «Довольно лизаться» (194)
14  «...довольно, довольно лизаться, -- проворчал Буратино...» (245)
15  «жирный кот, с надутыми щеками в золотых очках -- он служил при губернаторе тайным нашептывателем в ухо» (243)
16  «Это был не тот кот, которого Буратино встретил вчера на улице, но другой -- тоже Базилио и тоже полосатый.» (198)
17  «спесивая лисица, державшая в лапе цветок ночной фиалки.» (214)

CHAPTER FOUR

2. Illustration by A. Kanevsky (edition of 1950)

These repetitions and doublings are too frequent to be accidental. The numerous examples demonstrate that the author experienced, at least unconsciously, the presence of a "two–tact" rhythm in his fairy tale. It is very hard to subsume these doublings under a "common signifier." Some of them embody contrast (the theaters of Buratino and Karabas) and some resemblances, which in a number of cases brings contrasting characters closer together (Buratino and Pierro, thieves and rulers). In some cases, these repetitions reveal the evolution of a character (Pierro's beatings), but this is more the exception than the rule—the vast majority of the doublings add nothing to what is already known of a character.

Furthermore, the doublings nearly *displace*, or hide, the "rule-of-threes," which is far more characteristic of the fairy-tale genre and apparent here only in the instance of Buratino receiving three gifts: the alphabet book from father Karlo, the money from Karabas and, finally, the golden key from Tortilla. Despite their surface resemblance to fairy-tale conventions, these plot devices differ from the fairy-tale model. The gifts follow no hierarchy of purpose: Buratino loses the first two gifts, keeping only the third, the golden key, which leads him to the ultimate goal, unknown to Buratino until the very last scene. The incidental way Buratino loses some gifts but acquires others is closer to the plot twists of an adventure novel than to the rigid logic of symbolic exchange we find in fairy tales.

Even more significantly, in *Zolotoi kliuchik* receiving and losing gifts is hardly ever linked to the motif of *trial and testing*, which normally plays a key role in the structure of a fairy tale. If in the fairy-tale tradition "the hero must exhibit kindness, humility, quick thinking and politeness, and most often—the knowledge of certain 'rules of the game,'" which grant him "magical things of value from a mythical other world, from miraculous creatures and the like" (Meletinskii, Nekliudov, Novik 18, 19), in *Zolotoi kliuchik*, strange as it might seem, Buratino is rewarded for *incorrect behavior*—or, put differently, for *transgressions*. Certainly these transgressions are much more innocent than those associated with the mythological trickster, or even those that mark the path of Ostap Bender, but let us not forget that *Zolotoi kliuchik* is a work *for children*. This is why Buratino's transgressions seem more like child's play. Thus, father Karlo heads out to sell his coat and buy the alphabet book after Buratino is almost killed by the rat Shushara for his tomfoolery. Karabas gives Buratino money after he, "screeching into his ears," makes an inherently stupid claim—namely that he cannot get into the fireplace because the last time he tried, "he only poked a hole in it"[18] (Tolstoy 1960:8: 197). Finally, Tortilla decides to give Buratino the golden key after he breaks the idiomatic fairy-tale *code of conduct*: on finding himself in the pond, he reacts crudely, though rather honestly, to the offered hospitality: "Buratino sniffed and tried the frog's delectables—I am nauseous—he said—this is so gross!"[19] (ibid., 217)

Indeed, if one applies the principles which in a fairy tale guarantee the hero's success to *Zolotoi kliuchik*, the outcome of the comparison is rather negative: Buratino "does not exhibit *goodness*...in relation to gift-givers, animals, old women, etc." (Meletinskii, Nekliudov, et al, 51–2). Instead he unwittingly gives valuable information to Karabas, accidentally learns of the golden key from Pierro, and ignores the good advice and interdictions of the wise Cricket, father Karlo, Mal'vina and many other well-wishers. The only rule of fairy-tale conduct Buratino seems to obey is "unfailingly choosing the most unworthy object, the most dangerous path, in principle the worst...option" (ibid., 51). However, the choice of "the most unworthy object" as an indication of altruism does not apply

---

18 «и только проткнул дырку.» (197)
19 «Буратино понюхал, попробовал лягушиное угощение. -- Меня стошнило, -- сказал он, -- какая гадость!» (217)

to Buratino, since he reacts aggressively even to an innocent arithmetic problem: "I won't give my apple to anyone even if he fights me for it!"[20] (Tolstoy 1960:8: 210) On the other hand, "the most dangerous path, in principle—the worst option" is not only an apt description of Buratino's adventures, but is also reinforced by his own declaration (perhaps the sole expression of his "worldview"): "More than anything in the world, I love terrible adventures. Tomorrow at first light I am going to run away from home—climb over fences, despoil birds' nests, mock boys, pull dogs' and cats' tails...I'll think of worse things yet!..."[21] (ibid., 187).

The morphology of the fairy tale fails to explain these particularities of *Zolotoi kliuchik,* but the *model of mythological mediation* can be applied to them. This model, if transformed, is preserved in the structure of the folkloric fairy tale (see Meletinskii, Nekliudov, et al, 41–7), but in *Zolotoi kliuchik,* mediation takes center stage and alters the fairy-tale logic of trials and rewards. Multi-leveled doublings, which fail to submit to a unifying interpretation, fill out the space between the distinct opposition of *one's own* and *the other,* which is realized in *Zolotoi kliuchik* through the juxtaposition of Karabas'theater and the theater won by Buratino. The logic of this process is quite close to that described by Claude Lèvi-Strauss as the logic of myth, which proposes overcoming opposites by replacing the "main" opposition with less distant "pairs" which collapse in the figure of the mediator-trickster. Buratino thus acquires the functions of the mythological mediator-trickster precisely through his misbehavior and his counter-systemic actions. Many fairy-tale heroes are genetically linked to the trickster, so it is not surprising that Tolstoy arrived at this mythological semantics while writing his fairy tale.

The mediation enacted by Buratino appears in many incarnations. He is at once wooden and alive, he can be used for firewood, cannot be drowned, but is easily blown around by gusts of wind—and at the same time he is constantly hungry, he gets bruises, he can be pinched ("the puppets again began to hug, kiss, push, pinch and once more hug Buratino, who so remarkably escaped a terrible death in the fireplace"

---

20  «Я же не отдам некту яблоко, хоть он дерись!» (210)
21  «Больше всего на свете я люблю страшные приключения. Завтра чуть свет убегу из дома -- лазить по заборам, разорять птичьи гнезда, дразнить мальчишек, таскать за хвосты собак и кошек... Я еще не то придумаю!..» (187)

[Tolstoy 1960:8:197–8]²².) He is a doll, a marionette and at the same time, a real little boy. This juxtaposition of traits seems particularly original when compared with Yurii Olesha's *Tri tolstiaka* (*Three Fat Men*, 1924/28), where the opposition between the child and the doll is also central. Olesha uses this model as a source of conflict and plot development: the living Suok must pretend she is a doll in order to save Prospero, and swapping places with a doll saves her own life in turn; Tutti, the heir of the ruling clique of the Three Fat Men, is convinced in the course of the plot that he has a human and not a mechanical heart etc. Tolstoy's work is devoid of these dichotomies: the charm and strength of his hero lies precisely in the lack of conflict between his human and puppet features.

The mediator traits inherent to Buratino generate more complex but analogous fusions of opposites. Thus, when Buratino is newly made, having been named only yesterday, he is immediately *recognized* on arrival at the theater: "The living Buratino!—cried Pierro, waving his long sleeves around [...] It's Buratino! It's Buratino! He's come to us, the happy little rogue Buratino!"²³ ( ibid., 194). This paradoxical and unexplained situation may only be understood as a result of conjoining the biographic traits of the "novelistic" or adventure hero (Tolstoy initially wanted to call his fairy tale a "novel for children and adults") and the *mythological* hero, who is always already known to everyone. Furthermore, he is not only known, but also recognized as a trickster— "the happy little rogue Buratino."

It would be wrong to contend that Tolstoy replaces the fairy tale with the myth. Rather, he unites the two models, creating something that evokes syncretic fairy-tale myths.²⁴ Furthermore, Tolstoy systematically excludes any sort of mythological seriousness from the stylistic spectrum of his fairy tale, never allowing the reader to forget that his cast is made up of puppets, not humans, and that his plot depicts a game, not real life. In essence, the plurality of doubles discussed above reinforces the

---

22 «...куклы опять начали обнимать, целовать, толкать, щипать и опять обнимать Буратино, так непонятно избежавшего страшной гибели в очаге.» (197-8)

23 «Живой Буратино! -- завопил Пьеро, взмахивая длинными руками (...) К нам, к нам, веселый плутишка Буратино!» (194)

24 "In syncretic myth-fairy tales ... the theme of marriage was secondary to the acquisition of mythical (cosmic) and ritual objects, or the discovery of guardian spirits..." (Meletinskii, Nekliudov, et al., 16)

logic of myth, which visibly accentuates the artificiality and playfulness of the action—if in life everything only happens once, a game, as noted by Johan Huizinga, always implies doublings (see chapter 2 of *Homo Ludens*). If Tolstoy mythologizes anything, it is the game itself—theatrical, full of pranks and tomfoolery—and what emerges as a result is the paradoxical myth of the fairy tale world.

It is necessary to underline the fact that Tolstoy is not consciously recreating and emphasizing the logic of mythological mediation. Rather, this structure emerges on its own, from the "memory" of the fairy-tale form through Tolstoy's attempt to reconcile, or mediate, between the cultural traditions of Russian modernism and Soviet culture and the official and the unofficial. It is Buratino's status as trickster, with its underlying archaic mythological semantics, that allows Tolstoy to turn a fairy-tale novel into a specific kind of artistic manifesto or, more precisely, a utopia based on the mediation between the absence of political freedom and the freedom of the artist.

## BURATINO AS AN ARTIST

Elena D. Tolstaia identifies the central theme of *Zolotoi kliuchik* as the "plot of a foolish but lucky wooden man, who escapes into the freedom of art from an evil puppet-master—a sort of authorial alter ego" (38). That which Tolstaia calls "the freedom of art" is embodied by the motif of *one's own theater*, won by Buratino as the prize for all his adventures. In Tolstoy's mind the idea of one's own theater is, paradoxically, associated with Stalin. This is clearly evident in the manuscript to the play *Zolotoi kliuchik*, written in 1936, when Tolstoy was simultaneously working on *Khleb*. Tolstoy wrote the script for the play in a thick notebook, using one side of the page. The reverse of each page is usually left blank, though several times a doodle or drawing appears. The first instance is opposite Mal'vina's words (omitted in the final edit): "I miss the theater. If I could only have my own puppet theater [...] We could write our own plays, sell tickets ourselves ... all without Karabas' lash" (Tolstoy's archive II: 60). Here Tolstoy drew the profile of a mustached man (fig. 1).

A similar profile (fig. 2), adorned with the characteristic pipe, appears once more in the manuscript, after almost a hundred pages, opposite the scene of the opening of the very theater Mal'vina had dreamed of: "*The voices of children:* Buratino, Buratino,/ The happy Buratino himself/ Is opening his own theater,/ the best in the world for children./ Engaging plays [...]/Written by puppets themselves/ who dance and sing" (ibid., 152; this scene is also tellingly omitted from the final edit of the play).

Fig.1                                    Fig.2

The repeated association between the motif of "one's own theater" and a face reminiscent of Stalin allows for the proposal that Tolstoy is mentally appealing to the dictator for his dream of his own theater—i.e., the right to play by his own rules. It is Stalin, absolute power personified, who can liberate the artist from the petty rule of various "Karabases-Barabases" and allow true creative freedom, albeit under well-defined conditions. Let us remember that, at first, many interpreted the Writer's Union, which seemingly liberated "fellow-travelers" from the terror of the RAPP (Russia's Association of the Proletarian Writers), as filling this function.

From this perspective the whole project "Buratino" can be read as a kind of utopia—the paradoxical if not oxymoronic *utopia of the free marionette.* Scholars of Tostoy's work have observed the most minute discrepancies between *Zolotoi kliuchik* and Collodi's fairy tale, but have somehow failed to notice the colossal and heavily emphasized difference between Buratino and Pinocchio: although Pinocchio and Buratino both come into the world with a long nose, Pinocchio's nose is only elongated when he lies, making his original nose relatively small. This motif does not feature in *Zolotoi kliuchik* and hardly because Buratino never lies. Quite the contrary: lying initially defines this character!

At the same time, as M.A. Chernysheva notes, *Zolotoi kliuchik* removes the antithesis of the doll/puppet and the human, the game and life, so vital for *Pinocchio*: "In *Zolotoi kliuchik* [...] the doll is human, the game is life" (117). If we accept the hypothesis that Buratino is Tolstoy's alter ego, his long nose acts as a declaration of the artist's *credo*, which for Tolstoy does not consist of the obligation to tell the truth, as the Russian cultural tradition demands, but consists instead of the very opposite—*lying*, creating amusing fibs. Tolstoy replaces the artist-prophet with the artist-Buratino, who remains at all times in the space of the game, in virtual reality. The only thing Tolstoy needs for the realization of this artistic goal is the right to *lie freely*, for for his own pleasure, and not for fear of the lash.[25] The fate of the puppet here loses all its tragic undertones: if life is a theater, it is the ideal setting for *games*—for misbehavior, for pranks, for fibs and adventures—the very things Buratino does best.[26]

The traits of the trickster and the mediator exhibited by Buratino shed a new light on Tolstoy's utopia. In this utopia, the cynicism of adapting to repressive political conditions is rendered as the kynicism of a self-sufficient lying-game. The artist-Buratino is an artist-trickster, moreover, an artist-kynic who freely plays with social and cultural conventions. He submits to no moral court because he belongs to no system completely. By playing around, he transforms the laws of existential survival into the rules of a game. In this sense the gestures of the trickster—his lack of place and propriety and even his artistic amorality—confirm the artist-Buratino's creative freedom.

The artist-Buratino's self-realization poses no threat to established

---

25  In the 1930's collection *Kak my pishem* (*How We Write*) Tolstoy was aready insisting: "The words 'make-belief" (here I appeal to the readers) shouldn't be treated as unserious, for instance if it's written from life it must be the truth, and if made-up, only 'literature'..." (10:136). It is interesting that at an official speech at a meeting with young writers, in April 1934, Tolstoy sincerely formulated analogous ideas: "The more make-belief the better. It is real creativity.[...] You cannot write at all without make-belief. The whole of literature is make-belief" (Tolstoy 1960: 10:247). It is enough to replace "make-belief" with "lying" and we get the program of the writer-Buratino.

26  Elena D. Tolstaia formulated this precisely: Tolstoy's "puppet 'finds itself' in the very fact that it is a puppet and an actor, it is as if it were doubly framed, playing itself, acquiring, on its magical path, the freedom of action—or rather the illusion of freedom. Self-realization does not occur by the means of the escape from the world of conventions and into the world of immanent values, as in *Pinocchio*, but through the creation of conventions of a second order and mastery over them—this decision is post-symbolist, and far more novel than the fairy-tale's purely adventuristic depsychologized plot" (Tolstaia 31).

authority, which fears truth and exposure above all else. This is why Stalin's profile appears in Tolstoy's manuscript—it is the embodiment of the hope in power, which is capable of granting the artist the right to his own reality, his own theater—conditional upon unadulterated lying or, put differently, upon the artist's non-involvement in political affairs.

This utopia may be understood as a unique attempt to reconcile modernism with the conditions of the "Soviet night." After all, is not the proposal that art is a lie an obvious, if oversimplified (via the conventions of the children's fairy tale), iteration of the modernist concept of the autonomy of art, and the understanding of art as a free game unrelated to the political, social, and ideological aspects of reality? From this perspective, the many associations with the culture of the Silver Age that can be found in *Zolotoi kliuchik* acquire an entirely different meaning. Petrovskii first revealed this powerful associative layer in Tolstoy's fairy tale, discussing aspects related to Vsevolod Meyerhold's theatre, Aleksandr Blok's *Balaganchik*, Andrei Bely, Valerii Briusov, *The Satyricon*, Moris Meterlink's mystical plays, and fin de siècle interest in the occult (see 175–88), while Tolstaia has contributed additional and convincing corroborations to Petrovskii's hypothesis.

However, it is not entirely clear why Tolstoy would write a *veiled* parody of the Silver Age in 1935, when modernist experiments were officially branded "formalism" and denounced as bourgeois decadence. For instance, Petrovskii interprets Karabas' theater as a parody of Meyerhold, with his theory of the actor as a super-marionette, and even sees the lightning bolt on the curtain of Buratino's theater as a reference to the seagull on the Moscow Art Theater [MAT] curtain. However Tolstoy, who had been close to the Meyerhold circle in his youth, had openly polemicized with the director in the 1920s and early 1930s. Using *Zolotoi kliuchik* to covertly attack Meyerhold, who by 1935 was already a major target of the official campaign against "formalism," appears meaninglessly anachronistic.

A different assumption offers itself: Tolstoy may have used veiled associations with Meyerhold and Symbolism to evoke the aesthetic experience of modernism and the avant-garde and to *reinstate* the essentially Meyerholdian understanding (especially in his early period) of art as a free disinterested game, the "theatrical theatre," and joyful self-expression of the liar-artist. Irony appears in Tolstoy's fairy tale as a reaction against the *overly serious* realization of this program. Seriousness leads to the purposeful isolation of the artist (inner or outer emigration); his or her escape from the cruel theater of life comically depicted in *Zolotoi kliuchik* as Mal'vina's doll garden or the cave where Mal'vina and Pierro hide from their pursuers.

In Petrovskii's view, Tolstoy's text cruelly parodies Blok and other great Russian poets who chose the path of emigration—both outer and inner—in this quatrain pronounced by Pierro:

> We will live all summer
> Right atop this shrub
> Oh, in total solitude
> To everyone's surprise...
> (Tolstoy 1960: 8: 233.)[27]

In the logic of Tolstoy's fairy tale, Buratino is inherently freer than Mal'vina and Pierro. Here "the brainless, trusting little fool with short little thoughts" takes the most unpleasant of circumstances as mere guidelines to a game, and if he plays then he applies himself fully, drawing all the theatrical effects he can from any situation. Buratino does not take survival seriously: his motto is "Enjoy the show!" Which is precisely why his final reward is not actual power or wealth but *his very own theater*. This theater becomes the "temple," the topos of the paradoxical sacred ritual of the freely played game adopted by Tolstoy's hero.

However, the opposition between Buratino and Mal'vina or Pierro is not absolute: no wonder Buratino "would even give up the golden key to see his friends again"[28] (Tolstoy 1960: 8: 243). Just the same, Tolstoy's ironic attitude towards modernist themes and motifs borders on an *attempt at self-justification*—before himself, before his past, and before that circle of ideas and people he was so close to, and broke with so decisively, on his path to official Soviet recognition.

---

27  «Будем жить все лето // Мы на кочке этой, // Ах, - в уединении, //Всем на удивление...»
28  «отдал бы даже золотой ключик, чтобы увидеть снова друзей.»

3. An illustration by Leonid Vladimirskii (edition of 1956)

## BURATINO AS A CYNIC

Project "Buratino" does not merely embody the kynical utopia of the free marionette, but also that utopia's collapse, as kynical free play transforms into cynical conformism. In his notebook from 1936, used by Tolstoy to gather historical materials for *Khleb*, there is a surprising entry related to Buratino:

> "In addition—put on leeches three times.
>     Sparkle bright the candles
>     Dance the little men
>     So why aren't I happy [crossed out]
>     Hanging low my head [crossed out]
>     Our owner nimbly

─────── CHAPTER FOUR ───────

Jerks the strings" (Tolstoy's archive I: 7)[29]

This poem, not included in either the play or the film script, is the clearest example of the author's self-identification with Buratino, both as the hero and the puppet on a string. In these lines of verse, written after the completion of the prose version of the fairy tale, one senses the admission of the bitter failure of the central hope manifested in *Zolotoi kliuchik*: the liberation from the rule of the tyrannical puppet master and the acquisition of one's own theater become dubious victories—despite outward rejoicing, the puppet-master still "nimbly jerks the strings."

It is telling that the poem appears in immediate proximity to, and seemingly as a surprising development of, the thought of leeches and therefore of Duremar. The meaning of this image is relatively transparent in the fairy tale, the play, and the film script alike: Duremar is a servile intellectual with a certain amount of learning, who readily submits to those in authority. It seems as if while working on *Khleb*, Tolstoy could not escape the thought of the role he had taken on by agreeing to insert a commissioned and thoroughly false novella into a novel dear to him. In other words, had he not become the sell-out cynic Duremar, instead of the indomitable kynic Buratino, playing his own game in his own theater?

Certainly, the word "owner" or "master" ["khoziain"], especially in context with *Khleb*, directly points at Stalin as a parallel to Karabas Barabas. It should not be assumed, however, that Karabas is a direct parody of Stalin. As we have shown, Stalin's profile in the manuscript appears connected to the dream of one's own theater, or in other words, as the antithesis of Karabas' authority. However, while Tolstoy is working on *Khleb*, Stalin appears to merge with the image of Karabas. Why?

The innately modernist utopia of the free marionette, the utopia of the artist-liar, the artist-Buratino presupposes the latter's lack of interest in truth, and his non-involvement in political affairs, as has been mentioned. When Tolstoy agreed to work on *Khleb*,

───────

29 «Это вдогонку - пиявки надо поставить раза три. Сверкают ярко свечки// Пляшут человечки//Что же мне не весело [зачеркнуто]// Голову повесил я [зачеркнуто]// Наш хозяин прытко // Дергает за нитки.»

he entered the direct and unambiguous domain of the authorities' interests. It became clear that power demands more than the artist's loyal non-involvement into its affairs. It requires the artist to participate actively in its own spectacles; he must play to its tune. Furthermore, in *the sphere of political authority, the artist's make-believes immediately acquire the status of the real,* and it is only natural that those in power cannot allow the artist to *control the real*—that is authority's prerogative. It is simpler and more profitable to control the artist, who thus enters a far more rigid dependency than before. This is why the figure of the benevolent patron, the foundation of Tolstoy's hopes for his own theater, and his own game under the protection of the authorities, transformed, over the course of his work on *Khleb,* into the figure of the new and far tougher puppet master, Karabas.

More precisely, the utopia of the free marionette presupposes the *fairy tale* or, in Propp's words, "purposeful and poetic invention" (81) as its optimal creative model, demanding no faith but only entertainment. Totalitarian power needs no fairy tales but only myths, constructs of reality that inspire faith and are given and accepted as the "higher" truth. The totality of myth is the source of totalitarian power. By agreeing to write *Khleb*, Tolstoy stepped out of the modality of the fairy tale and into the modality of myth, and he immediately sensed the change in his own status. (It is strangely ironic that the initials of the fairy tale's title coincide with the abbreviation ZK ["*zakliuchennyi kanaloarmeets*"—an imprisoned member of the labor army of canal-builders]—a term born at the White Sea- Baltic Sea Canal construction site/concentration camp, where, as we recall, Tolstoy went in the summer of 1933, before beginning project "Buratino.")

This perhaps rather abstract proposal is confirmed by the transformation of the finale of *Zolotoi kliuchik* in the editions of the fairy tale, the play, and the film script. In the text of the fairy-tale novel, for the most part written even before Tolstoy's conversation with Voroshilov, the heroes open the secret door to find a magical theater, on whose stage a *garden, Africa,* and *a city* appear in sequence—devoid, notably, of any trace of "social construction," depicting a city in general (matte street lamps ... a toy tram car ... an ice-cream vendor ... a newspaper seller" [Tolstoy 1960: 8:

255]). Furthermore, the scene emphasized the *toy-like* character of these worlds: "In little trees with gold and silver leaves sung wind-up starlings as big as a finger-nail"[30] (ibid.); "A plush bear with an umbrella shambled back and forth"[31] (ibid.); "A rhino galloped by—a rubber ball on his sharp horn for safety"[32] (ibid., 256), "A bicyclist rode by, on wheels no bigger than a little jam saucer. A newspaper man ran by—a leaf from a tear-away calendar folded four times—that's how big his newspapers were"[33] (ibid., 256). This toy world is the ideal setting for a fairy-tale game, completely isolated from reality.

In the finale of the play, written, at the same time as *Khleb*, we first see a magical book, whose words become real and whose pictures come to life—a sort of "device laid bare": we are invited to enter a mythological narrative, not a fairy-tale one. The magical book throws Karabas Barabas "into Tartarary," while Buratino and his friends get a flying ship (another image with a rich mythological "memory"), which carries them into the "land of happiness." The description of this happy land, the "land of happy children" is utterly unambiguous: "here is the sea, and the pioneer camp in the mountains, and fields for reaping, and airplanes in the sky ... towers above resembling the Kremlin, behind them the rays of the sun"[34] (ibid., 314). Tolstoy demonstratively destroys the boundary between the theatrical reality of the game and all that which lies beyond its borders: Buratino turns to the audience, asking them for the name of this "land of happy children," gets the uniform response "the USSR!" and begs for permission to "stay with you, learn and play."[35] This finale directly testifies to Tolstoy's rejection of the fairy-tale

---

30  «На маленьких деревьях с золотыми и серебряными листьями пели заводные скворцы велечиной с ноготь (255)»

31  «Переваливаясь, проковылял на задних лапах плюшевый медведь с зонтиком (255)»

32  «Проскакал носорог, -- для безопасности на его острый рог был надет резиновый мячик (256)»

33  «Проехал велосипедист на колесах -- не больше блюдечка для варенья.» «Пробежал газетчик, -- вчетверо сложенные листки отрывного календаря -- вот какой величины были у него газеты (256)»

34  «здесь и море, и пионерский лагерь в горах, и поля, где жнут, и самолеты в небе... наверху башни, похожие на Кремль, за ними -- лучи солнца" (314)»

35  «остаться у вас, учиться, веселиться.»

utopia in favor of ideological mythologies, presumably representing (but actually forming) reality.

The finale of the film script (1937) strongly resembles the finale of the play, but includes an additional and significant detail, which completes the mythological model, pushing out the utopia of fairy-tale freedom. Instead of a flying ship, a "steel red-winged bird" emerges from the book, and from it emerge "three men wearing leather," who "flick away" Karabas and Duremar and fly Buratino and friends into the "happy land" (Tolstoy's archive III, 74–81). The airplane and the idiomatic "leather jackets" symbolically represent the authority that *violently* guarantees the might of the triumphant world. In total accordance with this logic, Aleksandr Ptushko's film includes a mustached captain with a pipe among the pilots, his resemblance to Stalin quite apparent. As Alexander Prokhorov notes:

> The clear hierarchy of Buratino's mentors determines the Soviet mythological aspect of Ptushko's cinematic fairy tale. The axis of the film's action is the journey of the hero to the magical door, in the course of which Buratino changes several mentors, finally finding the true one, who flies in from the Kremlin, wears a mustache and smokes a pipe. (2008: 158)

The transformation of the personal utopia of the free marionette playing in its own theater into the faceless official mythology of "the land of happy children" is impossible to blame in its entirety on the vileness of totalitarian culture. In my view, it reveals the pitfall of the modernist discourse. The essence of Tolstoy's utopia of the free marionette may be described as the attempt to limit the universalism of modernist discourse with a fairy-tale creation of fiction, with a game lacking in ontological status. But modernism *is ontological in its very nature*—it bestows a universal character on the game (everyone has to play, the whole world is involved in *my* game). Modernism always transforms every locality into the symbol of everyone's state-of-being, and so inevitably and unceasingly it generates myths. Even the initial text of the fairy tale—as the analysis demonstrates—undergoes an unintentional, but thorough, mythologization, granting the fairy-tale hero an archetypal depth. In this sense, the author of *Zolotoi kliuchik* is not only a hostage of totalitarian culture, but also a hostage of modernism. And in this context, project "Buratino" turns into an impressive, and surprisingly successful, experiment on the borderline of both discourses.

# CHAPTER 5
## VENICHKA: A TRAGIC TRICKSTER

It was written between January and March, in 1970, and circulated in samizdat typescripts and "tamizdat" editions. Some readers memorized it word for word. It was first published in Russia only in 1988, in the newly established magazine *Sobriety and Culture* (though it is hard to imagine a less suitable work for a propaganda campaign against alcoholism), and re-released in a separate edition in 1990, priced 3 rubles 62 kopeks—the exact cost of a 500 ml bottle of vodka in the 1970s. Even today Venedikt Erofeev's prose poem *Moskva-Petushki* (*Moscow to the End of the Line* or *Moscow Circles*, to cite different translations) possesses a unique status: in all likelihood, no other text of the unofficial culture has had greater resonance. There are now several hundred critical publications on *Moskva-Petushki*, including at least one monograph, two collections of articles, and two line-by-line book-length commentaries.[1] Trips from Moscow to Petushki and back on Erofeev's birthday have become a popular outing for bohemian youth and an opportunity for creative happenings.

The poem and its author became symbols of the Russian underground of the 1970s—symbols that hardly idealized the counterculture, presenting it as repulsive and appealing at the same time. Erofeev gave a new *philosophical* meaning to the image of the trickster, accentuating his liminality and a certain, expenditure-driven sacrality, thus creating an exemplary image of the kynic, perhaps the strongest and most expressive in Russian culture of the twentieth century.

This combination embodied the philosophical and behavioral model

---

1   See: Geisser-Schnittmann, Ryan-Hayes, Fomenko, Vlasov, Levin.

of the underground artist, which could also be seen in other actors of the unofficial culture of the 1970s and 1980s, first and foremost the Mit'ki group, Dmitrii A. Prigov, the rituals of "Collective Action," and "Medical Hermeneutics." Furthermore, by giving trickster qualities a grotesque and hyperbolic scope while reinforcing their philosophical dimension, Erofeev willingly or unwillingly revealed the tragic meaning of the trickster's pleasure and his kynical disruption of all authoritative goals and values.

## THE TRICKSTER AS THE UNDERGROUND AUTHOR

Erofeev's protagonist is marginal by definition: an unemployed alcoholic with no permanent address (at the beginning of the poem he awakens in a building hallway). He is depicted en route—literally betwixt and between—and the scope, both topographical and symbolic, of his journey from Moscow to Petushki is constantly changing. His route, while geographically determined (the first USSR book edition in 1990 was illustrated with a map of the Vladimir train line on which the station of Petushki is located), expands into a journey from hell to heaven and back: if Petushki is truly heaven ("Petushki is the place where the birds never cease singing, not by day or by night, where winter and summer the jasmine never ceases blooming. Perhaps there is such a thing as original sin, but no one ever feels burdened in Petushki" [Erofeev 1997: 43]), then the Kremlin is directly associated with hell (Kuritsyn). At the same time, Venichka Erofeev's journey includes a brief overview of world culture from the perspective of drunkenness, a tale of his fantastic wanderings around Europe, and the story of the revolution in the village of Cherkasovo, to say nothing of the numerous mythological themes and plots that come to life in the hero-narrator's tale. Venichka's train car becomes a genuine liminal zone, at first inhabited by relatively realistic characters ("the woman of a difficult fate," "black-mustache," Mitrich and grandson, the conductor Semenych). Later, on the road back to Moscow, the train car is possessed by totally fantastic characters: Satan, King Mithridates, hordes of Erinyes, (saint?) Peter, the statue of the Worker and the Kolkhoz Laborer, and the Sphinx. The liminality of Venichka's chronotope is especially apparent in the final section of the book, where time disappears: "What do you need the time for, Venichka? ... Once you had a heavenly paradise, you could have found out the time last Friday, but now your heavenly paradise is no more, what do you need with the time?"(1997: 155), and the space is constructed through oxymoronic fusions such as: "Petushki. Sadovy Circle" and "Petushki. The Kremlin."

As Laura Beraha aptly notes about Venichka, "this marginal hero spends most of his time hovering in liminal spaces: in the much-discussed 'unfamiliar/unidentified front hallway'; on the platform between two railcars that witnesses his gagging resurrection with the first dose of the day [...] Since thresholds, as Bakhtin pointed out so many times, are charged with the atmosphere of crisis and the straining towards decisive change, one threshold after another signals one change after another, a movement which eventually leads, via the logic of *plus ça change*, to the perverse stability of constant flux that is the hallmark of the picaresque." (Beraha, 25) Having carried out a detailed comparison between *Moskva-Petushki* and the picaro's novel, as well as between the poem's protagonist and the figure of the rogue, Beraha nevertheless comes to the conclusion that despite a surface resemblance to the picaresque ("a peripatetic, marginal hero; a pointedly loose, episodic structure overloaded with interpolated tales and short on psychological development; a first-person quasi-autobiographical form" [ibid., 19]) in Erofeev's poem "the picaresque is evoked and erased" (ibid., 23); "it is this picaresque dynamic that, doubled back on itself, empties out time, space, language and destiny to suspend them in the multi-layered void of *Moskva-Petushki*." (ibid., 47)

The likely cause of this transformation is the fact that the liminality of the environment in Erofeev's poem emerges directly from the complex stylistic and discursive game, which organizes the protagonist's (and author's) consciousness, highlighting his unique trickster-like ambivalence. Venichka represents the "rock bottom" of life, but at the same time his "polyphonic monologue" (in the words of Svetlana Geisser-Schnittmann [272]), woven from a wide range of quotations and references, demonstrates his cultural erudition and even *control* over a vast spectrum of layers and spheres of Russian and European culture, which allow him to define himself as a "self-motivated Logos." (1997: 104)[2] Still, even this self-definition is immediately followed by a demotion: "'You're a fool, Erofeev, and no kind of Logos. Get!' he

---

2   «...самовозрастающий Логос» (Erofeev 1990: 84).

screams. Get out of our Sorbonne, Erofeev" (1997:104)[3].

Venichka is at once part of the perpetually drunk "masses" ("I like my people. I'm happy that I was born and grew up under the gaze of their eyes" [1997: 28][4]; "Now, after 500 grams of Kubanskaya, I was in love with those eyes, in love like a madman" [ibid., 72][5]), and their symbolic ruler, "the little prince," a brigadier drawing up charts of alcohol consumption, so as to "examine with care, intently and close up, the soul of every shitass" (ibid., 40)[6]. Critics (Altshuller, Lakshin) have described Venichka as a "representative" of the people's descent into alcoholism, or alternatively, as the "typical face" of the nonconformist intelligentsia (Pomerants, 1995 and 1995a)—but in my opinion, both approaches are unproductive precisely because the hero emphatically belongs to neither camp; both sides mistake him for the other. The waiter at the Kursk station restaurant kicks Venichka out, treating him as a drunk who has gone to the dogs, while his dormitory roommates berate him for being an overly effete intellectual. Notably, Venichka is accused of "superhuman" arrogance (his roommates compare him with "Cain and Manfred" [1990: 28]) after he refuses to go to the toilet at their suggestion, despite having been drinking beer for several hours.

Similar oscillations between the "high" and the "low," the bodily carnivalesque and the sublime characterize the ambivalent positions of Venichka the hero and Venichka the narrator. In Erofeev's narrative, the high and the low do not negate or annihilate one another, but instead form an ambivalent unity of meaning. In fact, all of the most stylistically vivid passages are built on the ambivalent conflation of high and low discourses and registers: from the famous words about spitting on each step of the social ladder to the chapter on cocktails, from the description of the "the most beloved of trollops" (1997:43[7]), to the meditation on the theological nature of the hiccup. Even the parodic story of unrequited love for the famous Soviet harpist Olga Erdely (where the

---

3   «Дурак ты, - говорит,—а никакой не Логос! Вон,—кричит,—вон Ерофеева из нашей Сорбонны!» (ibid., 84).
4   «Мне нравится мой народ. Я счастлив, что родился и возмужал под взглядами этих глаз» (ibid., 27).
5   «... после пятисот кубанской я был влюблен в эти глаза, влюблен, как безумец» (ibid., 60)
6   «...душу каждого мудака рассматривал со вниманием и в упор»" (1990: 35).
7   «...любимейшая из потаскух» (ibid., 38).

harpist is substituted with a one-ruble "hag of a woman, not so very old, but drunk as they come" [1997: 92-3][8]) realizes the high theme of resurrection through love, which was invoked a few pages before in Venichka's story about his own resurrection. And the comic list of writers and composers who drank in the name of art and for love of the people (only "Privy Counselor Goethe did not drink a gram" [1997: 84][9], according to Venichka) becomes a kind of authorial confession that paves the way for the poem's end: "He [Goethe] remained alive but it was as if he committed suicide. And now was completely satisfied. This is even worse than real suicide" (ibid.)[10]. It is no accident that "the man with the black moustache" says the following about Venichka: "with you, it's not like with other people, it's like Goethe"(ibid., 87)[11].

The same ambivalence is emphasized when Venichka places his personality and journey into a biblical context. Irina Paperno and Boris Gasparov note:

> Each event exists simultaneously in two dimensions. A hangover is interpreted as an execution, death, crucifixion. Getting a hair of the dog that bit you—that's resurrection. After resurrection life begins: the gradual intoxication that ultimately leads to a new execution. The hero speaks openly about this at the end of the story: "For isn't the life of man a momentary booziness of the soul as well?" However, such an interpretation of these everyday events in turn has the opposite effect on the story's biblical motifs. They often take on the tone of parody, jokes, and puns: the high and the tragic are irrevocably tied together with the comic and the obscene. Moreover, this gives the biblical text a cyclical character: the very same chain of events is repeated again and again... The reversed order of events points to the vicious circle within which they move. (Gasparov and Paperno, 389–90)

---

8   «...бабонька, не то чтоб очень старая, но уже пьяная-пьяная» (ibid., 75).
9   «... тайный советник Гете не пил ни грамма...» (ibid., 69).
10  «Он остался жить, но *как бы* покончил с собой и был вполне удовлетворен. Это даже хуже прямого самоубийства, в этом больше трусости, и эгоизма, и творческой низости...» (ibid., 69).
11  «А у Вас все не как у людей, все, как у Гете!..» (ibid., 72).

## CHAPTER FIVE

The poem's references to the New Testament are intentionally ambivalent and ambiguous: they can be interpreted as blasphemy or as reenactments of myth. We should note that some of the New Testament parallels are deliberately distorted. Thus, for example, it is not Venichka/Jesus who resurrects Lazarus, but Venichka himself who is resurrected by a "bad woman": "twelve weeks ago I was in a coffin, I had been in a coffin for four years already, so that I had already stopped stinking. And they said to her, `Look, he's in a coffin. Resurrect him, if you can' (1997: 90)[12]; similarly the reference to the star of Bethlehem occurs only immediately *before* his tragic death, which is comparable to the crucifixion.

An especially significant detail is located in Venichka's principled ambivalence with regard to the positions of the author and the protagonist. Not only do author and protagonist share the same name, they also are united by a number of autobiographical elements, such as references to the places where the poem was written ("While working as a cable fitter in Sheremetievo, Autumn, 1969" [1997: 164][13]) right next to a description of this same cable-fitting job in the tale of Venichka's short career as a foreman (the chapters "Kuskovo-Novogireevo," and "Novogireevo-Reutovo"). The unsolvable paradox of this ambivalent position is accentuated by the concluding phrase of the poem: "I didn't know that there was pain like that in the world. And I writhed from the torture of it—a clotted red letter "ю" spread across my eyes and started to quiver. And since then I have not regained consciousness, and I never will." (1997: 164)[14]

This final phrase implies a whole spectrum of mutually exclusive interpretations. Petra Hesse believes that it creates a paradox that contradicts the laws of literature: the subject of the speech in Erofeev's poem is revealed as a "gap in the depiction of the space traversed by the hero": "That which until the last page seemed to be the motivating force behind the phantasmagoric beginning or the alcoholic delirium is finally

---

12   «Вот я, например, двенадцать недель тому назад: я был во гробе, я уж четыре года лежал во гробе, так что уж и смердеть перестал. А ей говорят: "Вот – он во гробе. И воскреси, если сможешь"» (ibid., 74).
13   «На кабельных работах в Шереметьево-Лобня. Осень 69 года» (ibid., 129).
14   «Я не знал, что есть на свете такая боль, и скрючился от муки. Густая красная буква "Ю" распласталась у меня в глазах, задрожала, и с тех пор я не приходил в сознание и никогда не приду» (ibid.).

exposed as the absence of the narrator in his own book—a contradiction of Nabokov's adage: The I in the book cannot die in the book" (227).

Irene Lukšić, on the other hand, argues that in Erofeev's poem "a consciousness appearing in the role of the demiurge has no other (ontological) basis than the literary, the written[...] his sole actuality is the ceaselessly occurring, growing and changing text" (264).

1-2. A monument to the heroes of Moskva-Petushhki, Moscow, Ploshchad' Bor'by. Sculptors V. Kuznetsov and S. Mantselev. Photos by Mark Lipovetsky.

In my opinion, the meaning of the concluding phrase is inseparable from Venichka's position of a trickster, with its inherent ambivalence. It places him in a state of permanent fluctuation between life and death, silence and voice, and, eventually, the logos and its radical negation. The last phrase defines the source of the narrative as precisely the liminal zone that transforms the text of *Moskva-Petushki* into the most effective model of cultural and philosophical liminality.

The poem also underlines the natural artistry of the trickster. The various sections on the inseparability of creativity and drunkenness are especially telling. The chapters "Esino-Friazevo" and "Friazevo—61st kilometer" and the recurring metaphor insist with an almost folkloristic persuasiveness that one should drink "throwing back [one's] head like a pianist, conscious both of the grandeur of the fact that it was just beginning and of what lay ahead" (1997:44[15], see also 53, 78) shows us art and drunkenness as interrelated. Other examples include: "Perhaps, I was rehearsing something out there?... Perhaps, it was the immortal drama of *Othello, the Venetian Moor*? I was playing it alone—all the roles at once" (1997: 29)[16]. It is not surprising that the very process of the drunken journey is described in the terminology of literary studies: "The devil knows in which genre I'll arrive to Petushki. All the way from Moscow it was memoirs and philosophical essays, it was all poems in prose, like Ivan Turgenev. Now the detective story begins" (ibid., 73, translation altered)[17].

In light of the final phrase, it becomes clear that Venichka does not simply relate the trickster's ambivalence and liminality to the creative act of the artist, but grants a *metapoetic meaning to the very position of the trickster*. Erofeev's poem presupposes that free—or underground— art can only be created by a trickster who inhabits a liminal zone, is hopelessly ambivalent, and interweaves the high and the low, the comic and the tragic. His art is disconnected from the "cultural context," at the same time creating this very context. Only the trickster can "hang suspended" between life and death. He can die, lose his consciousness and voice (the awl is driven into the hero-narrator's *throat* for a reason), and yet still narrate his own death.

The understanding of the underground author/artist as a meta-trickster, whose tricks unfold in the domain of language and consist of an irreverent game with opposing discourses—a game whose

---

15 «... запрокинув голову, как пианист и с сознанием величия того, что еще только начинается и чему еще предстоит быть» (ibid., 38-39)

16 «Может, я там что репетировал?... Может, я играл бессмертную драму «Отелло, мавр венецианский»? Играл в одиночку и сразу во всех ролях?» (ibid., 27)

17 «Черт знает, в каком жанре я доеду до Петушков... От самой Москвы все были философские эссе и мемуары, все были стихотворения в прозе, как у Ивана Тургенева... Теперь начинается детективная повесть» (ibid., 61)

major precondition is "living *vnye*" (outside)—was formative for the late Soviet underground. Alexei Yurchak, in his aforementioned book *Everything Was Forever Until It Was No More: The Last Soviet Generation*, analyzes numerous cultural practices, including many belonging to underground culture, arguing that the vast majority was marked by a "refusal to accept any boundary between seriousness and humor, support [for the regime] and opposition, sense and nonsense" (243). Especially telling is the behavioral/artistic strategy of the Leningrad group which called itself Mit'ki, and whose motto was: "The Mit'ki don't want to defeat anyone" ("Mit'ki nikogo ne khotiat pobedit'"). Through their ironic "life-construction" they created a "zone between the inside and outside of the boundaries drawn by Soviet authoritative discourse... a zone that refused the boundary between bare and political life and constituted the world of *vnye*. The Mit'ki rejected the *sociopolitical* effect of this boundary, refusing to fit either of the two subject positions that it created, the pro-system 'activist' and the anti-system 'dissident.'" (idem., 249) Despite its seeming "harmlessness," this position was rich in anti-authoritarian and anti-hierarchical potential. For instance, Dmitrii A. Prigov, one of the leaders and theoreticians of the Moscow conceptualist circle, writes, recalling the end of the 60s:

> [W]e were totally critical. Any discourse that entered our field of vision we immediately linked to the discourse of power. For instance, we regarded Pushkin and Mayakovsky as ordinary representatives of the Soviet regime. Furthermore, from our perspective figures like Akhmatova and Pasternak, who had been ethical guideposts for the previous generation, fell into the discourse of power as soon as they were published. (Prigov and Shapoval, 94–95)

In this sense, underground culture formed a liminal zone in which each and every pretension to power—symbolic, rhetorical or political—was undermined. One might say that the underground formed a peculiar "black market" in culture, and that the activists of the underground of the 1960s–1970s were forced to assume the trickster's position by the liminal semiotics of their activities.[18]

The merging of the free underground artist and the trickster inherent in the construction of Erofeev's poem also acquires a certain ethical dimension. The ethical philosophy emerging from this position is a principled lightness: "They, they're serious, they understand, and I'm a lightweight and I'll never understand it... *Mene, tekel, parsin*, that is, you are weighed upon the scales and found wanting—that is *tekel* [...] If there are scales there or not—there, we lightweights will outweigh and overcome. I believe in this more firmly than you believe in anything." (1997: 156, 157)[19]

This lightness is apparent in the eccentric "mircosermons" interspersing Venichka's narrative:

> Everything should take place slowly and incorrectly so that man doesn't get a chance to start feeling proud, so that man is sad and perplexed (1997:14);[20]

> Oh, if only the whole world, if everyone were like I am now, placid and timorous and never sure about anything, not sure of himself nor of the seriousness of his position under the heavens—oh, how good it could be. No enthusiasts, no feats of valor, nothing obsessive! Just universal faintheartedness. I'd agree to live on the earth for an eternity if they'd show

---

18  It should be noted that this "black market" was more than a merely symbolic formation but had a very literal economic aspect. Thus, Solomon Volkov recalls the terms "dipart"—the market side of underground art patronized by diplomats and other foreigners: "Dip Art (art for diplomats and other foreigners) burgeoned in the early 1960s changing the position of unofficial culture [...] We can only guess why the ubiquitous secret police looked the other way as the Moscow Dip-Art scene (followed by Leningrad) expanded and flourished. It is a fact that this unofficial guild, which at its peak had at least several dozen participants (probably around two hundred people), gradually turned into a tempting alternative to the state system of rewarding artists."(258).

19  «Они серьезные, они понимают, а я, легковесный, никогда не пойму... Мене, текел, фарес, то есть "ты взвешен на весах и найден легковесным", то есть текел. [...] Есть весы, или нет весов – там мы легковесные, перевесим и одолеем. Я прочнее в это верю, чем вы во что-нибудь верите» (Erofeev 1990: 123).

20  «Все на свете должно идти медленно и неправильно, чтобы не сумел загордиться человек, чтобы человек был грустен и растерян» (ibid., 16)

me first a corner where there's not always room for valor. 'Universal faintheartedness.' Indeed this is the panacea, this is the predicate to sublime perfection. (ibid., 20–21)[21]

And so I solemnly announce that, till the end of my days, I shall not undertake anything the like of my sad brush with eminence. I'll remain below and from below I'll spit on their social ladder. Right, spit on every rung of it. In order to climb it, it's necessary to be forged steel-assed from head to toe. And this I'm not. (ibid., 41)[22]

You have to have the ability to choose your work; there aren't any bad jobs or bad professions; one must respect every calling. It's necessary, just after waking, to drink something right away, or, no, I'm lying, not 'something' but precisely the same thing that you were drinking the day before—and drink every forty or forty-five minutes so that toward evening you have drunk 250 grams more than the day before. Then there won't be any queasiness or shyness and you will have such a white face it'll look as though it hasn't been

---

21  «О, если бы весь мир, если бы каждый в мире был бы, как я сейчас, тих и боязлив и был бы так же ни в чем не уверен: ни в себе, ни в серьезности своего места под небом - как хорошо бы! Никаких энтузиастов, никаких подвигов, никакой одержимости! - всеобщее малодушие. Я согласился бы жить на земле целую вечность, если бы мне прежде показали уголок, где не всегда есть место подвигам. "Всеобщее малодушие" - да ведь где это спасение ото всех бед, эта панацея, этот предикат величайшего совершенства!» (1990: 21)

22  «И вот - я торжественно объявляю: до конца моих дней я не предприму ничего, чтобы повторить мой печальный опыт возвышения. Я остаюсь внизу и снизу плюю на всю вашу общественную лестницу. Да. На каждую ступеньку лестницы - по плевку. Чтоб по ней подыматься, надо быть жидовскою мордою без страха и упрека, надо быть пидорасом, выкованным из чистой стали с головы до пят. А я - не такой.» (1990: 36)

kicked around for six months. (ibid., 59–60)[23]

These micro-sermons are impressive not only because of their specific sort of kynical "shamelessness," though it is certainly apparent: universal apathy is placed above the romantic imperative stipulating that "in life there is always a place for heroism." The knight without fear and fault becomes "a kike's mug without fear and reproach... a faggot forged from pure steel from head to toe," harmony with society demands a regular increase in alcohol intake. Far more important is the fact that these categorical anti-imperatives embody that which Sloterdijk defines as the essence of kynical reason: "insight into the original purposelessness of life... a critical, ironical philosophy of so-called needs, in the elucidation of their fundamental excess and absurdity [...] the knowledge —decried as nihilism—that we must snub the grand goals. In this regard we cannot be nihilistic enough" (194). The resemblance is striking: "insight into the original purposelessness of life, limiting the wish for power and the power of wishing" directly applies to the maxim: "Everything should take place slowly and incorrectly so that man doesn't get a chance to start feeling proud, so that man is sad and perplexed"; "a critical, ironical philosophy of so-called needs" corresponds to "universal faintheartedness" as "a predicate to the predicate to sublime perfection"; "we must snub the grand goals" translates as "I'll remain below and from below I'll spit on their social ladder"; while an ever-increasing dose of alcohol as a criterion of progress parodies such goals of socialist construction as "the steady rise of the individual above himself."

It is with equal cynicism (kynicism?) that Venichka mocks a whole range of authoritarian discourses and their corresponding grand goals. Thus, the single phrase "To climb this ladder you have to be a kike's mug without fear and reproach, you have to be a faggot forged from pure steel from head to toe" (to use a literal translation) contains a travesty of Herzen's famous line about the Decembrists: "These are some sort of warriors, forged from pure steel from head to toe," which relates to,

---

23  «Надо уметь выбирать себе работу, плохих работ не бывает. Дурных профессий нет, надо уважать всякое призвание. Надо, чуть проснувшись, немедленно чего-нибудь выпить, даже нет, вру, не "чего-нибудь," а именно того самого, что ты пил вчера, и пить с паузами в сорок-сорок пять минут, так, чтобы к вечеру ты выпил на двести пятьдесят больше, чем накануне. Вот тогда не будет ни дурноты, ни стыдливости, и сам ты будешь таким белолицым, как будто тебя уже полгода по морде не били.» (ibid., 50)

first, the idealization of the Decembrists that was typical for the "antisystemic" discourse of the Soviet liberal intelligentsia in the 1960s, and second, to Lenin's article "To the Memory of Herzen" (the discourse of the revolution as an ideological dogma). As a result, the phrase itself became idiomatic (the corresponding fragment from Lenin's essay was assigned for rote memorization in Soviet high schools). At the same time, Venichka undermines the revolutionary rhetoric through clichés of anti-intelligentsia rhetoric: the terms "kike's mug" and "faggots" are closely associated with "popular" attitudes towards the intelligentsia, as well as to official discourse in the 1960s (i.e., the discourse of the "system" of party bureaucracy)—after all, "fags" was the label Khrushchev applied to the avant-garde artists exhibiting at the infamous 1963 show at the Manezh.

Another link to kynicism is apparent in the fact that Erofeev's poem and his hero-narrator express the idiosyncratic wholeness of the kynical position—the transformation of the cynical transition from one social mask to another in a *metamorphosis*, the artistic flexibility of a subject engaging body and mind. Kynical metamorphosis takes place in at least two layers of the poem. It is apparent in the organization of the colorful stylistic, discursive and referential pluralism of Venichka's speech. This aspect of the poem is perhaps the one most thoroughly investigated. Thus, for instance, Geisser-Schnittmann emphasizes such stylistic schemata of *Moskva-Petushki* as the biblical layer, the numerous traditional literary styles, each cast in the light of parody ("faux-romantic, symbolist, pseudo-Gogolesque"), Venichka's philosophically detached manner, "historical citations," parodies of ideological and media stamps, folklore and vulgarity (see 250–257). The breadth of the poem's intertextual field is unprecedented, which is why there are at least two weighty commentaries on virtually every line of *Moskva-Petushki* (see Vlasov, Levin).

At the same time, the apparent diversity of the referential mosaic is overcome because the various stylistic registers, and the direct and discursive quotations in the poem's narrative, do not clash, but transform into one another. For example:

> And later (listen carefully), later, after they had found out why Pushkin died, I gave them Alexander Blok's poem *The Nightingale Garden* to read. There, at the center of the

poem—if you throw out all of the perfumed shoulders, the unilluminated mists, the rosy towers in smoky vestments—there at the center of the poem you find the lyric hero dismissed from work for drunkeneness, whoring, and absenteeism. I told them, "It's a very contemporary book." I told them, "You'll find it useful." And so? They read it. But, in spite of everything, it had a depressing effect on them—Freshen-up disappeared immediately from all the stores. It's impossible to say why, but blackjack was forgotten, vermouth was forgotten, Sheremetievo International Field was forgotten, and Freshen-up triumphed. Everyone drank only Freshen-up. Oh, to be carefree! Oh heavenly birds, who neither sow nor reap. Oh, the lilies of the field are dressed more beautifully than Solomon! They drank up all the Freshen-up from Dolgoprudny Station to Sheremetievo International. (1997: 37)[24]

This passage's stylistic trajectory is best described as a downward parabola. The beginning features an ironic imitation of Symbolist style ("the perfumed shoulders, the unilluminated mists, the rosy towers in smoky vestments"), only to descend sharply, first into vulgarity ("for drunkenness, whoring, and absenteeism") and then into the Lenin quote ("It's a very contemporary book"). But the final part of this passage is a provocative return to the poetic key. Moreover, the name of the "Freshen-up" cologne is semantically associated with Alexander Blok's "Nightingale Garden" ("Freshen-up triumphed") and placed within a stylistic context that is biblical ("Oh, the lilies of the field are dressed

---

24  «А потом (слушайте), а потом, когда они узнали, отчего умер Пушкин, я дал им почитать «Соловьиный сад», поэму Александра Блока. Там в центре поэмы, если, конечно, отбросить в сторону все эти благоуханные плеча и неозаренные туманы и розовые башни в дымных ризах, там в центре поэмы лирический персонаж, уволенный с работы за пьянку, блядки и прогулы. Я сказал им: «Очень своевременная книга, — сказал, — вы прочтете ее с большой пользой для себя». Что ж? Они прочли. Но, вопреки всему, она сказалась на них удручающе: во всех магазинах враз пропала вся «свежесть». Непонятно почему, но сика была забыта, вермут был забыт, международный аэропорт Шереметьево был забыт, — и восторжествовала «Свежесть», все пили только « Свежесть».

О, беззаботность! О, птицы небесные, не собирающие в житницы! О, краше Соломона одетые полевые лилии! — они выпили всю «Свежесть» от станции Долгопрудная до международного аэропорта Шереметьево!» (1990: 33)

more beautifully than Solomon..."). The result is a metamorphosis of several stylistic and discursive registers. The collision of the parody of symbolist style with vulgarity and ideological clichés produces an effect that is at once comically debasing and elevating: the emotional impact of poetry finds expression in an increased consumption of the cologne "Freshen-up," and the circumstances are retold in the language of the biblical "Song of Songs."

Second, metamorphosis is the only explanation for Venichka's relationships with the characters depicted in the second part of the poem. If "Black-Mustache," "Decembrist," Mitrich and grandson, "the woman of difficult fate," and the controller Semenych each appear to be independent of Venichka's consciousness to some degree; their reflections in the second part, i.e., Satan, the Sphinx, the Princess from Ivan Kramskoi's painting *Inconsolable Grief*, "my valet" (1997: 145[25]), Peter and King Mithridates are all unquestionably Venichka's own hallucinations (which cannot be said for certain of either Venichka's beloved, waiting at the Petushki station, or of the child "already knowing the letter 'ю'"). Nevertheless, Venichka enters a complex dialogue with these characters and in so doing undergoes a metamorphosis, remaining his own person and simultaneously manifesting a different, and even a stranger's, consciousness. The greatest unresolved problem is the question of the angels and Venichka's murderers—how far *removed* are they from the hero? In other words: to what degree are they the result of the hero's consciousness, affected by the influence of alcohol?

All these metamorphoses, as well as the trickster's meta-position embodied by the hero, and Venichka's kynical ethics stem from a common source—a shared notion of the sacred.

## RITUALS OF EXPENDITURE

The sensational popularity of the poem was further fuelled by the development of postmodern theory in Russia. Erofeev's work appeared to many critics as a very early and still unintended manifestation of Russian postmodernism. *Moskva-Petushki* cheerfully, yet tragically, demonstrated the collapse not only of the Soviet utopia, but also of the entire modernist conception of the *self*. The circular composition of

---

25   «мой камердинер» (ibid., 114).

the poem reads as the sarcastic transformation of the myth of progress (or vice versa, the myth of escaping civilization into "nature") into the carnival procession of the hero's visitors and drinking buddies, monsters, and murderers. The ongoing linguistic game collides fragments of very different discourses (whose sources range from the Old Testament to *Pravda*) within the confines of a single phrase, leaving only ruins of the faith in the word's power that was so common in the epoch of modernity. The hero's constant intoxication, on the other hand, openly defies modernity's worship of reason.

However, reading the demythologization of the Soviet (and not only the Soviet) ideology of modernity in Erofeev's poem, we must bear in mind that during the eighteenth to twentieth centuries in Russia the cult of reason, paradoxically as this might seem, was always colored by a notion of religiosity. This is the origin of the traditional Russian *literature-centrism*, which barely changed during the Soviet period. From this point of view, the unofficial culture of the 1960s–80s constituted a specific kind of secularization, linked to the critique of the myths of reason and progress. This is why Gianni Vattimo's conception of postmodern secularization is particularly relevant to Russian culture: "A secularized culture is not the one that has simply left the religious elements of its tradition behind, but one that continues to live them as traces, as hidden and distorted models that are nonetheless profoundly present." (Vattimo, 40)

However, it is precisely the religious element of the Russian literary tradition, sacralizing the word and literature, that gives the secularization in the underground its intense and dramatic character, distinguishing it from parallel and thematically similar tendencies in Western literature contemporary to Erofeev—in particular the novels of Ken Kesey and Jack Kerouac and the literature of the beatniks (see Reingol'd on this). On the one hand, Soviet unofficial art of the 1970s and 1980s subjected fragments of the Soviet notion of the sacred, as represented by Socialist Realism and official Soviet ideology, to grandiose carnivalesque deconstruction. On the other hand, this practice in no way implied disillusionment with the "transcendental signified" or the rejection of the search for the latter.

In the 1970s (and still today), the Soviet experience was understood by many as a *distortion* of the "normal" path of Russian culture—which some saw foreshadowed in the literary classics of the 19th century and others in the modernism of the 1910–1920s—and consequently a *replacement* of the true "transcendental signified" by false simulacra. This understanding explains the allure of a return to "uncorrupted" trajectories and becomes the source of many illusions in unofficial and official late Soviet art. This is also why new, unofficial and nonconformist art of the 1970s often combined deconstruction of the Soviet myth with a certain interest in the transcendental. Pertinent examples include Joseph Brodsky's half-ironic sacralization of language and its creative force, Andrei Tarkovsky's dialogue with Christian symbolism, and the non-canonical religiosity of the entire Leningrad unofficial culture, including Leonid Aronson, Mikhail Eremin, Viktor Krivulin, Elena Shvarts, and Boris Kurdiakov (see Stepanov, Golynko-Vol'fson, Ivanov), as well as the half-parodical, half-serious "holy foolery" of the Mit'ki group. For this reason, the central conflict of unofficial Russian culture in the 1970s–1980s is the conflict between a de-sacralizing discourse and a discourse searching for and aiming to renew transcendental values.

*Moskva-Petushki* is particularly significant in this respect, as it is one of the few narratives—especially in unofficial culture—to directly *enact* this intense collision. Not only did this collision play an important role in the process of Russian culture's liberation from Soviet (quasi) religiosity, but the poem also poses some of the key questions of postmodern culture as a whole: namely, whether or not art is possible without transcendence, and what happens to sacred meanings after the collapse of the modern utopia, "after Auschwitz"? The answers to these questions emerge from the philosophical position embodied by the figure of the trickster-kynic.

Scholars of Erofeev's poem have thoroughly traced his play to Old Testament and New Testament mythologems, the archetype of the holy fool and other religious discourses.[26] However, it is fundamentally important that all these themes and motifs are not only inscribed into the process of alcoholic intoxication, but grant the very process of getting drunk ritual meaning.

The reader witnesses a *ritual of expenditure* in the purest sense: all meanings involved in the process are directed towards the same goal—

---

[26] See: Geisser-Schnittmann 114–151, Gasparov and Paperno, Prokhorov G., Smirnova, Verkhovsteva-Drubek.

getting wasted—and the logical conclusion becomes the poem's finale. Aleksandr Genis considers drunkenness a primary motivation (in the sense the Russian formalists gave to the term) of the poem: "As soon as we honestly read the poem *Moskva-Petushki* we will be convinced that the vodka needs no justification—it justifies the author instead. Alcohol is the axis of Erofeev's plot. His hero goes through every step of intoxication [...] the poem's composition is built in strict adherence to this path." (Genis, 51) All this happens precisely because Erofeev demonstratively and provocatively *replaces transcendence with vodka and alcohol (and the concomitant self-destruction)*, thus accomplishing ritualistic expenditure.[27]

Venichka seems to *literally* live out Bataille's philosophical program: "This useless consumption is *what suits me*, once my concern for the morrow is removed. And if I thus consume immoderately, I reveal to my fellow beings that which I am *intimately*. Consumption is the way in which *separate* beings communicate. Everything shows through, everything is open and infinite between those who consume intensely." (1988: 58) To put it briefly, the hero of *Moskva-Petushki* consumes a very definite, though universal, product, which is his means of getting wasted.

Expenditure grants the symbolic power that is visible in the roles Venichka assumes over the course of the tale—not only "the little prince," Hamlet, "Cain and Manfred," and the holy-fool, but also Scheherazade, when he entertains the controller Semenych with his speech, the leader of the *symposium* in the train wagon, the leader of the

---

27  See also comparison between Erofeev's poem and magical rituals, as described in the books of Carlos Casteneda proposed by Viktor Pelevin: "The Russian means of eternal return differ from the Mexican only in the different names of the populated centers through which fate carries the heroes and those psychotropic devices with whose aid they cross the boundaries of the mundane world. For Mexican magicians and their disciples it is the hallucinogenic cactus peyote, psilocybin mushrooms, and complex mixtures prepared from datura. For Venichka Erofeev and the many thousands of adepts who follow his teachings it is "kubanskaia" vodka, fortified rosé and complex cocktails made from nail polish and cures for sweaty feet. Actually in total accordance with the practices of shamans, each of these mixtures permits the exploration of a particular aspect of reality. Mexican magicians deal with various spirits, and Venichka Erofeev meets some suspicious gentleman, all in blue lightning, laughing angels and a shy railroad Satan. Perhaps here what matters is not so much spiritual essences but various traditions of experiencing the supernatural in different cultures" (Pelevin 2005: 288–289; the essay was initially published in *Nezavisimaia gazeta*, 1993, January 20: 5).

Cherkasovo revolution, a European intellectual who used to argue with Sartre and Simone de Beauvoir, and finally, a shaman conducting an esoteric ritual, conversing with angels and dining with God. Ultimately, Venichka is a tragicomic double to the Messiah: "Trembling all over, I said to myself, *Talife cumi*, that is, 'Get up and prepare for the end ...' This isn't *Talife cumi*, it's *lama savahfani*, as the Savior said ... That is, 'Why hast thou forsaken me?' (1997:162)[28]

Venichka's drinking cannot be reduced to romantic escapism, which in turn is a direct outcome of the transcendental project. The drunkenness in *Moskva-Petushki* is no more compatible with the romantic tradition than the naturalistic logic of *chernukha* (dark and grim discourse), which focuses on the terrible residents of the underbelly of Soviet and post-Soviet society. Erofeev's work emphasizes the *ironic inadequacy* and the shock effect created by the replacing of God with vodka, through the contrast between the names of the cocktails, the rituals of their preparation, and their unlikely ingredients, as well as the comical comparison between another dose of coriander vodka with St. Teresa's stigmata and other playful blasphemies. Obviously, vodka is not identical with God, but due to the nonidentity of the substitution, vodka is capable of embodying God by the manifestation of expenditure as the sole path to transcendental intimacy with the world.

It is the *gaps* in Venichka's being and consciousness that point most strongly to the transcendental dimension of drunken expenditure. The transcendental semantic of gaps and ruptures is the focus of one of the quasi-philosophical fragments of the poem—the description of hiccups as epiphany. In this fragment, drunken hiccups, a chain of unpredictable convulsive ruptures, are equivalent to God's omnipotent hand:

> *It* is [hiccup] indiscernible and we are helpless. We are deprived of freedom and are in the power of the arbitrary which has no name and from which there is no escape
> 
> We are mere trembling creatures while *it* is omnipotent. It—that is, the Right Hand of God (*Bozh'ia desnitsa*) which is raised above us all and before which only cretins and

---

28  «Весь сотрясаясь, я сказал себе: "Талифа куми!" [...] Это уже не «талифа куми», то есть «встань и приготовься к кончине», -- это «лама савахвани», то есть «для чего, Господь, Ты меня оставил»?» (Erofeev 1990: 127).

## CHAPTER FIVE

rogues do not bow their heads. He is incomprehensible and therefore He is. (1997: 65, Erofeev's italics[29])

Here, as in a number of other fragments related to not-seeing and darkness, one suspects an intertextual reference to the tract "The Mystical Theology" by the fifth- and sixth century Christian thinker Dionysius the Areopagite, which had a wide circulation in the Moscow samizdat during the 1960s and 1970s. This tract asserts the apophatic idea that communication with God requires complete negation of all intellectual and sensual faculties, since He transcends human experience; thus communication with the Divine, according to Dionysius, requires plunging "into the Darkness of Unknowing":

> I counsel that, in the earnest exercise of mystic contemplation, thou leave the senses and the activities of the intellect and all things that the senses or the intellect can perceive, and all things in this world of nothingness[...] and that, thine understanding being laid to rest, thou strain (so far as thou mayest) towards an union with Him whom neither being nor understanding can contain [...] thou shalt be led upward to the Ray of that divine Darkness that exceedeth all existence (ibid., 192–3)

It is not difficult to see the link between Venichka's drunkenness and the tract's logic of realizing God via "oblivion" (granting that Dionysius the Areopagite, like Venichka many centuries later, handles the categories of drunkenness and hangover as though they were metaphysical). Drinking allows Venichka to reach "mental incognition and unknowing" and thus dive into the darkness conceived as the appearance of God, following Dionysius's recommendation: "For the more that we soar upwards the more our language becomes restricted to the compass of purely intellectual conception, even as in the present instance plunging into the Darkness which is above the intellect we shall find ourselves

---

29  "...о н а [икота] неисследима, а мы беспомощны. Мы начисто лишены всякой свободы воли, мы во власти произвола, которому нет имени и спасения от которого -- тоже нет. Мы -- дрожащие твари, а о н а -- всесильна. О н а, то есть Божья Десница, которая над всеми нами занесена и пред которой не хотят склонить головы одни кретины и проходимцы. О н непостижим уму, а следовательно, О н есть» (ibid., 55).

reduced not merely to brevity of speech but even to absolute dumbness both of speech and thought." (ibid., 197–8)

This context explains many of Venichka's sermons and meditations on the good of "the universal faintheartedness" («всеобщее малодушие»), in Dionysius's terminology equivalent to "renunciation" and "inaction"; and the suggestion that one should "honor the dark reaches of the another's soul [...] even if there's nothing there, even if there's only trash there. It's all one; look and honor, look and don't spit on it" (1997: 94)[30]—immersing oneself into "that super-essential Darkness" (Dionysius, 196), where darkness features as the equivalent of "a knowledge that exceeds his understanding." (ibid., 194) From this point of view, drinking as a chain of ruptures in consciousness and existence and intoxication as a regular arrhythmic plunging into the dark and chaos together form the poem's narrative and the hero's ragged being as a consistent means of approaching God. The fact that Venichka never makes it to Petushki, losing his beloved and the infant, the fact that he remains alone—first in an empty train and then in an empty Moscow—even the loss of his life at the end can all be read as the systematic reflection of the apophatic logic of Nothingness as the major attribute of the transcendental. In concordance with this logic, the emblem of the purest character in the poem—the infant, Venichka's son—becomes a bloody sign of death in the finale: "a clotted red letter 'Ю' spread across my eyes and started to quiver." (1997: 164)

The problem is the fact that this logic does not quite agree with Erofeev's poem *as a whole*. The paradox of *Moskva-Petushki* consists in the fact that the entire finale—after Venichka has missed his stop at Petushki—reads as an insistent refutation of the apophatic cognizance of God, superimposed on "altered" evangelical scenes and the chain of "renunciation of thyself and all things." (Dionysius, 191–2) It is not by an accident that the words "…what blackness and, beyond blackness—is that rain or snow? Or is it just that I'm looking through tears into the dark? Oh, God…" (1997: 130)[31] are followed immediately by the voice of Satan, not God as might well be expected. The darkness outside the

---

30 «… надо чтить потемки чужой души [...] пусть даже там и нет ничего, пусть там дрянь одна – все равно: смотри и чти, смотри и не плюй» (ibid., 77).
31 «о, какая чернота! и что там в этой черноте – дождь или снег? или просто я сквозь слезы гляжу в эту тьму? Боже...» (ibid., 103).

window no longer calls up the recollection of God, but awakens the "black thought": "So there remains only one way out: accept the dark." (ibid., 132)[32] The hope for apophatic transcendence comes to nothing: "All your guiding stars are rolling toward the horizon and, if not, they are barely glimmering—and even if they are, they aren't worth two gobs of spit." (ibid., 157)[33] The darkness at the poem's finale materializes not as an appearance of God but as his deafening silence and the mocking laughter of the angels. This also proves that apophatic transcendence in Erofeev's poem is just *an isolated case* of expenditure, while the latter is truly universal, encompassing God, the hero and his word alike. (The suggestion that the logic of expenditure is not accidental for Erofeev's oeuvre is confirmed in the analogous finale of his "tragedy in five acts" *Val'purgieva noch', ili Shagi kommandora* [*Walpurgisnacht or the Steps of Commander*], with another trickster, Gurevich, in the lead.)

### "I WILL NOT EXPLAIN TO YOU WHO WERE THESE FOUR …"

The genius of *Moskva-Petushki* consists, perhaps, in its nature as a unique sort of metaphysical (or post-metaphysical?) detective story. The reader is presented with the corpse of the hero (or author?) and the very understanding of the poem, as well as the philosophical experiment that stands behind it, demands that the murder be solved. There is a reason why Erofeev purposefully evokes associations with another famous metaphysical detective story: Sophocles's *Oedipus Rex*. Venichka meets the Sphinx: "There, in Petushki, what's wrong? The pestilence? Did somebody get betrothed to his own daughter there?" (ibid., 136)[34]

Strange as it might seem, despite the abundance of published interpretations, the central question of any detective story (in this case *"who killed Venichka Erofeev?"*) remains open. Even if one considers the murder as a pure outburst of absurdist aggression, it is necessary to understand the powers that gave rise to this aggression.[35] Let us note that the hero states that he knows his killers *with certainty*: "I recognized

---

32  «Значит, остается один выход -- принять эту тьму» (ibid., 104).
33  «Все ваши путеводные звезды катятся к закату... а если и не катятся, то едва мерцают, а если даже и сияют, то не стóят и двух плевков» (ibid., 123).
34  «там в Петушках, – чего? моровая язва? Там кто-то вышел замуж за собственную дочь, и ты...? – Там хуже, чем дочь и язва» (ibid., 107).
35  See Tiupa and Liakhova, 36.

them at once—I won't tell you who they were." (ibid., 158)[36]

Every interpretation of *Moskva-Petushki* seeks an answer to this question; however, each existing version considers only a few of the killers' characteristics, while ignoring the others completely. Thus the suggestion that the four murderers are Marx, Engels, Lenin, and Stalin is reinforced by the statement that the killers look "not at all like brigands—rather, there was a touch of something classical about them" (ibid., 158)[37], as well as the phrase "Where, in what newspapers, did I see their repulsive mugs." (ibid., 159)[38] This version heavily stresses the importance of the proximity of the murder site to the Kremlin.

"Something classical," albeit with no more references to the line about newspapers, is understood as a reference to the four Roman legionnaires who crucified Jesus. This proposal is supported by the words about the apostle Peter: "warming himself by the fire, together with *them*" (ibid., 158, emphasized by the author).[39] The apocalyptic atmosphere makes us think of the four riders of St. John's Revelation.[40] Other scholars have commented upon the recurrent motif of four antagonists (fellow-drinkers in the brigade, neighbors at the dormitory, etc), which turns the killers into the embodiment of an aggressive social sphere.[41] The last, and perhaps most original, version is associated with a particularity ascribed to the fourth assassin: "the fourth looked like ... actually, I will tell you later, whom he resembled." (ibid., 124)[42] As Vitalii Tiupa and Elena Liakhova believe, "this is none other than the infant who did not wait for his father's gifts (and so joined the choir of angels)" (39).

However, as has been said, none of these hypotheses takes into consideration *all* of the characteristics of Venichka's assassins. If they are the classics of Marxism-Leninism, then why do they warm themselves by the fire with Peter? If they are the riders of the Apocalypse, then where are their horses and why do they run so badly? The version that proposes a materialized aggressive social sphere does not hold, since

---

36   «Я сразу их узнал, я не буду вам объяснять, кто эти четверо» (1990:124).
37   «... совсем не разбойничьи рожи, скорее даже наоборот, с налетом чего-то классического» (ibid., 124)
38   «Где, в каких газетах я видел эти рожи?» (ibid.,125).
39   «грелся у костра вместе с этими». (ibid.,124).
40   See Bethea, Tumanov.
41   See Tiupa and Liakhova, 38.
42   «А четвертый был похож... впрочем, я потом скажу, на кого он был похож» (ibid.,124).

## CHAPTER FIVE

Venichka immediately *recognizes* his killers. If one of the killers is the child and the others are angels, then how does one explain the line about newspapers? And why does Venichka beg the angels to help him ("Angels of heaven, they're coming up, what should I do? What should I do, now, so as not to die?"(1997: 162)[43], if they are the ones killing him? Another characteristic of the fourth assassin hardly fits the infant, "the fiercest and most classical profile." (ibid., 163)[44] Finally, none of these versions accounts for the last detail: when the four climb the stairs barefoot immediately before the murder, holding their shoes in their hands. The narrator tries to find a pragmatic explanation: "Why was that necessary? So as not to make noise in the hall? Or in order to sneak up on me unnoticed? I don't know, but it was the last thing I remember." (ibid., 163)[45] But then why does Venichka accentuate his surprise, and why is "this very surprise" his last recollection, immediately followed by the "a clotted red letter 'Ю'"?

Let us take as our starting point one of the least contradictory suggestions (though one that still does not answer all our questions)—Vlasov's linking of the murderers to the four beasts before the throne of God in the New Testament Book of Revelation.[46] Vlasov seems to have the following fragment in mind:

> Around the throne, and on each side of the throne, are four living creatures, full of eyes in front and behind: the first living creature like a lion, the second living creature like an ox, the third living creature with a face like a human face, and the fourth living creature like a flying eagle. Each of the four living creatures had six wings and was covered with eyes all around, even under his wings. Day and night they never stop saying: "Holy, holy, holy is the Lord God Almighty, who was, and is, and is to come." Whenever the living creatures give glory, honor and thanks to him who sits on the throne and who lives for ever and ever. (Rev 4: 6–8)

---

43  «Ангелы небесные! они поднимаются! что мне делать? что мне сейчас делать, чтобы не умереть?» (Erofeev 1990: 127).
44  «...с самым свирепым и классическим профилем» (ibid., 128).
45  «... для чего это надо было? чтобы не шуметь в подъезде? или чтобы незаметнее ко мне подкрасться? не знаю, но это было последнее, что я запомнил.» (с. 128)
46  See Vlasov, 257.

Vlasov's commentary does not make clear what, besides their number, connects these heavenly beasts to the four that kill Venichka.

However, it is important to note that the New Testament passage compiles two separate Old Testament descriptions. The first is from Isaiah: the famous passage about the seraphim:

> In the year that King Uzziah died, I saw the Lord seated on a throne, high and exalted, and the train of his robe filled the temple. Above him were seraphs, each with six wings: With two wings they covered their faces, with two they covered their feet, and with two they were flying. And they were calling to one another: "Holy, holy, holy is the Lord Almighty; the whole earth is full of his glory." (Isaiah, 6:1–3)

"The beasts' in the fragment from Revelation are akin to the seraphim in their places around the throne, their songs of praise, and certainly their six wings. Note, however, that Isaiah does not tell the number of the seraphim; whereas, Revelation emphasizes that there are four.

The second description is from Ezekiel, and it is particularly close to the depiction of the "beasts" of the Apocalypse:

> 1.⁴ I looked, and I saw a windstorm coming out of the north—an immense cloud with flashing lightning and surrounded by brilliant light. The center of the fire looked like glowing metal, ⁵ and in the fire was what *looked like four living creatures*. In appearance their form was that of a man, ⁶ but each of them had four faces and four wings. ⁷ *Their legs were straight; their feet were like those of a calf and gleamed like burnished bronze.* ⁸ Under their wings on their four sides they had the hands of a man. All four of them had faces and wings, ⁹ and their wings touched one another. Each one went straight ahead; they did not turn as they moved. ¹⁰ Their faces looked like this: Each of the four had the face of a man, and on the right side each had the face of a lion, and on the left the face of an ox; each also had the face of an eagle. ¹¹ Such were their faces. Their wings were spread

───────── CHAPTER FIVE ─────────

out upward; each had two wings, one touching the wing of another creature on either side, and two wings covering its body. ¹² Each one went straight ahead. *Wherever the spirit would go, they would go, without turning as they went.* ¹³ *The appearance of the living creatures was like burning coals of fire or like torches.* Fire moved back and forth among the creatures; it was bright, and lightning flashed out of it. ¹⁴ The creatures sped back and forth like flashes of lightning. ¹⁵ As I looked at the living creatures, I saw a wheel on the ground beside each creature with its four faces. ¹⁶ This was the appearance and structure of the wheels: They sparkled like chrysalides, and all four looked alike. Each appeared to be made like a wheel intersecting a wheel. ¹⁷ *As they moved, they would go in any one of the four directions the creatures faced;* the wheels did not turn about as the creatures went. ¹⁸ Their rims were high and awesome, and all four rims were *full of eyes all around.* ¹⁹ When the living creatures moved, the wheels beside them moved; and when the living creatures rose from the ground, the wheels also rose. ²⁰ Wherever the spirit would go, they would go, and the wheels would rise along with them, because the spirit of the living creatures was in the wheels. ²¹ When the creatures moved, they also moved; when the creatures stood still, they also stood still; *and when the creatures rose from the ground, the wheels rose along with them, because the spirit of the living creatures was in the wheels.* [...]

2.¹ He said to me, "Son of man, stand up on your feet and I will speak to you." ² As he spoke, the Spirit came into me and raised me to my feet, and I heard him speaking to me. ³ He said: "Son of man, I am sending you to the Israelites, to a rebellious nation that has rebelled against me; they and their fathers have been in revolt against me to this very day. ⁴ [...] ⁷ You must speak my words to them, whether they listen or fail to listen, for they are rebellious. ⁸ But you, son of man, listen to what I say to you. Do not rebel like that rebellious house; open your mouth and eat what I give you." ⁹ Then I looked, and I saw a hand stretched out to me. In it was a scroll, ¹⁰ which he unrolled before me. On both sides of it were written words of lament and mourning and woe. (Ez.,1: 4–19, 2:1–7; italics are mine - *ML*.)

This fragment presents us with "four living creatures," whose "form was that of a man." Both Revelations and Ezekiel describe the same set of "faces": the eagle, the bull, the lion, and the man. The creature's wings is another recurrent motif (though in the latter case there are four wings, while the first two visions listed their number as six). Finally, it was this description that gave the New Testament account the mysterious detail of being "full of eyes all around." As follows from the fragment, it is not the beasts themselves that are "full of eyes," but rather their symbolic shadow or extension—their wheels or *ofannim*.

Considering the parallels between these three texts, it is perhaps more accurate to use the ancient Hebrew term "hayyot" (written otherwise as "hayott" and "hayoth"), living beings, which Ezekiel uses explicitly and which refers exclusively to these beings throughout the Old Testament. As we know from various sources, the "hayyot" and the "seraphim" play practically the same role in biblical theology: they are closely interrelated angels of the highest rank: winged half-men, half-beasts, standing next to the throne of God. Statues of the "hayyot" decorated the temple of Moses and David while their outstretched wings formed the throne of Yahweh. (Isaiah 25: 18–22) The inseparability of the "hayyot" and God's throne is also noted in the Book of Ezekiel:

> Spread out above the heads of the living creatures was what looked like an expanse, sparkling like ice and awesome. [...] And when they went, I heard the sound of their wings like the sound of many waters, like the thunder of Almighty, a sound of tumult like the sound of the host; when they stood still they let down their wings. And there came the voice above from the firmament over their heads... And above the firmament over their heads there was the likeness of a throne, in appearance like sapphire; and seated above the likeness of a throne was a likeness as it were of a human form [...] I saw as it were the appearance of fire, and there was brightness round about him... (Ez, 1:22, 24–27)

Perhaps it is the closeness of these creatures to God's throne that Erofeev parodied in the poem's topography. After all, the murderers first find Venichka by the walls of the Kremlin. At the same time, in Revelation the "beasts" precipitate the appearance of the Lamb-Christ and they traditionally serve as symbols of the four evangelists, making their unseen presence in other scenes of the New Testament possible, including Peter's renunciation. The qualities of Ezekiel's "hayyot" in conjunction with the traits of the seraphim in the book of Isaiah, apparent in the description of the apocalyptic "beasts," seem to explain the other peculiarities in Erofeev's killers. In my understanding, these peculiarities most vividly express the meaning of the poem's tragic finale, which is itself at odds with the now classical interpretation of *Moskva-Petushki* as an apophatic (holy-fool-like) affirmation of the Christian "transcendental signified" in the midst of drunken hell and universal chaos.

Let us now turn to these peculiar assassins. First of all, there are the eyes. None of the existing interpretations of Erofeev's poem noted the expressive description: "But the eyes of all four—have you ever sat on the toilet in the Petushki station and do you remember how, far below the round openings, that reddish-brown piss-water splashes and glitters? That's the kind of eyes they all had." (1997:158[47]) It is doubtful that this characteristic can be applied to the eyes of Venichka's child; yet even in other interpretations the passage clearly has a decorative role. At the same time, the description indicates that Erofeev assigned a particular weight and meaning to the *eyes* of his murderers.

The "hayyot," as the aforementioned passages demonstrate, are *full of eyes* (symbolizing Divine omniscience). Their entire image is associated with fire: "The appearance of the living creatures was like burning coals of fire or like torches. Fire moved back and forth among the creatures; it was bright, and lightning flashed out of it. The creatures sped back and forth like flashes of lightning." (Ez. 1:13) This trait also links the "hayyot" with the "seraphim"; the very word "seraphim" derives from the ancient Hebrew verb "to burn" or from a noun denoting a fiery flying serpent—and thus to both the chthonic and celestial domains (which agrees with the aesthetic of *Moskva-Petushki* as a whole). Fire and light are the major characteristics of the seraphim's eyes, inflamed with the

---

[47] «...но в глазах у всех четырых – вы знаете? вы сидели когда-нибудь в туалете в Петушинском вокзале? Помните, как там, на громадной глубине, под круглыми отверстиями плещется и сверкает эта жижа карего цвета – вот такие были глаза у всех четырых» (1990:124).

love of God, burning with loyalty to His will. The image of the flaming or glowing eyes is inverted in Erofeev's description of the terrifying slush *sparkling* in the depths of a public toilet. The presumably "decorative," anti-aesthetic detail holds a paradoxical reference to the semantics of the image of the "hayyot" and the "seraphim." (Let us not forget that the name Lucifer literally means "light-bringer," and that before his fall, Lucifer was one of the four leaders of the seraphs.)

We can assume that Erofeev's *inversion* of all the powers and capabilities of the "hayyots'" eyes is conscious: fire becomes slush, top turns into bottom, and light into fecal matter. At the same time, it is important to emphasize that the angelic does not turn into the demonic, but rather *incorporates* its opposite or negation into itself. The inseparability and impossibility of distinguishing between good and evil, angelic and demonic, is in this case made particularly clear.

Second is the matter of the assassins' feet. Venichka notes that the murderers "can't run at all." (1997: 161)[48] Moreover, the feet of the murderers get a final, maximally accentuated "close-up": "And I had already caught sight of the four of them, they were climbing up from the floor just below. But when I saw them, I was really more surprised than afraid. All four of them were climbing the stairs barefoot, with their shoes in their hands [...] [I]t was the last thing that I remember. That is, this feeling of surprise." (1997: 163)[49] The parallel with the "hayyot" explains this oddity: "Their legs were straight; their feet were like those of a calf" (Ez.,1:7)  Maimonides explains this description of the "hayyot": "in his view their legs do not bend because they have no joints, since the "hayyot" never sit, serving as the living chariot for God." (Maimonides, 252–5) "They also guard the entrance to Eden" (Gen., 3:24), again prohibiting rest. From the point of view of Erofeev's poem, each of these details can explain why Venichka's killers are such bad runners.

The strange scene of the assassins climbing barefoot, shoes in hand, also evokes the image of the "hayyot." It is unlikely that pragmatic motifs play any role here: if the purpose is stealth, why do the murderers make

---

48 «...совсем не умеют бегать» (ibid., 128).
49 «А этих четверых я уже увидел – они подымались с последнего этажа... И когда я их увидел, сильнее всякого страха (честное слово, сильнее) было удивление: они, все четверо, подымались босые и обувь держали в руках – для чего это надо было? [...] не знаю, но это было последнее, что я помнил. То есть вот это удивление» (ibid., 128).

so much noise when they strangle Venichka? Are they afraid he will run away? But Venichka has nowhere to run: he "climbed up to the top landing" (1997: 162)[50], the murderers "were climbing up from the last floor."[51] Perhaps what we see here is a direct, if ironic, materialization of the part of the "hayyot's" description that speaks of their "rims" or "wheels" (*ofannim*): "As they moved, they would go in any one of the four directions the creatures faced; the wheels did not turn about as the creatures went. Their rims were high and awesome, and all four rims were full of eyes all around." Venichka's pursuers use their "wheels" to look for Venichka—it is also important that in youth slang of the 1960s "wheels" (*kolesa*) meant footwear (see Mokienko and Nikitina, 270). Moreover, in accordance with Ezekiel's description of the "hayyot," they follow the wheels, are *led* by them: "When the creatures moved, they [the wheels] also moved; when the creatures stood still, they also stood still; and when the creatures rose from the ground, the wheels rose along with them, because the spirit of the living creatures was in the wheels." (Ez., 1:21)

Third is the fact that there were *four* killers. Though four "beasts" also appear in Revelation, in Ezekiel the number "four" recurs several times: four angels, with four faces and four wings each, moving in four different directions. As commentators have noted, the symbolism and meaning of the number four in these fragments derives from the four corners of the earth, the four archangels, or the four letters of the sacred name YHVH.

Finally, the "beasts" of Revelation are often directly associated with the four Gospels (four versions of the word of Christ) and even the four Evangelists. Curiously, John is associated with the Eagle, the one with "fiercest and most classical profile." And it is John who introduced the equation between God and Logos—which perhaps explains why this figure is distinguished among the assailants as the one who "pulled a huge awl with a wooden handle out of his pocket" (1997: 163–4)[52] and stuck it into Venichka's throat. Illuminatingly, wooden statues of the Eagle, Lion, Ox, and Human as symbolic depictions of evangelists are displayed in Suzdal Sviato-Efimievsky monastery (see figs. 1–4) Since

---

50   «... дополз до самой верхней площадки...» (ibid., 127).
51   «... поднимались с последнего этажа» (ibid., 128).
52   «... вытащил из кармана громадное шило с деревянной рукояткой» (ibid., 128).

the monastery was opened as a museum in 1967, when Erofeev resided in Vladimir, in close proximity to Suzdal, it is quite possible that he was have been inspired by these very images. Tellingly, among them, the eagle has the most sinister look.

1.

3.

2.

3. Figs. 1-3. Details of the altar from the village church of Resurrection. Museum of the Sviato-Efimievsky Monastery, Suzdal. Photos by Stephan Mizha.

## CHAPTER FIVE

4.

5.

4. Figs. 4-5. Details of the altar from the village church of Resurrection. Museum of the Sviato-Efimievsky Monastery, Suzdal. Photos by Stephan Mizha.

But if Erofeev's murderers are the "hayyot" and/or seraphs, how does one understand the phrase: "where, in what newspapers have I seen their repulsive faces?" (1997: 159) One possible interpretation is that the profiles of the lion and eagle really do trigger associations with the medal-like profiles of political leaders on the front pages of Soviet newspapers.[53] However, from this interpretation, it is impossible to infer the popular reading of the poem's finale, which asserts that the work's ultimate meaning lies in the fact that a drunken genius is murdered by the Soviet regime.

The identification of various symbols of Divine power with the iconography of Soviet power is highly telling: one might even suggest symmetry with Dmitrii A. Prigov's declaration:

> [A]ny language is capable of becoming Soviet power. I surprised myself when I understood this from literally a single phrase (I can't remember whose) "Stalin is

---

53 Readers who have not had the chance to experience the Soviet period, should remember that practically all central newspapers were decorated with medals which graced the title page—thus Lenin's medal-like profile accompanied the headlines of every issue of *Pravda* and *Izvestiia*.

Pushkin today." Everyone laughed: how audacious—comparing Pushkin to Stalin. But I understood that any language that strives for supremacy is affected by the cancerous tumor of power. [...] My ... generation was able to translate a negative attitude towards Soviet power into a negative attitude towards any power. We lost the illusion that there is such a thing as good power." (Prigov and Shapoval, 95)

Erofeev comes to an analogous conclusion which, moreover, spreads to his idea on Divine power, his faith in the absolute, and the transcendental signified. This is exactly what Venichka speaks about at the beginning of the poem:

> I'm not saying that now truth is known to me, or that I've approached it close up. Not at all. But I've gotten close enough to it so that it's convenient to look it over.
> And I look, and I see, and for that reason, I'm sorrowful. And I don't believe that any one of you has dragged around with himself this bitter, bitter mishmash. I'm in a quandary over saying what this mishmash is composed of, and, all the same, you would never understand, but mostly there's 'sorrow' and 'fear' in it. 'Sorrow' and 'fear' most of all and, then, muteness..." (1997: 46) [54]

In this fragment, sorrow and fear are directly linked to the sight of the transcendental truth, or rather with the *sight of its inevitable repressiveness* ("any language that strives for supremacy is affected by the cancerous tumor of power"). Here is the source of the motif of *silence* and *muteness*, which is vital to the whole poem, but especially to the finale. Before the very end Venichka thinks that he will die

---

54  «Я не утверждаю, что мне – теперь – истина уже известна или что я вплотную к ней подошел. Вовсе нет. Но я уже на такое расстояние к ней подошел, с которого ее удобнее всего рассмотреть. —И я смотрю и вижу, и поэтому скорбен. И я не верю, чтоб кто-нибудь еще из вас таскал в себе это горчайшее месиво – из чего это месиво, сказать затруднительно, да вы все равно не поймете – но больше всего в нем "скорби" и "страха". Назовем хоть так. Вот: "скорби" и "страха" больше всего, и еще немоты» (Erofeev 1990: 40).

"without accepting this world, perceiving it close up and far away, inside and out, perceiving but not accepting it" (1997:154)[55], and that he will be *silent* before the face of God "with that muteness familiar to everyone who knows the outcome of a hangover after many days of hard boozing." (ibid., 155, altered)[56] This silence at the point of death can be read retrospectively as a response to God's silence in the scene of Venichka's murder: "the heavenly angels laughed at me. They laughed, and God stayed silent." (ibid., 163)[57] Silence, or rather, the abolition of the voice, is written into the very circumstances of Venichka's murder.

It is likely that Erofeev, just as Vlasov proposes, really uses the description of the "beasts" of Revelation with the intent of imbuing the entire murder with an apocalyptic atmosphere. However, in the course of the work—intentionally or not—the appearance of the assassins highlights those traits that connect the New Testament "beasts" with the Old Testament seraphim and "hayyot." As a result, the apocalyptic semantic of these images merges with its opposite: in all three contexts these creatures *prepare the coming of God*: His throne, His glory, His voice, and His word (Logos). There is a reason why Erofeev links his killers not only to the esoteric "hayyot," but also to the seraphim, known to every schoolchild as the ones entrusted with passing the divine word to prophets in classical literary culture. But in emphasizing this semantic field, the finale of the poem radically changes it: Venichka's terrible death *embodies* (without substituting for) the appearance of God.

In other words, Venichka, the seeker after God, finds that which he sought and is *convinced in the Divine presence*. The killers who pursue Venichka prove this. The biblical God (and the Logos associated with him) appeared not only in the burning bush, but in the storm, the whirlwind and the pillar of fire, as in the passage from Ezekiel cited above. Erofeev renders the appearance of God immanent in the murder of the poem's hero. *An awl into the throat is Erofeev's theophany!*

It is crucial that the divine messengers do not kill Venichka with a

---

55  «... так и не приняв этого мира, постигнув его вблизи и издали, снаружи и изнутри постигнув, но не приняв...» (ibid., 121).
56  «... и эта немота знакома всем, кто знает исход многодневного и тяжелого похмелья» (ibid., 121).
57  «...небесные ангелы надо мной смеялись. Они смеялись, а Бог молчал...» (ibid., 128).

blow to the heart (where Mithradates already stabbed Venichka with his knife), but with a blow to the throat—the organ of speech. This murder might seem like a paraphrase of Isaiah—the very episode interpreted by Pushkin in his "Prophet":

> And I said: 'Woe is me! For I am lost; for I am a man of unclean lips, and I dwell in the midst of a people of unclean lips; for my eyes have seen the King, the LORD of hosts.
> Then flew one of the seraphim to me, having in his hand a burning coal which he had taken with tongs from the altar. And he touched my mouth, and said: 'Behold, this has touched your lips; your guilt is taken away, and you sin is forgiven. And I heard the voice of the Lord saying: 'Whom shall I send and who will go for us?' Then I said, "Here I am! Send me.'" (Is., 6:5–8)

But in Isaiah, as well as in Ezekiel and in Pushkin, man becomes the messenger of God (an analogous role is assumed by the vision of the "beasts" in Revelation, only the messenger there is also the narrator). Erofeev depicts God's messengers or, more radically, the Logos, the Word of the absolute (transcendental) truth, as killing *the individual voice*, in accordance with the logic of power.

The divine Logos striving for absolute supremacy deprives the hero of his own voice, precisely because Venichka's discourse transforms sacred and pseudo-sacred orders and dissolves the boundaries between the sacred and the profane, the high and the low, and the transcendental and physiological, and, trickster-like, undermines any sort of power—including the absolute. Characteristically, the "clotted red letter 'ю'" which literally clouds Venichka's sight and being, is at once a reminder of the infant (and thus of the existential and transcendental meanings in Venichka's life), and an ideogram of the murder ('ю'—the "stick" as the sewing needle's handle, the linking dash as the blade and the "oval" as a stylized human head). At the same time, it is significant that "ю"—a letter, an element of the language and of the Logos—becomes the sign and *weapon* of death.

It emerges that God and the Logos are able to show their presence—and supremacy—in one way only: *through the murder of the individual voice and consciousness*. This is why Venichka is not a holy fool: unlike the classical holy fool, he does not represent God, but is *betrayed by him*. This betrayal is embodied in the figures of the assassins: by symbolically expressing the presence of God and the granting of the Divine Logos to the hero, they viciously and *cynically* obliterate the hero and his word.

The cynicism is vividly accentuated in the part of the poem that immediately precedes Venichka's death and overtly corresponds to Christ's prayer of the cup:

> Trembling all over, I said to myself, *Talife cumi*, that is "Get up and prepare for the end..." This isn't *Talife cumi*, it's *lama savahfani*, as the Savior said... That is, "Why hast thou forsaken me?"
>
> The Lord was silent.
>
> Angels of heaven, they're coming up, what should I do? What should I do, now, so as not to die? Angels!
>
> And the angels burst out laughing. Do you know how angels laugh? They are shameful creatures... should I tell you how they burst out laughing just now? A long time ago, in Lobnia—at the station—a man was cut by a train, cut up in an unbelievable way: his whole lower half was crushed to smithereens and scattered over the road bed, but his upper half from the belt up remained as if alive, and stood by the tracks, the way busts of various pigs stand on pedestals. The train pulled away but he—that half of him—remained standing there, and on his face there was a sort of perplexity and his mouth half open. A lot of people couldn't stand to look at it and turned away, pale, with a deathly weariness in their hearts. But some children ran up to him, three or four children, they had picked up a lighted cigarette butt from somewhere and stuck it in the dead man's half-open mouth. And the cigarette butt continued to smoke and the children ran around roaring with laughter.
>
> That's how the heavenly angels laughed at me then.

They laughed and God was silent. (1997: 162–3)[58]

The extended comparison between the angels' laughter and the laughter of children defiling the body of a human being who has been cut in half, while the hearts of onlookers fill "with a deathly weariness," fully conveys the cynicism of the angels' reaction. Tellingly, in the Gospel of Luke, the plea for respite (*lama savahfani*) is answered: "an angel from heaven appeared to him and gave him strength." (Luke, 39:43)

The laughter of the angels in the finale of Erofeev's poem not only reverses the role played by the "heavenly angels" in the Gospels, but points accusingly at God, whose silence is no less cynical than the laughter of the angels. Not only does God refrain from helping Venichka and, moreover, supporting him in his trial, but the murderers that pursue him actually *embody his power*, paradoxically enabling the encounter with God that Venichka sought throughout his journey. At the same time, God's silence testifies to the genuine source of his power, uncovered as violence, not Logos. "The genuine heart and secret soul of the sacred consists of violence" wrote Rene Girard (43), as the author of *Moskva-Petushki* and other representatives of the underground seem to have guessed as well.

The silence of God obviously recalls the silence of Christ in Dostoevsky's "Legend of the Grand Inquisitor," which in the context of Erofeev's poem is subordinate to the logic of carnivalesque inversion. God himself becomes the Grand Inquisitor, whom Sloterdijk,

---

58   «Весь сотрясаясь, я сказал себе: "талифа куми", то есть встань и приготовься к кончине... Это уже не талифа куми, я все чувствую, это *лама самахвани*, как сказал спаситель... То есть: "для чего, господь, ты меня оставил?" Для чего же все-таки, господь, ты меня оставил? Господь молчал. И ангелы рассмеялись. Вы знаете, как смеются ангелы? Это позорные твари, теперь я знаю — вам сказать, как они сейчас рассмеялись? Когда-то, очень давно, в Лобне, у вокзала, зарезало поездом человека и непостижимо зарезало: всю его нижнюю половину измололо в мелкие дребезги и расшвыряло по полотну, а верхняя половина, от пояса, осталась как бы живою, и стояла у рельсов, как стоят на постаментах бюсты разной сволочи. Поезд ушел, а он, эта половина, так и остался стоять, и на лице у него была какая-то озадаченность, и рот полуоткрыт. Многие не могли на это глядеть, отворачивались, побледнев со смертной истомой в сердце. А дети подбежали к нему, трое или четверо детей, где-то подобрали дымящийся окурок и вставили его в мертвый полуоткрытый рот. И окурок все дымился, а дети скакали вокруг и хохотали над этой забавностью... Вот так и теперь небесные ангелы надо мной смеялись. Они смеялись, а бог молчал...» (ibid., 127)

symptomatically, brought into his "cabinet of cynics." In the opinion of the author of the *Critique of Cynical Reason*:

> The actual result of the Grand Inquisitor's cynical reasoning is not as much the self-exposure of the church politician, but the discovery that the good and evil, end and means can be interchangeable. This result cannot be overemphasized. With it, we slide inevitably into the area of cynicism. [...] The absolute anchoring is gone: the age of moral teetering begins. Beyond good and evil we by no means find, as Nietzsche assumed, a radiantly vital amoralism but rather an infinite twilight and a fundamental ambivalence. Evil becomes so-called evil as soon as it is thought of as a means to good; good becomes so-called good as soon as it appears to be something disruptive (Jesus as disrupter [— or Venichka for that matter, *ML*]), destructive in the sense given to it by institutions. (188)

One is inclined to think that this characteristic fully applies to the metaphysical heroes of *Moskva-Petushki*: to God, the angels and the murderers (hayyot), as cynical representatives of the absolute, presented by Erofeev as an institution of metaphysical authority, indistinguishable from any other power, symbolic or political, including the Soviet one. This is the reason why, if one "translates" Erofeev's poem into the language of the images of Bulgakov's novel *The Master and Margarita*— which was first published just a few years before *Moskva-Petushki* was written (1966–67), and which Erofeev emphatically rejected[59] —we discover that in *Moskva-Petushki* the ritual murder is not performed by "Woland," but by "Yeshua," and those sacrificed are not the cynical Berlioz and Maigel, but the "Master" (whose "Margarita" remains alone on the Petushki platform), and it is not even a human sacrifice, just a base and casual murder in the entrance of a building.

The latter circumstance is very important. The fact that the final chapters do not depict a ritual sacrifice, but a mere murder that is devoid

---

59 "He couldn't stand Bulgakov. He hated *The Master and Margarita* with a passion" ("Булгакова на дух не принимал. *Мастера и Маргариту* ненавидел так, что его трясло") (Murav'ev, 93).

of the promise of resurrection or even revenge, seems to require no further proof. This means that Venichka fully corresponds to the label *homo sacer* according to Giorgio Agamben: "*homo sacer* belongs to God in the form of unsacrificeability and is included in the community in the form of being able to be killed" (82). The state Venichka has reached at the end of the poem represents the extension and price of the ritual expenditure which, as we have seen, commands the logic of discourse and plot. *Moskva-Petushki* takes the philosophical freedom of the trickster-kynic to its ultimate limit. Freely wasting the symbolic capital of each and every authoritarian discourse and any social position, the trickster reaches total freedom in the state of the *homo sacer*—exempt from all legal or religious order and deprived of all human or divine value, and therefore "permitted to be killed without committing homicide and without celebrating a sacrifice." (idem., 83) This ultimate freedom also expresses the ultimate meaning of the trickster's notion of the sacred, which paradoxically negates the very category of the sacred, since it appears to be based upon his/her "unsacrificeability." And it is the "unsacrificeability" of Venichka's life, originating in his tragic freedom, which is epitomized in the poem's last, magnificent sentence: "And since then I have never regained consciousness, and I never will." (1997:164)

However, the fact that God and his angels appear in the guise of super-cynics testifies to a new phase of development in the conflict between the trickster and the society of cynics described in preceding chapters. Erofeev's poem was not only written after Stalinism, but after the collapse of "Thaw-era" attempts at destalinization. It was at this time that cynicism, which was previously only attributed to the political authorities and social elites, began to be seen as a *universal principle* of the social order: Erofeev just translated this sensation into the language of "metaphysics." According to him, there is no alternative to cynicism on earth and in heaven, in society and in consciousness: this is the testimony inscribed into the tragic finale of *Moskva-Petushki*.

According to Sloterdijk, the universal presence of cynicism testifies to the transformation of modernity from a project into the *state of society*: "For as soon as the metaphysical distinction between good and evil becomes outmoded and everything that exists appears neutral in a metaphysical sense, only then does modernity, as we refer to it, really begin: it is the age that can no longer conceive of any transcendental morality and that, consequently, finds it impossible to distinguish neatly between means and ends." (189–190) This state of modernity was indeed reached by the Soviet society in the 1970s —the decade which was called "developed socialism" (*razvitoi sotsializm*), only to be later renamed the "period of Stagnation" (*zastoi*).

# CHAPTER 6

## TRICKSTERS IN DISGUISE:
## THE TRICKSTER'S TRANSFORMATIONS IN THE SOVIET FILM OF THE 1960s–70s

"REFORMED" TRICKSTERS IN THE COMEDIES OF THE SIXTIES
The trickster trope in "official" Soviet culture underwent serious transformation only after the end of the Thaw, between the late 1960s and early 1980s. I think one can rule out any possible influence Erofeev's prose poem might have had, especially since the mutations of the "official" trickster lacked philosophical weight and, in all likelihood, constituted a reaction to the conformism of the intelligentsia and the widespread distribution of "shadowy" economic practices, which acquired de-facto legality to an unprecedented degree. Yegor Gaidar defines these processes in the following terms:

> When total state ownership still appears to be the norm, certain 'shadow' movements begin to stir within it. An exclusively 'bureaucratic' market comes into being. Deep within the protective sac of state ownership—or more accurately, 'pseudostate' ownership—the embryo or quasi-private or ur-private ownership begins to develop, still hidden from the view but potentially powerful. (Gaidar, 62)

These processes affected the nomenclature and ordinary people alike. Essentially, the nomenclature simply took the "favors of access" (Ledeneva), which were crucial to the Soviet social model in the 1930s–1950s, to their logical limit, so that by the 1960s and 1970s the "shadow economy" had become the unwritten law of "socialist society":

> The use of public resources for private (even if not selfish)

purposes reflected a paradoxical feature of the Soviet regime: the character of state property. State property was declared to be public and supposed to be guarded by everyone. [...] But "public" also could be interpreted as quasi-private, which was reflected in everyday sayings such as: "'public' means that part of it is mine," "one gets what one guards [*chto okhraniaiu—to i imeiu*]." (Ledeneva 2000: 185)

It is no accident that the Soviet 1960s and 1970s were the golden age of *blat*, the system of quasi-goodwill exchanges of social and economic connections and favors that in reality amounted to corruption. As Alena Ledeneva notes: "Although from a legal perspective, *blat* could be most adequately viewed as 'anti-systemic' behavior [...] structural (both economic and cultural) forces or constraints of the Soviet overcontrolling center resulted in the flourishing of *blat*: life became impossible *unless* the rules were broken." (1998: 50, 46) These socio-economic practices along with the formalization of the official discourse and deterritorialization of the entire system of Soviet values[1] are responsible for the formation of "the cynical reason of late socialism," to use Alexei Yurchak's apt formula (see Yurchak 1997, also Kharkhordin, 270-78).

In the years of the Thaw, the novels of Il'f and Petrov, republished after an official interdiction, immediately became a sort of "quotation book": "Someone who knew Il'f and Petrov's books well enough could discuss any topic with the help of a few quotes from these books"—note Petr Vail' and Aleksandr Genis. (Vail' and Genis, 674) At the same time, the trickster became, first and foremost, a free and happy man, losing the previous stigma of the "subversive element" in accordance with the overall atmosphere of the Thaw era: "There was a new understanding that only a joyful man is good. Laughter sang praises to freedom in the sense that it opposed everything immobile, stagnant, repressed: the unfree." (ibid., 671)

When the famous film director Mikhail Shveitser filmed the first movie

---

1  This process is detected and analyzed by Yurchak in his book *Everything Was Forever Until It Was No More*: "This internal displacement of the system's dominant discourse was different from the dissident kind of opposition and was not articulated in oppositional terms; indeed it did not preclude one from feeling personal affinity to many values that were explicitly or implicitly central to the socialist system [...] Unlike the dissident strategies of opposing the system's dominant mode of signification, deterritorialization reproduced this mode at the same time as it shifted, built upon, and added new meaning to it" (2006: 115, 116).

based on Il'f and Petrov's *Zolotoi telenok* (*If I Had a Million Rubles* in American release, 1968), he staged it as the second half of a peculiar diptych on the 1930s, whose prequel was based on Valentin Kataev's 1932 novel *Vremia, vpered!* (*Time, Forward!*) (*Vremia, vpered!* 1965). Both films starred Sergei Iurskii, who played more or less the same character, a joyful and free man: in *Vremia, vpered!*, the engineer David Margulies, who sets a Stakhanovite record at "building communism," and in *Zolotoi telenok* the con artist Ostap Bender, who admits that he is bored by the socialist construction.[2]

## Gaidai's Tricksters

1. Aleksandr Demianenko as Shurik (*Kavkazskaia plennitsa*)

Shurik (Aleksandr Dem'ianenko), the protagonist of Leonid Gaidai's comedies *Operatsiia 'Y' i drugie prikliucheniia Shurika* (*Operation "Y" and Shurik's Other Adventures*, 1965) and *Kavkazskaia plennitsa, ili Novye prikliucheniia Shurika* (*The Prisoner of the Caucasus, or Shurik's New Adventures*, 1968), based on screenplays written by Iakov Kostiukovskii and Moris Slobodskii, became one of the symbols of the sixties.

The immense popularity of Shurik, in many ways the face of the 1960s Soviet generation, can probably be explained by the hybridization of tropes of the trickster and the simpleton, Ivan the Fool, the rogue and the honest Komsomol member. This very hybridization proved a new development to Soviet culture. Although Andrey Sinyavsky proposed a

---

2  Along with Iurskii, there were other actors playing in both *Vremia, vpered!* and *Zolotoi telenok*. For instance, Leonid Kuravlev played the construction manager (*prorab*) Korneev in *Vremia, vpered!* and Shura Balaganov in *Zolotoi telenok*. Tamara Semina (Olia Tregubova in the former, Raechka in the latter), Mikhail Kokshenov (Kanunnikov and the secretary), and Igor' Iasulovich (Vinkich and a young amateur driver) also participated in both films, enhancing the effect of interconnectedness between them.

particularly cogent interpretation of Ivan the Fool, suggesting that Ivan is a sort of passive trickster (see 46–49), this view hardly fits the context of Soviet culture. A close reading of a number of texts reveals that where one finds a trickster one also finds an archetypal fool who helps define the trickster by providing a contrast; thus, next to Ostap Bender we see Ippolit Matveevich and Shura Balaganov, near Woland and his host we see Ivan Bezdomnyi, and near Buratino there is Pierro, etc. Evidently, in Soviet culture the trickster was necessary as a personage that is opposed to the "naïve" hero, a modified Ivan the Fool whom official culture depicts as the main benefactor of the revolutionary— see for instance Aleksandr Tvardovskii's *Strana Muraviia* (*The Land of Muraviia*, 1936); Aleksandr Zarkhi's and Iosif Kheifets' *Chlen pravitel'stva* (*The Great Beginning*, 1939); and Grigorii Aleksandrov's *Svetlyi put'* (*The Radiant Path*, 1940). In nonconformist culture the same character was represented as the primary victim of the Soviet social order as in Aleksandr Solzhenitsyn's *Odin den' Ivana Denisovicha* (*One Day in the Life of Ivan Denisovich*, 1961); Vasilii Belov's *Privychnoe delo* (*The Habitual Deal*, 1966); and Vasilii Shukshin's *Do tret'ikh petukhov* (*Before the Third Rooster's Cry*, 1974), and others.

2. A scene from *"Navazhdenie"* (*Operatsiia 'Y' i drugie prikliucheniia Shurika*), Aleksandr Demianenko and Natalia Selezneva.

3. A scene from *Kavkazskaia plennitsa*, "Coward", "Seasoned", and "Dummy" (*Georgii Vitsin, Evgenii Morgunov* and *Yurii Nikulin*)

Thus the hybridization of the trickster with the naïve fool, exemplified by Gaidai's Shurik, was actually aimed at "cleansing" the trickster of his associations with cynical culture. Simultaneously, the kynical energy of the trickster was to be utilized as a powerful weapon in the hand of the idealistic youth. Similar to the appropriation of the trickster trope by the Stalinist culture (as exemplified by Petr Aleinikov's cinematic heroes, by the character Maxim from Kozintsev's and Trauberg's trilogy, as well as by Aleksandr Tvardovskii's Vasilii Tyorkin), the liberal culture of the '60s tried to enhance its appeal by using the trickster, yet in a selective way that emphasized some aspects and reduced—or eliminated—others.

Shurik retains such tricksterish traits as the capacity for mediation and metamorphosis (particularly evident in the first film, and in the novella *Navazhdenie* [*Obsession*]). Here Shurik, while zealously preparing for an examination and reading shared lecture notes, inadvertently transforms into the heroine's girlfriend and even lies in bed with her half-naked (a daring sexual scene for Soviet comedy in the 1960s). However, his utter lack of cynicism means he is frequently deceived, or finds himself in the role of the simpleton. In the view of Alexander Prokhorov: "Shurik's nerdiness, however, was only a contemporary disguise for the popular hero of Russian fairy tales, 'Ivan the Fool.'" (2003: 486) The most important difference is Shurik's total lack of ambivalence: he is honest and positive; not only does he not strive to undermine social values but, on the contrary, he defends them against the assaults of wicked (and cynical) tricksters, mainly in the guise of the comedic triad Coward—Dummy—Seasoned (Trus-Balbes-Byvalyi, played by Georgii Vitsin, Yurii Nikulin and Evgenii Morgunov respectively), as well as from such characters as the lazy and crude Fedya (Aleksei Smirnov) from the novella "Naparnik" ("The Partner") in *Operatsiia 'Y,'* or the conniver and demagogue-in-authority "comrade Saakhov" (Vladimir Etush) in *Kavkazskaia plennitsa*. However, in order to defend these values, Shurik has to *temporarily* wear the mantle of the trickster and to use deception and manipulation against the comical villain-tricksters. The trickster's ambivalence and subversive energy, which are repressed in the protagonist, find an outlet in the cinematic language of his comedies. As Prokhorov argues: "Gaidai carnivalized the very economy of Soviet comedy's narrative. For him any narrative provided an excuse to set up a series of attractions: narratives led to the gags instead of gags reinforcing the narrative. [...] Visual jokes

[were] intended to undermine narrative flow and substitute Logos with visual carnival." (2003: 457, 465)

Before the Shurik comedies, Gaidai attempted to create a trickster film in his version of O'Henry's story "The Ransom of Red Chief," released in 1963 as a part of the movie *Delovye liudi (Business People)*. Here the child, as the paradigmatic hero of Thaw cinema, the embodiment of humanity and sincerity, was represented as "A subversive clown, challenging the physical stability of the adult world; his major asset is his ability to put the world around him into an unpredictable spin, which the filmmaker can channel into yet another visual joke." (ibid., 467) The precondition for this film's success was the "exclusion" of the protagonist from the Soviet social sphere, accentuated by his age and also by the tacit understanding that the film was only a retelling of a classic American short story whose action takes place at a great temporal and spatial distance. For Gaidai, decreasing this distance by turning to Russian literary sources proved full of insurmountable obstacles, as becomes apparent in the films he made in the 1970s, in particular *Dvenadtsat' stuliev (Twelve Chairs, 1970)* (after Il'f and Petrov) and *Inkognito iz Peterburga (Incognito from Petersburg, 1977, after Gogol's Revizor)*. In creating cinematic versions of such classic Russian and Soviet tricksters as Ostap Bender and Khlestakov, Gaidai tried to find a compromise between the familiar language of slapstick comedy and the literary humor of the original sources. As a result, his gags became illustrations and lost their carnivalesque vividness, while at the same time reducing the multiplicity and ambivalence of the protagonist-tricksters and turning them into banal thieves who are driven exclusively by pragmatic interests. Critics and viewers did not fail to notice this, and they compared Gaidai's works with the familiar originals in tones of disappointment and rejection.

## *Riazanov's Detochkin*

The hybrid Gaidai discovered in Shurik—the idealist and trickster-by-necessity—acquires a wholly different status in El'dar Riazanov's *Beregis' avtomobilia (Beware of the Car, 1966)*, based upon an earlier eponymous novella by Riazanov and Emil' Braginskii (1963). As Prokhorov notes, the protagonist of the comedy, Yurii Detochkin (Innokentii Smoktunovskii) was not only depicted as a naïve grown-up child (suggested by his last name, derived from the diminutive form of the Russian word for "child"), as a modern-day Robin Hood, and as a Russian holy fool, but was also associated with Prince Myshkin and Hamlet, roles earlier played by Smoktunovskii. Within the film, Detochkin also plays Hamlet in an amateur production, something that certainly surrounds this character with the aura of idealization.[3] At the same time, we must bear in mind that the sense of justice Detochkin championed in his eccentric way is profoundly Soviet: essentially, Detochkin's criminal actions leads to the officially declared, "war on income not generated by labor" (*bor'ba s netrudovymi dokhodami*) and thereby comes to resemble the Socialist Realist underground revolutionary, whose actions assert social justice—tellingly, the hero's revolutionary genealogy is emphasized by his mother's (Elizaveta Dobzhanskaia) heroic past and her singing of revolutionary songs. By stealing cars from those he considers to be thieves and blatmeisters, Smoktunovskii's hero becomes a mediator between official power and the criminal, but practically legitimate, "black market" of favors and exchanges.

4. A scene from *Beregis' avtomobilia*, Detochkin (*Innokentii Smoktunovskii*) and Militsiaman (*Georgii Zhzhenov*)

5. A scene from *Beregis' avtomobilia*, Detochkin (*Innokentii Smoktunovskii*) and Maxim Podberezovikov (*Oleg Efremov*)

Detochkin, an innovative thief, is also represented as an idealist, who sends all the money he acquires by stealing cars into the provincial orphanage where he was raised. This is why Detochkin can maintain a friendly relationship with the idealistic detective Maksim Podberezovik (Oleg Efremov), who upon learning the real motive for Detochkin's

---

3  See the detailed and insightful analysis of this film in Prokhorov 2007: 256-67.

crimes is prepared to release him. In Prokhorov's view, a Doppelgänger relationship also ties Detochkin to his antagonist Dima Semitsvetov, the department store owner who acquires and sells imported goods at a large mark-up (brilliantly played by Andrei Mironov). Dima's father-in-law (Anatolii Papanov) is a retired soldier and brute who threatens his son-in-law with the promise of imprisonment ("They'll lock you up, and you don't steal" [*Tebia posodiut* [sic], *a ty ne vorui!*]), but fiercely defends Detochrin at the trial. He is yet another comic double of the hero: despite his demonstrative loyalty to the economic system, which forbids commercial activity, he actively practices what is forbidden by growing strawberries at a summer house he purchased with "stolen" money and selling them at the market for high prices.

6. "They'll lock you up, and you don't steal!", Semen Vasil'evich, Semitsvetsov's father-in-law (*Anatolii Papanov*), Dima Semitsvetov (*Andrei Mironov*) and Inna, Semitsvetov's wife (*Tatiana Gavrilova*)

While formally acting as a trickster—a master car thief who evades the law—and performatively exposing the profound contradictions in the Soviet social system, whose conception of justice is incompatible with the social order or its de-jure criminal (but de-facto market-driven) foundations, in the course of the film Detochkin is forcefully "washed clean" from every trait inherent to the trickster. This is the source of the lofty associations with Myshkin and Hamlet as markers, of Detochkin's altruism, and even of the fact that his "tricks" are largely unintentional—his honesty and naiveté are taken for cunning. Even sexually, Detochkin is far from a triumphant trickster—his relationship with Liuba (Ol'ga Aroseva), as Prokhorov justly notes, resembles a mother-son bond more than a love affair. The trickster's "de-tricksterization" is probably linked to the fact that Detochkin is construed as the enemy of the new "consumer society" or rather, a society based on *blat* and "black market" networks—a society where cynicism is a mass phenomenon that is considered normal (confirmed by a gallery of minor cynical characters), and where it is impossible to tell a rogue from an honest man. It is not surprising that the film never makes it clear whether Detochkin stole his last car from a thief or from a respected scientist. Tricksters' traits are directly associated with this kind of cynicism, which is why Detochkin is so thoroughly "purged" of them over the course of the film.

At the same time, only the trickster possesses the deconstructive potential to undermine and performatively defamiliarize the corrupt and cynical system. This is why the authors of *Beregis' avtomobilia* created the previously unthinkable hybrid of trickster and idealist: according to the film's logic, the true Soviet idealism of the Quixotic variety demands trickster tactics, since without them it is doomed in a society of triumphant cynicism.

## *Daneliia's Buzykin*

7. Oleg Basilashvili as Andrei Buzykin in *Osennii marafon*.

This logic is deconstructed in the film *Osennii marafon* (*The Autumn Marathon*) by Georgii Daneliia (1979, based upon Aleksandr Volodin's eponymous play). Once again, on the surface, the role of the protagonist—the translator Andrei Buzykin (Oleg Basilashvili)—is reminiscent of the traditional trickster: he is "a servant of two masters," deceiving his wife Nina (Natal'ia Gundareva) and lover Alla (Marina Neelova), getting caught in funny and embarrassing situations, only to extricate himself using lies that are not convincing and obvious to all parties involved. However, the psychological portrait of this role is more tragic than comic—small wonder then that the initial title of the film read "The Bitter Life of the Rogue" (*Gorestnaia zhizn' pluta*).

## CHAPTER SIX

Just like Detochkin, Buzykin is an *involuntary trickster,* and worse—an unsuccessful one. Within the confines of the film, he is the only hero willing to *give away himself and his time,* while most of the characters around him—not only his wife and his mistress, but also the visiting Danish translator Bill (played by German journalist Norbert Kuchinke); the incompetent translator and old friend Varvara (Galina Volchek); and the brilliant trickster, Buzykin's neighbor, the plumber (Evgenii Leonov)—are only trying to take and even *own* Buzykin, his time, his personality, and his talent. Essentially, *Osennii marafon* transfers the notion of the society of cynical consumption represented in *Beregis' avtomobilia* into the domain of ethical and psychological relationships, highlighting the cynicism of the late Soviet world *beyond* the economic sphere, at the very heart of friendships, love affairs, neighborly relationships, and more.

The tricksterish function of mediation is emphasized in Buzykin—it is no accident that he is a literary translator. His complicated relationships with women appear subject to his (albeit naïve) refusal to inflict pain or hurt another's dignity. Yet, the resulting effect appears as a sad double to the model of a "free marionette": in an attempt to stay true to his good nature and humanity, Buzykin constantly finds himself enslaved by those whom he loves, pities, and helps.

Unsurprisingly, critics readily placed Buzykin in the context of the Russian classics, just like Detochkin. Neia Zorkaia and A. Zorkii wrote:

> Buzykin is marked by features that are inherent to the intelligentsia: cultured behavior, delicacy, pity, compassion, and the fear of hurting another person. For good or for ill, these same traits were always common to many Russian literary heroes, who suffered in anguish but could not change themselves, did not listen to wise advisors and could not deliver the saving cold hard truth. Andrei Bolokonskii couldn't honestly tell his wife Lisa that he did not love her, and when she died he mourned long and hard, hardly rejoicing in his new-found freedom. [...] And Prince Lev Nikolaevich Myshkin? Wasn't his weak-willed oscillation between Aglaia Epanchina and Nastaya Filippovna duplicit? Wouldn't it have been more correct to put Aglaia in her place and to give Nastasya Filippovna

a hint about her shameful past without ever intending to become engaged to her? Finally why do Chekhov's heroes so often submit to people who are strong and crude, why do they suffer so from the pressure of the self-confident and the know-it-all?! (Zorkaia and Zorkii)

It is telling, however, that Daneliia's hero not only resonates with the ethos of the Russian classics, but equally with popular discourses (and even campaigns) of literary and cultural criticism during the late 1970s–1980s. It was the period when "kindness" was declared the highest value and utilized as a primary *aesthetic* criterion. Thus Valentin Kataev, Yurii Trifonov, and the prose of the "forty-year-olds" (Vladimir Makanin, Anatolii Kim, Ruslan Kireev, and others) were faulted in part for their "lack of kindness," i.e., the authors' lack of compassion towards their heroes, or in other words, for the harshness and critical clout of their artistic views. In the sarcastic words of the literary critic V. Kardin: "In the 'five mark' grading system for literary works, the highest grade was awarded for *kindness*. It was cloyingly discovered in poets and prose writers, playwrights and publicists. The Union of Writers could be easily renamed the Union of the Kind" (236, author's emphasis).

In *Osennii marafon*, the kindest, warmest, and most talented character—Andrei Pavlovich Buzykin,—fully embodies this elevation of kindness, to the supreme value. He uses trickster methods in order to avoid *hurting* anyone, but in the end sacrifices his *freedom*. As such, this film centers on the conflict between the mediating strategies of the trickster-idealist and freedom, his most important value. Though Detochkin has his freedom taken away and is sent to jail, he remains true to himself. In the Sisyphus-like finale of the film we see that Buzykin is doomed to expending *himself* tragically, which inevitably reminds us of the finale of *Moskva-Petushki*.

*Beregis' avtomobilia* and *Osennii marafon* are classic examples of the genre of "sad comedy" (to follow Daneliia's prompt). This genre embodies the new ambivalence of a trickster-like protagonist. Both Detochkin and Buzykin act like tricksters without enjoying their own tricks (instead they suffer from the need to lie, being ill-suited to their "calling") and gaining little, if any, pragmatic value from their deceptions. The latter facility distinguishes these characters from the numerous cynics featuring in both films. At the same time, the lack of pleasure they derive from their trickery distinguishes Detochkin and Buzykin from kynics. Symptomatically, Detochkin's and Buzykin's trickery is not an "art" that marks them as outstanding, unique individuals. Instead, it is a necessary facility that permits these odd heroes to *participate* in the very social practices from which they hope to free themselves. Furthermore, unlike kynics who disregard long-standing, let alone idealistic, goals, both Detochkin and Buzykin are driven by idealism that is represented as "old-fashioned," yet in fact reflects their faith in mainstream social values. Detochkin and Buzykin suffer for the very values that were most actively promoted in mainstream Soviet culture: the battle against "non labor-generated income" in the 1960s, the cult of "kindness" in the 1970s and early '80s.

The sad humor of the films can be seen as a symptom of the radical transformations in Soviet social semiotics that happened in the 1960s–1970s. While the tricksters of the 1920s–1930s illuminated the discursive nature of Soviet reality through the performative juggling of social signifiers, the protagonists of the "sad comedies" of the 1960s and 1970s perform their tricks in an attempt to achieve the opposite goal, i.e., to restore the signifieds behind confusing networks of social signifiers, while their comical failures demonstrate the irrelevance of these attempts. These films soundly testify to the crisis that befell Soviet cynicism when it became total and lost all alternatives, including kynicism and idealism, thus turning on itself.

The kynical impulse returns to a trickster-like character only with Mark Zakharov's Munchhausen in the TV feature *Tot samyi Miunkhauzen* (*That Very Munchhausen*, 1979, based upon Grigorii Gorin's eponymous play). The protagonist of this film, played by the masculine, ironic, and self-confident Oleg Iankovskii, represents an inversion of the traditional image of this trickster, exemplified by Raspe's Munchhausen, who utters numerous tall tales but swears that he never lies. The most important feature of Munchhausen in Gorin/Zakharov's film was associated with the fact that their Munchhausen *really did not lie*, although his truth remained far removed from the dull pragmatism of the cynical world.

Gorin and Zakharov gave their Munchhausen the traits of the free artist who not only creates his own artistic reality, but also lives in it and follows its rules. In the context of this free reality, created by the Baron himself, all his fibs—the deer with the cherry tree growing from its head, or the ducks shot dead through a chimney—become truth. Certainly, this image of Munchhausen draws on the romantic and modernist conception of the artist as the creator of autonomous worlds and alternative "truths." But within the confines of the film, rich in ironic nods to the culture and politics of the 1970s and 1980s,[4] Munchhausen becomes a metaphor for the underground artist or political dissident, true to his liberty and living by its principles, with no regard for the demands of the cynical outside world.

This trickster is also an idealist, but of a special kind: his idealism is anchored in his playful freedom. Munchhausen's ambivalence is defined by the status of his truth, which seems obvious to him and fantastic to others. The world created by Munchhausen for himself and around himself acquires the traits of the liminal space where everything is possible—from flights to the Moon to journeys in time—and which has to stay isolated from the world of "normal cynicism." The unpragmatic and playful nature of Munchhausen's realm not only expresses the freedom of the trickster-hero (or rather, the trickster raised to the rank of hero) but paints his world in joyful kynical colors. Amidst the cynics that surround him—his old friend-burgomaster (Igor Kvasha), his ex-wife (Inna Churikova), her lawyer paramour Ramkhof (Aleksandr Abdulov), the pastor (Vladimir Dolinskii), and even the Duke (Leonid Bronevoi)—Munchhausen is the only character in the first half of the film who never has to wear a mask or juggle social identities. He is always himself and always playing—hence the orchestra that follows him everywhere, turning each of his gestures into a happy theatrical performance. And hence Munchhausen's motto: "A serious face is not yet a sign of intelligence, gentlemen. Every idiocy on Earth is done with exactly that expression. Smile, gentlemen, smile!"

8. Oleg Iankovskii as Baron Munchhausen in *Tot samyi Miunkhauzen*.

---

4   See Moss on political undertones of the film.

One should note that Munchhausen's kynicism is somewhat reduced, even sterilized: this trickster is lacking all carnivalesque "impropriety"—all his transgressions attack only the cynical common sense and pragmatic logic, yet never undermine anything else. Munchhausen's world is safely set within a theatrical setting reminiscent of the 18$^{th}$ century and characteristically, all of Munchhausen's cultural "contacts" belong to the sphere of "high" (read: intelligentsia's) culture: Shakespeare, Sophocles, Newton, etc.

Attempts to overcome the liminality of Munchhausen's world, to "normalize" him, to create a compromise with the cynical outside world, all lead to the hero's defeat and his symbolic suicide and transformation into the utterly unimportant and undistinguished gardener Müller, while Munchhausen's name and legend are wildly exploited by his former persecutors. In the finale of the film, Munchhausen returns, and in order to prove that he never died, sets out for the moon. This final gesture is provocatively ambivalent—on the one hand, Munchhausen climbs an endless ladder to the sky, proving his superiority over the society of cynics; on the other hand, this is yet another suicide. To confirm his unique position, this trickster-idealist has to enact a radical gesture of *expenditure*—he must abandon everything, above all his beloved Marta (Elena Koreneva), for whose hand he once renounced himself—but in so doing he keeps himself and his kynical freedom. Once again, this finale seems to resonate deeply with *Moskva-Petushki*.

***

The philosophical tragedy of the trickster's position exposed by Erofeev's poem, and the socio-psychological dramatization of the trickster trope in the cinema of the 1960s–1970s, testify to an internal conflict between two of the major functions of the trickster in Soviet culture: the provision of aesthetic justifications for strategies of survival and mimicry in the Soviet world and the exposure of the ambiguity, cynicism, and internal contradictions of that world. In Erofeev's poem, as in the aforementioned films, the trickster provides the basis for the creation of certain myths of the Soviet (anti-Soviet, a-social) intellectual and his/her relationship to the socio-cultural regime of the post-Stalin era. A vital trait of this new order is the normalization of cynicism ("the cynical reason of late socialism") and those socio-economic relations—*blat*, the "black market", the unofficial economy of favors and privileges—that were seen as dangerous transgressions in the preceding period, thus requiring symbolic justification by the trickster. In the 1970s, these once dangerous games became a stable source of *jouissance*, after Slavoj Žižek: "the surplus-enjoyment via the magic reversal-into-itself by which the very material texture of our expression of pain [...] gives rise to enjoyment." (1997:47)

Erofeev's hero-trickster offers a far more radical answer to this conflict. His vitality is never dependent on the cynical social order—from the very beginning, it lies outside the boundaries of the intelligentsia's "norm"—but exists in relation with such philosophical and metaphysical categories as God and Satan, good and evil, logos and chaos. Cynicism here acts as a metaphysical principle of being, not a defect of the social system. The hopeless tragedy in the poem's finale logically arises from the position of the unrestrained trickster, who expresses his freedom through limitless expenditure which becomes the only possible and necessary path for him.

The films of Gaidai, Riazanov, Daneliia, and Zakharov propose more moderate, compromise-driven strategies for the intelligentsia's adaptation of the trickster's strategies. All of these films tapped the trickster for traits that would guarantee the intellectual a *viable* symbolic superiority over the society of cynics. And if in Gaidai' and Riazanov's films trickery is understood as a method, or more exactly, a technique for accomplishing the intelligentsia's romantic ideals (which were in reality rather Soviet), then in Daneliia's film the method and the goal are in contradiction, depriving the hero of his liberty. Gorin and Zakharov return to the value of freedom and non-belonging, prompted by the trickster trope, but turn it into a theatrical and refined convention, thus avoiding the question of the character's survival altogether.

For the most part, all these compromises lead to the tragicomic defeats of the protagonists and sometimes of their authors (as it can be seen in Gaidai's failures in the late 1970s and 1980s). However, the search for viable strategies for the intelligentsia-trickster bore fruit. Within the culture of late socialism emerged at least one version of the adaptation of the trickster trope for the self-identification of the Soviet intellectual that was utterly devoid of tragedy (or tragicomic effects) and, furthermore, outlived the Soviet epoch. This strategy was based on the trickster's game and/or the intelligentsia's collaboration with cynical power. It found its clearest expression in the image of the Soviet spy, first and foremost Stierlitz, a.k.a. Maksim Isaev from the miniseries *Semnadtsat' mgnovenii vesny* (*Seventeen Moments of Spring*, 1973) by Tatiana Lioznova, which produced another *cult* character whose popularity is comparable with that of Ostap Bender or Buratino.

## THE ART OF ALIBI: STIERLITZ AS THE SOVIET INTELLIGENT

Upon returning to Moscow after four years of absence in the summer of 2000, I was struck by the sight of a long row of banners in Kurskii Railway Station. They showed an advertisement for the cigarette brand "Otechestvo [Fatherland]" which included the image of a smoking SS officer.

Stierlitz,—I guessed.

No one froze under this ad to scoff or brandish their fists in outrage. Muscovites and visitors to the capital seem to take the SS officer next to the fatherland (or perhaps, the Vaterland?) as something natural.

*Semnadtsat' mgnovenii vesny* is a twelve-part TV series by Tatiana Lioznova based on the novel by Yulian Semenov (1931-1993), a renowned star of the Soviet spy genre, produced on direct order from the KGB[5] and evidently exceeding all expectations placed on it. The Soviet spy Maksim Isaev, in the guise of Standartenführer Max Otto von Stierlitz (played by Viacheslav Tikhonov) not only glorified "the contribution to the Victory of the soldiers of the unseen front," but he also created a powerful cultural myth, deeply embedded in the cultural imagination of the last Soviet generations as well as the first post-Soviet one. Curiously, in 2009 a new color version of the originally black-and-white film was produced in order to enhance its appeal to the new generations, who are apparently "corrupted" by Hollywood blockbusters. Notably, this version was broadcast on the First state channel during the week of the Victory Day celebrations.[6]

Many film spies that are popular among Soviet viewers pale next to Stierlitz, including: Aleksei Fedotov, a.k.a. the Nazi officer Henrich

---

5  Leonid Parfenov speaks about this in detail in the TV series *"Semnadtsat' mgnovenii vesny: Dvadtsat' piat' let spustia"* ("Seventeen Moments of Spring: Twenty Five Years Later," 1998). Yurii Andropov's deputy, general of the KGB Semen Tsvigun was a consultant for the filming (in the film's credit he was listed as general-colonel S. Mishin) in which capacity he was very active.

6  See "Semnadtsat' mgnovenii vesny..."

Eckert (Pavel Kadochnikov) in the "cult" film of the post-war years; *Podvig razvedchika* (*Secret Agent*,1947, directed by Boris Barnet); the elegant Nikolai Kuznetsov (Gunar Tsilinkis) from *Sil'nye dukhom* (*Strong with Spirit*, 1967, directed by V. Georgiev); the very handsome Captain Kloss (Stanislaw Mikulski) from the Polish TV series *Stawka wieksza niz zycie* (*More Than Life at Stake*, 1968, directed by Andrzej Konic); Weiss-Belov (Stanislav Liubshin) from the TV series *Shchit i mech* (*Shield and Sword*, 1968, directed by Vladimir Basov), based on the novel of the leading Socialist Realist writer Vadim Kozhevnikov; Ladeinikov (Donatas Banionis) in *Mertvyi sezon* (*The Dead Season*, 1969, directed by Savva Kulish); and the Soviet double-agent Skorin, brilliantly played by Oleg Dal' in the TV mini-series *Variant 'Omega'* (1975, directed by Antonis Vogiazos). Yet, only the White Army lieutenant Kol'tsov (Yurii Solomin) from the mini-series *Ad'iutant Ego prevoskhoditel'stva* (*Aide of His Excellence*, 1969, directed by Evgenii Tashkov) seems comparable to Stierlitz. Kol'tsov, like Stierlitz, bears the stamp of the intelligentsia's charm and intellectual brilliance and, just as in *Seventeen Moments*, the enemy's uniforms and aiguillettes in this film look most attractive in comparison to the baggy jackets and tunics of "our men," i.e., the Soviet military. However, for some reason Stierlitz has entered folklore while Kol'tsov has not. One possible reason is that by the late 1960s–early 1970s, the Civil War was a much less sacred field in the popular imagination than the Great Patriotic War and had therefore lost some of its potential to generate myths. The Great Patriotic War, on the other hand,—as an artificially separated "Soviet" part of WWII—is in the words of Lev Gudkov, "the most important element of collective identification for [Soviet and post-Soviet] society on the whole, the benchmark, the gauge, the source of a certain optics for assessing the past and also partially for interpreting the present and future. [...] In fact, this is the sole positive reference point for national identification in [Soviet and] post-Soviet society." (2005: 52)

Stierlitz is a trickster by trade, not by temper: he is not simply a Soviet spy in the upper echelons of the Third Reich, but a spy masked as a German intelligence officer—one may say a double trickster. Although the traits of the classical trickster, such as humorous playfulness and transgressive mischief, appear reduced in Stierlitz, certain trickster features underpin his role from the very beginning: these features are fully realized in the Stierlitz *anekdots* that appeared after the release of the mini-series (see below).

When compared to all the other film spies of the socialist mold, Stierlitz appears almost lethargic: strictly speaking, he performs a multi-staged governmental plot and serves many masters, gaining their unconditional trust and betraying them at the same time. Although he does not participate in exchanges of gunfire, does not blow anything up and does not run away from anything, Stierlitz immediately became an icon when the series was first broadcast. "The streets of Soviet cities were empty,"[7] according to a journalistic cliché. Photocards with the actor Viacheslav Tikhonov in the uniform of an SS Standartenführer immediately became a treasured adornment of girls' albums, and the series of extraordinarily original anecdotes that resemble neither those inspired by Chapaev nor those about Lieutenant Rzhevsky or any other jokes about a film character, only corroborates the mythological effect of the KGB-contrived PR operation: an effect that is long-term, as is now clear.

Symptomatically, scriptwriter Iulian Semenov tried to cast Archil Gomiashvili for the role of Stierlitz. This actor had already gained fame as Ostap Bender in *Dvenadtsat' stul'ev* by Leonid Gaidai (1971). The director, Lioznova, preferred Oleg Strizhenov for the part, the chief romantic hero of the 1960s, who had played the heroic Gadfly in the eponymous film by Aleksandr Faintsimmer and Nikolai Akimov (1954, based upon Ethel Lilian Voynich's novel of 1897), as well as the aristocratic Govorukha-Otrok in *Sorok pervyi* by Grigorii Chukhrai (*The Forty First*, 1956, based upon Boris Lavrenev's novella of 1924). The actor Viacheslav Tikhonov turned out to be a felicitous compromise; his previous performances allowed him to mediate between two polar versions of intelligentsia self-realization, namely the heroic-romantic and the picaresque (more on this later). From the trickster's repertoire,

---

7   "At the first showings of the film, the Soviet cities from Kaliningrad to Vladivostok died out in the literal sense of the words: buses ran empty, consumption of water fell to nothing, and the use of electricity—soared to critical rates. All the countries of the Socialist bloc bought up the mini-series, Tikhonov became the idol of Berliners and Warsawians, of the residents of Bucharest and Prague. [...]From 1973 to the present the series has been on the air 3-4 times per year, but there have been years, where the number of airings exceeded 10. Finally, this is the first and for now the sole series in the world, which is shown in a single day from morning to night without a break, all 12 episodes in succession" (Kichin). In regards to "the first and sole," the critic, of course, slightly exaggerates: this is a quite customary way of showing popular series, for example, on American cable channels, the airing of *Twin Peaks*, *Sex in the City*, *The Sopranos*, *Rome*, and many others.

Stierlitz first and foremost manifests *mediation,* which he implements on various levels and in a vast array of forms, both within and beyond the film's plotline.

9. Viacheslav Tikhonov as Stierlitz in *Semnadtsat' mgnovenii vesny.*

*Semnadtsat' mgnovenii vesny* suffers from many flaws: its composition is monotonous, it is tempting to fast-forward through drawn-out passages and tedious excerpts from official chronicles about the victories of the Soviet army, and the often comical dialogue cannot make up for this ("Call the car. I must be at the crematorium in 20 minutes," is said by Kaltenbrunner in the first episode, and the black humor of this exit line remains unexplained). And how ridiculous is the famous scene when Stierlitz, on the occasion of Soviet Army Day, is baking a potato and singing *Step' da step' krugom*? He sings silently, but with the accompaniment of an accordion!

But then again, many of the absurdities of the mini-series are fully intentional. First there are the anachronisms: The civilian attire of the heroes—shoulder pads and broad lapels—does not bring to mind the style of the 1940s. All of the clothes—men and women's alike—are tailored to conform to 1960s Western style: narrow lapels, shirts with small and sharp collars, absolutely no shoulder pads, everything is figure-hugging, neck kerchiefs colored "peacock eye" style, hats with narrow brims, etc. Stierlitz's maid wears a bouffant hairstyle and his wife and Gabi sport "perms." This anachronism, incidentally, applies also to the SS uniforms: in his TV commentary on the mini-series, Parfenov presents an immense wardrobe of Nazi attire, tailored in Defense Ministry special workshops especially for the series and looking staggeringly authentic, even in color, although the film was black and white ("everything was embroidered, as genuine as possible"). Yet all the same, even the SS uniforms are styled after 1960s fashion and look like "a Godard film." The same can be said about the sets. For example, the café in which Stierlitz meets with his new liaison in the twelfth episode does not even pretend to be from the 1940s (like, say, the café "Elephant"): this is a recognizably Baltic (i.e., Western, in the Soviet imagination) café of the 1960s and early 1970s, in minimalist, "Corbusian" design, with several levels and stylish lampshades. And a song by Èdith Piaf, which Stierlitz and Pastor Schlagg listen to on the radio, was composed twelve years after the end of the war, as the more meticulous among the fans have pointed out. However, even the contemporary Soviet automobile, which runs in the background on "the road to Berlin," does not ruin the effect. After all, without these anachronisms Stierlitz would not have become what he is in the Soviet cultural imagination.

10. Stierlitz and Frau Saurich (*Emilia Milton*)

It is for a reason that Stierlitz has entered folklore and outlived the epoch that produced him. This trickster manifests the paradoxical trope of *"our" man amongst "them"*: not just disguised as an alien but living the life of enemies, blending in with the "alien" social environment. The main key to the perception of Stierlitz lays in the contradiction between what we know about him and how he behaves. Vadim Rudnev even considers that "the series was such a staggering success because it showed an internal émigré, living among strangers, having half become like them... The double standard of the internal émigré was shown in this series." (Rudnev, 400) Although I agree with this definition, I would like to be more precise: *Semnadtsat' mgnovenii vesny* presents an inversion of the situation of internal emigration, not unusual for a spy novel. An internal émigré lives in an inwardly alien environment. In the case of Stierlitz everything is reversed. We know that Stierlitz is "our man" and that he works for "us." And yet, the way his suit and SS uniform fit him, how he speaks to his superior with dignity, travels in a luxury car, drinks coffee and cognac, and of course, smokes elegantly[8]—all these elements do not indicate "one of us," i.e., a Soviet man, but a Westerner or rather, a Westerner according to Soviet imagination. It is completely impossible to imagine Stierlitz in the uniform of a colonel of the NKVD. Tikhonov—maybe. Stierlitz—no. Stierlitz embodies such an archetypical Western feature as rationality (everyone remembers him sorting matches) combined with maximally suppressed emotionality (the seven-minute scene of his silent emotional "intercourse" with his wife), which constitutes an inversion of stereotypical representations of "Russianness." Thus Stierlitz turns out to be not so much an internal émigré as a projection of at least two of the most significant themes of the late-Soviet intelligentsia's culture—a longing for "the West" and contempt for the Soviet system.

Stierlitz's artistic mediation between Soviet and "bourgeois," war and peace, daily life and work for the system, closely corresponded to the cultural and social functions of the late-Soviet intelligentsia and even more so to its self-image. Moreover, Stierlitz raised mediation to a truly heroic scale that is devoid of any official pathos. *Semnadtsat' mgnovenii vesny* transferred the heroic connotations of the principal Soviet myth—the myth of the Great Patriotic War—into an enchanting myth about the mediator-intellectual or rather, a myth about the Soviet intelligentsia's "Orwellian" doublethink. This re-definition, paradoxically, cancels out neither the heroism nor the charm of the created image.

---

8   He only does this for seven minutes in the first episode of the series and no less than an hour of screen time in the entire twelve hour series—a promotional image later used for a commercial for cigarettes is well motivated by the mini-series.

―――――――――――――――― CHAPTER SIX ――――――――――――――――

*Who are you working for?*

By the beginning of the 1970s, Tikhonov had established a reputation as an "intellectual actor." First the figure of Prince Andrei Bolkonsky in Sergei Bondarchuk's film version of Tolstoy's *War and Peace* (1965–7) and then, paramount to the intelligentsia's consciousness, the figure of the teacher Ilia Semenovich Mel'nikov from *Dozhivem do ponedel'nika* (*We'll Live Till Monday*, dir. Stanislav Rostotskii, 1968) had replaced the memory of Tikhonov as a dashing lad in such films as *Delo bylo v Pen'kovo* (*It Happened in Pen'kovo*, dir. Stanislav Rostoskii, 1958), and *Ch. P.—Chrezvychainoe proisshestvie* (*Extraordinary Accident*, dir. Viktor Ivchenko, 1958). Moreover, Tikhonov's Stierlitz was reminiscent of both Prince Bolkonsky (a natural born military officer with a uniform that fit like a glove) and the teacher Mel'nikov—e.g., Stierlitz *thrice* in the course of the series makes his subordinates repeat his instructions like a lesson, and one of them ironically addresses the Standartenführer as "Teacher Sir" (*Gospodin uchitel'*). If we add to this that Stierlitz (as becomes apparent in the eighth episode) also has a degree in physics, we have the full set of intelligentsia heroes from the 1960s represented in a single individual—and in new quality.

11. Viacheslav Tikhonov as Andrei Bolkonsky in Sergei Bondarchuk's *War and Peace*.

Effectively, Tikhonov's Stierlitz is a personification of the ideal figure of the smart, reserved, and self-deprecating intellectual who lacks the stereotypical weaknesses of the Soviet intelligentsia. He is: an iron-hard intellectual; considerate towards those around him and at the same time impenetrable to outsiders' eyes; polite even while interrogating and manipulating the overwhelming majority of his informants with the help of pseudo-rational sophisms; a connoisseur of foreign books and ancient artwork; comfortable in a cozy sweater and in tail coats; and a player of chess and the piano.

Apparently, this is Stierlitz's *mask*, justified by his mission as a spy and allowing him to blend in with the *enemies*. However, the main paradox of the mini-series lies in the fact that this very mask becomes Stierlitz's face, and it is because of it that he can rise to the status of the intelligentsia's hero. He is actually a spy *from the intelligentsia* who tries to present his true self as his adopted identity.[9] It is for a reason that the two characters closest to Stierlitz turn out to be patent intellectuals, Pastor Schlagg (Rostislav Pliatt) and Professor Pleishner (Evgenii Evstigneev). And they display the stereotypical weaknesses associated with the intelligentsia in Soviet cultural mythology: impracticality, naïveté, and absent-mindedness.

12. Stierlitz and pastor Schlagg (*Rostislav Pliatt*)

13. Evgenii Evstigneev as Professor Pleishner

The conflict of the Soviet intellectual who experiences himself as a stranger in the midst of his own people and at home among strangers is central to the representation of Stierlitz, who catches himself thinking of the Germans as "our people." At the same time, the accentuated "otherness" of Stierlitz with regard to the Soviet experience is expressed in his undisguised delight in such things as the lounges of bars and restaurants where he spends time sipping French cognac, the clean alleyways through which he strolls, and the house in which he lives—

---

9   This aspect of the Stierlitz myth is reflected by the joke, "Müller: Stierlitz, I know: you—are Jewish! Stierlitz: No, how can you say that! I am Russian!"

equipped with both a fireplace and a garage. In this cozy setting, the viewers almost forget about the real situation at the end of the war in Berlin, with constant air raids, etc.—this happens in precise accordance with Roland Barth's observation that "myth is constituted by the loss of historical quality of things: in it, things lose the memory that they once were made." (Barth 142) However, the performance of history in *Semnadtsat' mgnovenii vesny* presents a somewhat greater complexity than the author of *Mythologies* was able to anticipate.

"Information for Contemplation" (Информация к размышлениям), which had set the tone and style of Russian pseudo-documentary discourse for many years in advance, was, of course, important not so much because it satisfied the hunger for historical detail, but as an exquisite exercise in Aesopian language. Pieces of "Information for Contemplation" in the form of sub-plots about the luxuries enjoyed by Göring; the sexual adventures of the chief ideologue with the appearance of an ascetic; the description of party secretary Bormann at the peak of his career and his behind-the-scenes power; or the role of Himmler in the founding of "camps for re-education"—inevitably evoked associations with the Soviet past that remained "unmentionable" in the 1970s and even more so with the Soviet present, or rather with the widely circulating legends and rumors about the lifestyle of the contemporary party nomenclature. No less charged with dangerous political parallels were the documentaries showing ceremonies for the Führer's next birthday, with folk choirs and symphony orchestras, all too reminiscent of late Soviet anniversary vigils. The general discourse of the film, which was peppered with such expressions as "he was remolded," "party apparatus," "dissident," "listened to western radio too much," "this is not a telephone conversation," and "his grandma is a Jewess" also inevitably triggered Soviet rather than Nazi associations. In such a context, even such an evidently "German" phrase as "We all are under Müller's pointy hat" ( «мы все у Мюллера под колпаком»—i.e., "we are all under the Gestapo's surveillance")—becomes *our* formula, with the "Nazi" defamiliarization only adding to its ironic charm.

Against this background, the dialogues between the Gestapo provocateur Klauss (Lev Durov) and Pastor Schlagg, Stierlitz and Schlagg, Stierlitz and his accidental train acquaintance, the Wehrmacht general (Nikolai Gritsenko), and in particular the words shouted by intellectuals—the astronomer (Yurii Katin-Iartsev) and the physicist

Runge (Grigorii Liampe)—beaten during Gestapo interrogations, articulated that which was in principle not a subject of public discourse, let alone on television: the "kitchen" conversations, intellectual and distinctly dissident questions about the people's support for the totalitarian regime, about the ignorance of the masses, about "the nation, reduced to a mute herd," about the (im)possibilities of resistance to state violence, about the stool pigeons and provocateurs... Incidentally, the fact that Stierlitz kills only one character *with his own hands,* and that this character is not a stereotypical Nazi, but the double-crossing professional informer Klauss, was an instance of the Soviet intellectual's "dream come true," of the same order as the ritual killing of Baron Maigel at Woland's ball in Bulgakov's *Master i Margarita*.

14. General Wolfe (*Vasilii Lanovoi*), Schellenberg (*Oleg Tabakov*), and Himmler (*Nikolai Prokopovich*).

Furthermore, the novelty of *Semnadtsat' mgnovenii vesny* consisted not solely in the fact that this series for the first time depicted Nazis as smart, but in the *charm* bestowed on them. Obviously, this does not amount to an esthetization of Nazism (although the similarity between the esthetics of *Semnadtsat' mgnovenii vesny* and *The Night Porter* (1974) by Liliana Cavani has been noted already).[10] If such an effect did arise it was unintentional. Nazis in Lioznova's film were emanating charm, first by virtue of the already mentioned admiration of the West, and second, thanks to the cast of actors, which was oriented towards the "internal," i.e., the Soviet intelligentsia's, set of values and associations. Almost

---

10   See Popova.

all of the actors in the series, while speaking contemporary language, invested symbolic capital from their own former—famous—roles as Nazi characters. Thanks to Oleg Tabakov and the image associated with this actor at the beginning of the 1970s, the chief of German counter-intelligence Walter Schellenberg appears as a former idealist of the 1960s who had incorporated into the system and became a master of party intrigue, but in spite of this maintained a certain semblance of intellectual freedom; it is for a reason that he emphatically smokes Camels. Behind General Wolfe (Vasilii Lanovoi) looms the shadow of Pavka Korchagin from the eponymous film by Aleksandr Alov and Vladimir Naumov (1956, based on the paradigmatic Socialist Realist novel *Kak zakalialias' stal'* (*How the Steel Was Tempered* by Nikolai Ostrovskii). Behind the straightforward Eismann (Leonid Kuravlev) lurks the naïvely charming Pashka Kolokol'nikov from Vasilii Shukshin's film *Zhivet takoi paren'* (*There is Such a Lad*, 1964). Then there is the quiet little mouse Gabi (Svetlana Svetlichnaia), clattering away on the typewriter (God knows whither or why; perhaps, she is copying out late Soviet *samizdat*?). Gabi, who loves Stierlitz with perseverance and devotion, is a contrast to the most famous role of this actress, Anna Sergeevna from *Brilliantovaia ruka* (*The Diamond Arm*, 1969 by Leonid Gaidai), the most prominent, albeit parodical, femme fatal of the Thaw period. In this context, the casting of 1960s idol Yurii Vizbor, the poet and singer, bard of "campfire smoke," as *Parteigenosse* Bormann does not seem strange at all.

Each of these roles reflects a metamorphosis of the generation of the 1960s, many members of which became part of the Soviet system—that is to say, behind each of these roles the viewer could feel a scenario of imagined preservation of one's authentic self, or at least one's individual interests, behind the mask of the "cog in the wheel." Incidentally, the reiteration of formulas supposedly borrowed from the characters' personal dossiers ("True Aryan. Merciless towards enemies of the Reich"/"Истинный ариец. Беспощаден к врагам Рейха"). in essence *revealed nothing* about the heroes, but instead underlined their ritual, façade character, which in turn became a brilliant metaphor for the formalization and depletion of the official discourse of late-Soviet culture.[11]

It would seem that Müller—in an unforgettable performance by

---

11  See on this Yurchak 2006: 36-76.

Leonid Bronevoi—does not follow this logic of representation. After all, Bronevoi was a virtually unknown actor when cast in this role, which then made him an instant celebrity. But he made a firm impression in the cultural consciousness precisely because he depicted the chief of the Gestapo using the matrix of a typical Soviet police-investigator—burning the candle at both ends, suffering from hypertension, and spending long nights at the office. However, what he created on this stereotypical foundation was the image of the intelligent, ironic, artistic yet profound—and because of that infinitely attractive—*cynic*. In essence, he plays *a super-cynic* who outfoxes even the clever Schellenberg. Müller turns out to be the only one who is on equal footing with Stierlitz: there is a reason why, at the end of the series, they conclude a pact of non-aggression and cooperation, or, taking into consideration the subject matter, agree to a separate peace.

15. Yurii Vizbor as Bormann

16. Vasilii Lanovoi as General Wolfe.

Thus, the whole system of characters unfolds here as the conflict between dissenting (Soviet) intellectuals and those intellectuals who have chosen to play by the system's brutal rules for the sake of self-realization, often at a considerable advantage for themselves (in variations ranging from Schellenberg to Klauss). In this regard, Stierlitz stands out as the ideal mediator, having succeeded in fusing an SS officer (or "Chekist") and a secret dissident-intellectual. Both sides consider him their own and are ultimately deceived by him.

## CHAPTER SIX

### The Imperial Mediator

In this context, the trickster trope (as represented by Stierlitz) firstly supports the ahistorical—or rather, counter-historical—nature of the entire mini-series; and secondly, it lays the foundation for rendering the spy motif as a powerful tongue-in-cheek metaphor for the Soviet intelligentsia. *Semnadtsat' mgnovenii vesny* substantiates and heroicizes the internal non-affiliation to the social and political system to which the hero physically and historically belongs, hence his carefully cultivated "otherness." In other words, Stierlitz convincingly demonstrated that one can combine service to "our people" with the lifestyle of those who are "not our people," and one can serve without belonging to either the communists (in lifestyle) or the Nazis (in the line of duty) while technically belonging to both.

However, the mediation accomplished by Stierlitz is possible only because all the "masters" he serves are united by imperial interest. After all, what is the point of Stierlitz's intrigue, which leads to the breakdown of negotiations between the Nazi General Wolfe (secretly supported by Himmler) and the US chief of intelligence Allen Dulles? If a separate agreement had been reached and the Germans had capitulated on the Western front, then the post-war map of Europe would look quite different; one would not find the GDR on it and the Soviet empire would not stretch from Kamchatka to Berlin.

At the same time, in *Semnadtsat' mgnovenii vesny* the imperial splendor of the Nazi regime *replaces* the image of the Soviet empire—this is why the Soviet intelligence officers are so faceless and expressionless (they even lack names and biographies, as opposed to their adversaries), and Hitler, though prominent in the documentary quotations, is practically absent in the mini-series itself (the sole exception is one inconsequential scene with him in the first episode). On the other hand, the scene in which Stalin solemnly dictates a letter to Roosevelt with mention of Soviet intelligence agents (this letter, Lioznova confesses, brought her to tears of ecstasy!) is lavishly presented and drawn out. It is noteworthy that Schellenberg and Himmler call Americans "the Allies" and representatives of the "West," as if their cabinets were not located in Berlin, but in the Kremlin.

17-18. Leonid Bronevoi as Müller

Owing to all these displacements, insignificant at first glance, and to the plot focus on the negotiations for a separate peace between Germany and the "West," the traditional war film conflict between Germans and Russians is replaced by a game of interests involving liberal democracies and empires—which obviously echoes the disposition of the Cold War. Furthermore, the Nazi and Soviet empires appear on screen to be fused into one, with the figure of Stierlitz situated where the fusion takes place. As a result, the meaning of the film's plot ultimately boils down to the following: on the eve of collapse of the Third Reich, Stierlitz rescues the imperial idea from Western democracy, entrusting it to the Soviet side.

In this regard, Stierlitz appears as a heroicized version of the Soviet intelligentsia's consciousness, and at the same time—much like other Soviet tricksters—embodies the deconstruction of this consciousness.

## CHAPTER SIX

Secret freedom turns out to be impossible without an SS officer uniform in the wardrobe. Apparently, the function of the intelligentsia as a mediator between "our people" and "the other," between the authorities and the dissidents, between the West and Russia, etc., preserves meaning only in an imperial context. Is it indeed so? The answer is probably yes, which explains why Stierlitz discovers the ultimate goal for his heroic and secret mission in saving the empire rather than ending the war (as the war could have ended much earlier through the aforementioned separate peace). Without the empire, Stierlitz's as well as the Soviet *intelligent*'s status appears precarious and highly problematic, which can be read as an unheard prophecy about the social and cultural crises of the intelligentsia following the breakup of the USSR.

Or rather, a prophecy that not only went unheard by its addressees, but was even uttered unintentionally. It is unlikely that Lioznova, in Parfenov's documentary, accidentally establishes a connection between the fame of *Semnadtsat' mgnovenii* and memories about the historical grandeur of Soviet civilization: "Time turns in such a way that, unfortunately, a lot has slipped through the hands of this great country. It seems to me that the majority of those who live on this land wish this country had the grandeur, the strength and the independence it once had... and which, not of our will, we have lost." And to leave no doubt which lost grandeur the film director mourns during this speech, Parfenov accompanies her tirade with picturesque footage of the Victory parade in 1945, with Marshall Georgii Zhukov prancing on a white horse—possibly the most striking visual symbol of the triumph of the Soviet empire.

Nothing exposes the imperialist lining of the myth about Stierlitz more clearly than the arrangement of the female characters. It was noticed long ago that the imperial logic of power and submission is duplicated and nourished by gender relations within the dominant culture.[12] It is curious that half of the female characters were added by the director in order to "warm" the figure of the hero. Besides, they all (with the exception of Barbara) pursue typical intelligentsia professions and exhibit the intelligentsia's style of behavior, fashion, and so on. The unfolding gender disposition turns into the formula of the patriarchal consciousness of the late Soviet intelligentsia. On the

---

12   See for example, McClintock.

highest level we find the mother—an archetype that is significant for any patriarchal culture, but particularly accentuated in the imperial context (Stalinism and Nazism agree to great extent in this question). In *Semnadtsat' mgnovenii vesny* this archetype appears in two guises: the young and fertile Kat (Ekaterina Gradova) represents the heroic aspect of motherhood, while the poignant Frau Saurich (Ekaterina Mil'ton) demonstrates the comical side through the figure of the eccentric old lady or helpless witch. (Significantly, she appears in the very beginning of the film next to Stierlitz and, what is more, in the *forest* scene, where he takes her every *spring*. It is also mentioned that she earns her bread by *fortune-telling*, a fact that triggers a wide spectrum of diverse mythopoetic associations.) On the lowest level among the female personages (it would be more precise to call them female gender roles) stands the SS officer Barbara (Ol'ga Soshnikova) who preaches sexual emancipation, but within matrimony. Despite this puritanical limitation her debauched ideology is proudly refused by Kat, while Barbara herself is compromised when she tortures a child. (The comical double to Barbara is the drunken lady in a fox fur cape in the last episode played by Irina Ul'ianova.)

Sexuality in general is consistently repressed in the film: it is also evident in the way Stierlitz defines himself as an "aging loner" («стареющий одинокий мужчина»)—despite the fact that when the series was shot Tikhonov was 45 years old!—while his "distanced sex" with his wife is safely confined to the pre-war past. The women who love Stierlitz—his wife (Ekaterina Shashkova) and Gabi—are trapped between the poles of mother and "debaucher." And they are the ones who are deprived of *discourse* in this intelligentsia thriller: they are only allowed to adore the hero *silently*.[13]

Yet, let us not forget that characteristics inherent to the imperial mythology, such as "the attributes of state heroic spirit and the providential route [...] the traditional hierarchical notion about society and man" in accordance with which "there is only one way prescribed to the individual: service to the great whole, absolute self-sacrifice" (Dubin 2001: 336),—appear *doubly estranged* in *Semnadtsat' mgnovenii vesny*. Firstly, by the chronotope of Western comfort, which is emphatically individualistic and thus opposed to the pathos of self-

---

13  See Prokhorova for the detailed analysis of the connection between imperial discourse and gender models of the ideal man, realized in the figure of Stierlitz.

sacrifice. Secondly, by the imperial glow of the uniforms and symbols of distinction that appear tangibly and visibly, while being associated with the *image of the enemy* and not with the supermen from the NKVD. Is it not this complicated dialectic of signifieds and signifiers that invokes the ironic spark that once in a while flashes in the eyes of Stierlitz/Tikhonov?

Once the imperial idea is saved, the next task, which occupies Stierlitz throughout all twelve episodes, is a more individualized, if not individualistic issue, namely the *issue of alibi*. Naturally, Stierlitz is anxious for Müller and Schellenberg to believe his alibi. But one should not lose sight of the metaphorical dimension of this issue, which was particularly relevant for the late-Soviet intelligentsia. Its "phantom existence" (Yurii Levada) presupposed both active solidarity with the despised authorities, which incidentally guaranteed the system of social privileges for the intelligentsia, and demonstrative intellectual disaffiliation from the Soviet ideologies, policies, and most importantly, life style. An alibi was required for the authorities as well as for one's close intelligentsia circle—each group required constant proof of loyalty and spectacles of belonging. Stierlitz's skill in resolving this issue may explain the supernatural popularity of this personage.

Put together, his aptitude for mediation between worlds that at first glance appear incompatible, for belonging/non-belonging, and finally for the art of alibi, amount to an *illusion of freedom,*—the trickster's freedom—as all these abilities promise the possibility of slipping away from fixed social roles, identities, obligations, and so on. The version of freedom embodied by Stierlitz was precious and unique precisely because it was gained *from within the system* as a result of virtuoso play with its internal contradictions. *Play* probably also provides the key to the character of Stierlitz as a professional trickster. For good reason he is famous among his SS colleagues as a master of radio-games and he emphasizes that "I am a player, but not a dummy!" («Я игрок, а не болван»). And the audience understands that the game which Stierlitz plays is considerably more difficult than his superiors can imagine.

### *Stierlitz's Afterlife*

As was noted earlier, tricksters are the favorite heroes of Soviet jokelore. Stierlitz occupies an honorary place among them, along with Chapaev,

Buratino, and Sherlock Holmes. Part of the reason why the genre of the *anekdot* flourished in Soviet culture is its inherently trickster functions, such as the transgression of borders, the profanation of the sacred, and the squandering of symbolic values. But why did Stierlitz enter Soviet jokelore? After all, what he lacks in the film is precisely a sense of humor and buffoonish energy, appearing serious, imposing, and reserved instead.

As Catharine Nepomnyashchy aptly mentions: "[T]he popularity of Stierlitz jokes and parodies are in some sense a function of the popularity of the original series itself, exposing it, and its 'positive hero,' as an inherently ambiguous text through which we can read the deeply rooted, unvoiced, and perhaps unacknowledged cultural allegiances and anxieties of its audience." (Nepomnyashchy, 3) *Anekdots* about Stierlitz target the aura of the intelligentsia's sophistication which surrounds the hero. Based on puns, these practically untranslatable jokes convert bookish literary formulae into their literal meaning («Штирлиц склонился над картой СССР. Его неудержимо рвало на родину»[14]) and transform Stierlitz from a subtle intellectual to a brutal simpleton («Штирлиц погладил кошку, кошка сдохла. «Странно»—подумал Штирлиц, поплевав на утюг»). Interestingly, at the same time, these jokes often employ the difference between written and oral speech ("Штирлиц выстрелил вслепую. Слепая упала")— once again, on another level, transgressing the borders of the intelligentsia's (logocentric) paradigm. It is also notable that in jokes about Stierlitz the oral formula is often realized through acts of violence that presuppose a subversion/inversion of the purely intellectual games of the film hero:

> «Штирлиц и Мюллер стреляли по очереди. Очередь быстро уменьшалась»;
>
> «Штирлиц хотел повесить занавеску. Но сделать это было непросто—Занавеску сопротивлялся и бил его по голове гантелей»;
>
> «Штирлиц топил буржуйку. Только через два часа ему удалось ее утопить.»

To some extent, the effect of Stierlitz jokes is similar to that of

---

14  All Stierlitz jokes are cited from Komandir Mochalkin.

the early prose of Vladimir Sorokin, in which the naturalization of the symbolic and the literalization of verbal and cultural metaphors constitute the central devices for the deconstruction of authoritarian discourses (see on this Lipovetsky 2000). Yet, unlike Sorokin's stories, Stierlitz *anekdots* not only deconstruct the intelligentsia's myth, but also convert the intelligentsia hero into a buffoon, an impetuous violator of conventions, by these means *saving* him from a tragic-serious aura and taking mediation to a new level: this time, it oscillates between intellectualism and silly clownage.

The combined—"filmic" and "jokelore"—mythology of Stierlitz seemed especially in demand at the end of 1990s, when the practical attempts to fuse Soviet lifestyle habits ("ours") with Western style and relations ("alien") revealed their, to put it mildly, questionable nature, when the Perestroika dream of Russia turning into Europe if only the communists were removed from power was repeatedly and painfully proved a failure. On the ruins of these utopias Stierlitz accrued unprecedented vitality as a model of successful—not intellectual but intuitive—synthesis of "ours" and "alien" values, discourses, and lifestyles.

19. Stierlitz and Frau Saurich (*Emilia Milton*)

More than this, the Russian collective unconscious elected Stierlitz as president, giving him preference over the mythologically weak archetypes of the strong but thieving Soviet manager (*khoziaistvennik*), the behind-the-scenes diplomat, the eloquent speaking intellectual, and the party secretary. It is Stierlitz who sheds light on the emphatically faceless Putin, whose only distinction from the other political figures of the late 1990s was a career as a professional spy and knowledge of the German language (here comes Stierlitz!). Just a hint of Stierlitz helped an inconspicuous *apparatchik* become the people's favorite and the "father of the nation," beating all records of popularity despite the official blessing from the other, extremely unpopular, "father" (Yeltsin). That Putin benefited so greatly from an archetype as powerful as Stierlitz is not surprising. As argued by Roland Barthes, "in the mythical signifier [...] its form is empty but present, its meaning absent but full" (124); Putin then became the signifier of the myth of which Stierlitz served as the mythical signified, cleansing its meaning of any unnecessary associations.

In 2000, I expressed a hypothesis on the effect of the Stierlitz myth in the election of Putin as president (see Lipovetsky 2000a). Not so long ago, I stumbled upon evidence that this supposition is not so far from the truth. In Ol'ga Darfi's play, *Trezvyi piar-1* (*Sober PR-1*) based on an interview with famous post-Soviet spindoctors, one may find the following fragment:

> [W]hen we understood that Yeltsin was completely finished and something needed to be done, we launched all kinds of polls throughout Russia, quantitative and qualitative, and one of the questions—your favorite personage, film hero—Stierlitz. That's all. It was unnecessary to invent anything, he [Putin] showed up in the right place at the right time, and with finishing touches [...] the rest is done. (Gremina and Ugarov, 41)

Of course, this is not a documentary, but a play. But all the same, a documentary play...[15]

As we see, Stierlitz has outlived the Soviet epoch with ease. And possibly he awaits new reincarnations (Sergei Ursuliak, made famous by the TV mini-series *Occupation*, has released in 2009 a new multi-episode film *Isaev* about young Stierlitz). But the matter is not so much the immediate appearances of this hero on the screen as his overall impact on post-Soviet culture by remaining part of it, not only as a memorial to a past era but also as a stable cultural trope which gives rise to recognized

---

15 See also Nepomnyashchy (13-14) for more on the parallels between Putin and Stierlitz.

rhetorical and discursive models. Why is he destined for such a long life? Possibly because the mediation he implemented preserves its vitality even after the disintegration of the Soviet empire. But maybe simply because, as General Wolfe—and the paradigmatic Soviet actor Vasilii Lanovoi—pointedly noted in the film, "among us everyone served in the SS" ("у нас все служили в СС").

# CHAPTER 7

## SPLITTING THE TRICKSTER: PELEVIN'S SHAPE-SHIFTERS

## THE SOCIETY OF SHAPE-SHIFTERS

The quest for post-Soviet transformations of the trickster inevitably leads to Viktor Pelevin (b. 1962), one of the most outstanding representatives of Russian literary postmodernism. Tricksters of different scale appear in such of his novels as *Chapaev i Pustota* (*Buddha's Little Finger/Clay Machine-Gun*, 1996), with Chapaev featuring simultaneously as a hero-trickster from a Soviet cycle of jokes and as a reincarnation of Buddha, and in *Generation 'P'* (*Homo Zapiens/Babilon*, 1999), the protagonist of which passes through a trickster school, so to speak, of post-Soviet commercialism and as a result becomes a living god, the embodiment of simulative capitalism, the magic of TV and advertising. We will focus on Pelevin's novel *Sviashchennaia kniga oborotnia* (*The Sacred Book of the Werewolf*, 2004; hereafter, *SKO*), where the theme of the trickster is central and, moreover, interpreted in a vein that is close to the logic of this study.

The narrator in *SKO* is a werefox, a traditional trickster from Chinese folklore, who lives in contemporary Moscow in the guise of an underage prostitute and goes by the name A Huli, which sounds obscene to a Russian ear. The fox is not the only shape-shifter in the novel; the reader will also find here her sisters, who are werefoxes as well: the werewolf Aleksandr Seryi (literally—Gray); a general of the FSB (The Federal Security Bureau—the successor to the KGB); and his assistant, the werewolf Mikhailych.

Pelevin discovered the artistic potential of the shape-shifter (*oboroten'*) motif long ago, though not without the promptings of western mass culture.¹ The shape-shifter is a metaphor for postmodern (and post-Soviet) *identity,* forever oscillating between opposite states, entwined in a single personality and leading to internal as well as external conflicts. Liza Novikova rightly remarks that the motif of the shape-shifter belongs to a series of leitmotifs running through all of Pelevin's works: "Nearly all characters in Pelevin's works were similar 'shape-shifters': he turns Komsomol workers into hard currency prostitutes and the heroes of *The Life of Insects* into mosquitoes and flies. [...] In *SKO* he sculpts solely shape-shifters. 'Werewolves from central Russia' have already attracted the attention of the writer once before." (Novikova, 12)

The last sentence of the excerpt quoted above hints at Pelevin's early story, "A Werewolf Problem in Central Russia"; in an interview with the newspaper *Izvestiia,* Pelevin subsequently acknowledged that *SKO* simply continues the theme of that old story.² The impetus that prompted Pelevin to write the novel was probably the propaganda image of the "shape-shifters in shoulder-boards" (*oborotni v pogonakh*)³ which was widely used for lampooning corrupt cops in the Russian media in 2002–2003. Using this as a starting point, Pelevin essentially created the image of a *society of shape-shifters.* The shape-shifters from *SKO* substantially differ from analogous characters in earlier works. In this novel, shape-shifting is *normalized and presented as an integral part of the fabric of society.* Only a few characters here are *not* shape-shifters. Against the background of the everyday status of shape-shifting the effect produced by the magical features of A Huli and her antagonist/

---

1   The motif of the werewolf is among the most prevalent in Hollywood film, starting with the classic film *Werewolf of London* (1935, dir. Stuart Walker), but especially in the cinematography of 1950-1990: consider the films *The Wolf Man* (1941, dir. George Waggner), *I Was a Teenage Werewolf* (1957, dir. Gene Fowler, Jr.), *An American Werewolf in London* (1981, dir. John Landis), *An American Werewolf in Paris* (1997, dir. Anthony Weller), and many others.

2   "Characters from previous books appear in my novels because they already exist, and I am pleased to meet them once again [...] I wrote a story about werewolves. Why should I invent a new werewolf, when I have one already prepared, who sits and waits to be given his freedom?" (Kochetkova,15).

3   On the genesis and semantics of this image see L'vovskii 2003. In particular, L'vovskii notes: "The image is ideal, instantly giving the understanding that the scrutinized—essentially are from another world, and the majority of employees in law enforcement, are at least as charming and honest (albeit simple too) as the heroes of the television series "Menty /Cops." At the same time, all with the help of two words, returning to the widest usage the quasi-religious mythology, associated with the secret service."

lover Aleksandr appears to be inverted: the fact that they can turn into animals is not as stunning as the fact that Alexander is a general of the FSB whose ability to turn into a wolf forms part of his service to the state (as he understands this service, of course). Even more dazzling is the fact that by the end of the novel, he begins to transform into the murderous dog Pizdets (Phuckup in Andrew Bromfield's translation) instead of a wolf—an effect of the estrangement is achieved here by the ironic substitution of the extraordinary (wolf) with the *less* remarkable (dog).

Critics habitually accused Pelevin of journalistic superficiality, ignoring the fact that all the political jokes and sarcastic comments on current affairs with which he, as always, generously peppered *SKO* soundly resonate with and expand on the plot motif of shape-shifting. It is not an accident that the political metaphors in the novel—just as in post-Soviet political rhetoric, which Pelevin uses to great effect—are saturated with animal references. Pelevin is not too lazy to deconstruct even the most trivial of political clichés tied to the animal kingdom— such as the image of a fish that "rots from the head" (a Russian idiom that suggests that society's corruption begins with the elites): "Every time the reforms begin with the declaration that the fish rots from the head, then the reformers eat up the healthy body, and the rotten head swims on. And so everything that was rotten under Ivan the Terrible is still alive, and everything that was healthy five years ago has already been gobbled up." (ibid., 85)[4] Another example of the "beastialization" of the symbolic is Pelevin's commentary on the emblem of United Russia, the ruling party or rather the party of bosses in Putin's Russia: "A bear is a witty choice too: it is the international symbol of economic stagnation, and there is also the Russian expression 'greasing the paw.' The Eskimos have thirty different kinds of snow, and modern Russian has about the same number of expressions to describe giving a bribe to a state official." (ibid., 86)[5] The literalized pun (the heroes of the novel read the word *"apparat"* as "upper rat") is transformed into an allegory of the post-Soviet uroborus—in *SKO* the rat replaces the serpent which

---

4 «...затем реформаторы съедают здоровое тело, а гнилая голова плывет дальше... поэтому все, что было гнилого при Иване Грозном, до сих пор живо, а все, что было здорового пять лет назад, уже сожрано...» (2007:103).
5 «остроумный выбор: это международный символ экономической стагнации, к тому же есть выражение "брать на лапу"» (ibid.).

eats its own tail: "[T]here are no clear boundaries between these two branches of power—one merges smoothly into another, forming a single immense, fat rat consumed by greedy self-pleasing." (ibid., 85, changed translation)[6] Other details of the narrative belong to the same order: from the magazine headline "America Ponders Mad Cow Strategy" to the dependence of the Russian economy upon a brindled cow or rather, upon its skull, from which FSB General Seryi keeps summoning oil by howling. Similar is A Huli's view of sexual relations, in which she detects shape-shifters, rather than zoological logic:

> Woman is a peaceful creature; she only hypnotizes her own male and inflicts no harm on birds and animals. Since she does this in the name of the supreme biological goal, that is, personal survival, the deception here is pardonable, and it's none of our business to go sticking our noses in. But when a married man who lives every moment in a dream planted in his head by his wife, complete with elements of nightmare and gothic, suddenly declares over a glass of beer that woman is simply a device for bearing children, that is very, very funny. (ibid., 77)[7]

In general, social categories are described by Pelevin as normalized transgressions. There are numerous examples of this, such as: "the strictly tabooed vocabulary employed for daily communication between people here, and laws under which the generally accepted way of life is a crime" (ibid., 86)[8]; the names of cocktails in a Moscow restaurant, the list of which develops into a spicy story featuring Bloody Mary, a screwdriver and a zombie ("Tequila Sunrise, Blue Lagoon, Sex on the

---

6    «нефтяная труба и висящая на ней крыса [...] поглощенная жадным самообслуживанием» (ibid., 104, 103).
7    «Женщина—мирное существо и морочит только собственного самца, не трогая ни птичек, ни зверей. Поскольку она делает это во имя высшей биологической цели, то есть личного выживания, обман здесь простителен, и на наше лисье дело в это лезть. Но когда женатый мужчина, постоянно проживающий в навеянном подругой сне с элементами кошмара и готики, вдруг заявляет после кружки пива, что женщина—просто агрегат для рождения детей, это очень и очень смешно» (ibid., 93).
8    «... строго табуированная лексика, на которой происходит повседневное общение между людьми, и законы, по которым общественный уклад является уголовным преступлением» (ibid., 104).

Beach, Screwdriver, Bloody Mary, Malibu Sunset, Zombie. A ready-made proposal for a movie" (ibid., 8)); tattoos equating god and the criminal/police authorities in the form of "SWAT, SWAT, SWAT tattooed under a blue cross [...] were not meant to be the name of the Los Angeles Police Department's special assault force, but the Russian phrase '*Svyat, Svyat, Svyat*' (meaning 'Holy, Holy, Holy!') written in Latin letters." (ibid., 124) Among these normalized transgressions one also finds the transformation of the ethical imperative "*Zhit' ne po lzhi*" (Live not by lies), coined by Aleksandr Solzhenitsyn in the 1970s as a motto for political resistance against the Soviet regime, into an advertising slogan ("Live not by lies. LG" / "*Zhit' ne po lzhi. LG*" [2007: 270]). The same paradoxical fusion of "sacred" and "profane," "spiritual," and "lewd" is also detectable in the "metaphysics" of Russian machismo: "[A] Russian macho man's life is like a permanent spiritual séance: while the body is wallowing in luxury, the soul is doing time in the prison camps. [...] Russia is a communal country, and when the Christian peasant commune was destroyed, the criminal commune became the source of the people's morality." (2008: 233)[9] The final example illustrates particularly clearly the most important idea of the novel: according to Pelevin, the source of morals and norms in contemporary Russian society lies in the social experience of groups situated outside the bounds of "official" morals and legal norms; from criminal mores and other similar "outcasted" areas—in a word, from the sphere of transgression.

The main plot is linked to a prophecy about the appearance of the "super-shape-shifter." This prophecy is fulfilled by both Seryi, who turns into the dog *Pizdetz* (the appearance of this apocalyptic personage was already predicted at the finale of *Generation 'P'*), and A Huli, who disappears from the material world and leaves for the Rainbow Stream. Underneath its mythological/fairy-tale shell, this plot hides the sufficiently serious issue of the balance of power and freedom in a society with changeable, phantasmal, and hybrid identities. In examining this problem, Pelevin plays out two contrasting scenarios of shape-changing—corresponding to the novel's two types of shape-

---

9 «...жизнь русского мачо похожа на спиритический сеанс: пока тело купается в роскоши, душа мотает срок на зоне... Россия—общинная страна, и разрушение крестьянской общины привело к тому, что источником народной морали стала община уголовная. Распонятки заняли место, где жил Бог—или правильнее сказать, Бог сам стал одним из "понятиев"...» (ibid., 268, 269).

shifter identity formation and neo-mythological transcendence.

Pelevin colors the "foundational myth" of the werewolf-general Seryi in sarcastic, even satiric tones. The werewolf-general is turning towards thanatological superpower, expressed through a hybridization of motifs of the Soviet obsession with death (marked by the character's association with the KGB) and ancient as well as new-age eschatological myths. This is why the general is identified with Fenrir—"an immense wolf who pursues the sun across the sky. When Fenrir catches the sun and devours it, Ragnarek will begin. [...] At Ragnarek he will kill Odin and be killed by Widar." (ibid., 114)[10] Curiously, Fenrir is a hereditary trickster, as it were—he is the son of Loki, the trickster-god of the Scandinavian pantheon.

After the transformation, which is triggered by A Huli's kiss, Seryi turns into the mythological dog, who goes by the name of *Pizdets* and who "happens" (*prikhodit*) to people. In the Scandinavian myths he is called Garm.[11] Seryi's friend and assistant, Mikhailych (also a werewolf, and a colonel in the FSB) deferentially addresses his boss as Nagual Rinpoche. In the pan-mesoamerican mythology, Nagual, from the Aztecan *nahualli,* is a human being who has merged with its spirit double and possesses the power of transformation. Here, the word is used in the sense known from Carlos Casteneda's mystical novel-treatise *The Eagle's Gift* (1982) and denotes the teacher, the leader of wizards or warriors

---

10   «Сын Локи, огромный волк, гонящийся по небу за солнцем. Когда Фенрир догонит и пожрет его—наступит Рагнарек. Фенрир связан до Рагнарека. В Рагнарек он убьет Одина и будет убит Видаром» (ibid., 135) "When he comes to Ragnarök, Snorri says simply that a wolf swallows the sun and another the moon, and it is apparent that he regards neither of these as identical to Fenrir, for only after describing the swallowing of the sun and the moon and a devastating earthquake does he report that Fenrir has gotten loose. But Fenrir's subsequent action echoes the swallowing of the heavenly bodies, for he 'goes about with a gaping mouth. And the lower jaw is on the earth and the upper against the sky—he would gape wider if there were room—fires burn from his eyes and nostrils' [...] In the series of duels that make up the gods' last stand against the forces of chaos, Odin fights with and is killed by Fenrir [...] 'Immediately thereafter Vidar will come forth and put one foot on the lower jaw of the wolf... With one hand he will take hold of the upper jaw of the wolf and tear apart his gullet, and that will be the death of the wolf'" (Lindow, 111-14). See also: E.M. [Meletinskii Eleazar], 561.

11   In the mythological fragments, which John Lindow cites, Garm is defined as the "best of hounds," just as Yggdrasil is the "best of trees," and Bragi is the "best of skalds." At the same time he [Garm] is called the "supreme monster." He loudly howls before Ragnarök, then breaks loose, in order to kill Týr, but kills himself in the process (see Lindow, 134-5).

who helps comprehend the unknown; the word "nagual" holds a double meaning in the books by Casteneda, also referring to transcendental reality, vast and unending, borderless and frightening, and inaccessible to direct interpretation by the senses. Rinpoche, literally meaning "precious one," is an honorary title in Tibetan Buddhism used for the most respected lamas or their reincarnations.

But this leadership, both on the level of the FSB and on the level of the mythological prototype (Seryi as Fenrir/Garm) is permeated by a longing for death—not only the death of "enemies," but also self-destruction. For this reason, Mikhailych consumes ketamine in incredible doses, and then the skull of the brindled cow, upon which, for some mystical reason, the well-being of the whole power apparatus ("upper rat" according to Pelevin's pun) depends, is on the brink of destruction. Thus the mythological contexts in the novel unequivocally establish werewolves as agents of Thanatos and chaos; but at the same time, they appear as pillars of the social order.

## GENEALOGY OF THE HEROINE

However, the semantics of chaos in mythology are extremely rich, and Pelevin's heroes use a variety of its aspects. The most important role in the novel is played by another shape-shifter, the Chinese fox A Huli—a being the mytho-folkloric tradition also identifies with the forces of chaos: "In the Chinese *yin/yang* dichotomy, *yin* is interpreted as negative, ghostly, evil, female, and impure, whereas *yang* is positive, celestial, virtuous, male, and pure. [...] The fox ...[is] associated with the world of the dead and darkness and thus the *yin* force. [...] The fox magic... ran against the natural cosmic order, which gave supremacy to the *yang* force and appropriated the *yin* as an indispensable but inferior opposite." (Kang, 18) Like any trickster cults, local Chinese cults of the fox reveal "centrifugal" forces in traditional Chinese and Japanese cultures: the fox stories are "particular, messy, idiosyncratic, and often contradict or de-center the elegant but simplistic shared meanings that describe the system." (Smyers, 208) "The people generally believe that [a] fox-demon... may enter into men and children and smite them with disease, insanity and even death. When the fox changes his form, it is as a pretty girl that he appears most frequently and does most mischief as a temptress," wrote Father Kennely (quoted by Day, 45).

──────────────── CHAPTER SEVEN ────────────────

As one of the most prominent female tricksters in world mythology, the Chinese fox is known as an ambivalent figure that simultaneously instills horror and respect. She functions as a mythological mediator who is free to pass between the poles of binary oppositions—between animal and human, good and evil, death and life, light and dark—and thereby overcomes their incompatibility. In the words of the Chinese writer and scholar Ji Yun (1724—1805): "Humans and things are different species, and foxes lie in between humans and things; darkness and lightness take different paths, and foxes lie in between darkness and lightness; divine transcendence and demons follow different ways, and foxes lie in between divine transcendence and demons." (Kang, 2) In Chinese folklore, the fox appears as a being that is simultaneously: a servant of evil, belonging to the world of the dead, and a patron of family and fertility; a source of temptation, and a wise councilor; a sexual demon (similar to succubi) and a highly cultured confidant (foxes frequently transform themselves into erudite men or students); and a perfidious deceiver as well as a defender of justice.

Certain elements of the novel are a direct paraphrase of Chinese sources. Pelevin cites a fragment from the famous anthology of stories *Anecdotes about Spirits and Immortals*, compiled by Gan Bao, a historian of the Eastern Jin Dynasty, which began in 317 and continued to 420. Hence Pelevein establishes a genealogical link between his heroine and the fox A Tsy, who has been said to once have been a dissolute woman. But there are even more direct borrowings: the name of the main heroine harks back to the name of the patron werefox Hu Li Tsing (Huli Jing). The researcher of Chinese mythology C.B. Day, who analyzed the figure of this goddess, writes that Chinese peasants worshiped a group of foxes known as the "Venerable Fairy Damsels": "The first tablet bears the inscription, 'eldest sister', Ta Ku, the second is entitled 'second sister', Erh Ku, while the third is inscribed 'third sister' San Ku." (Day, 45) This, of course, immediately reminds of A Huli's two sisters—I Huli and E Huli.

The paraphrase of ancient Chinese texts echoes in some of A Huli's remarks; for example, about the similarity and differences between foxes and ordinary women: "What a fox has in common with the most beautiful of women is that we live off the feelings we arouse. But a woman is guided by instinct, and a fox is guided by reason, and where a woman gropes her way along in the dark, a fox strides proudly forward in the bright light of day." (Pelevin 2008: 91)[12] Or: "A prostitute wants to get a hundred bucks out of a man for giving him a good time, but a respectable woman wants all his dough for sucking all the blood out of him." (ibid., 8)[13] Here is how the last thought looks in the original source, dating back to the Tang poet Bai Juyi (772 – 846), who wrote a poem in which he compared fox's magic to that of a woman:

> If false beauties may fascinate man in such a manner,
> The attraction exercised by genuine beauties surely will surpass it.
> Such false and such genuine beauties both can bewilder a man,
> But the human mind dislikes what is false and prefers what is real.
> Hence a fox disguised as a female demon can do but little harm,
> No can beguile a man's eyes for longer than a day or night;
> But a woman acting like a vulpine enchantress (*humei*) is the cause of absolute ruin,
> For the harm she does to a man's mind grows with each passing day.
> (Kang, 21)

Even the highly postmodernist aspiration of A Huli "to wander through the terra incognita of contemporary sexuality, studying its fringes" (Pelevin 2008: 239)[14], which shocks Seryi with his fanatic homophobia, in large part dates back to Chinese folklore, where a fox is able to transform into a man: "As men, foxes often appeared as young scholars who displayed elegant deportment, extraordinary talent, and impressive scholarship." (Kang, 25) As Guo Pu (a.d., 276–324) wrote:

> When a fox is fifty years old, it can transform itself into a woman; when a hundred years old, it becomes a beautiful female, or an adult male who has sexual intercourse with

---

12 «Лис объединяет с самыми красивыми женщинами то, что мы живем за счет чувств, которые вызываем. Но женщина руководствуется инстинктом, а лиса разумом, и там, где женщина движется в потемках и на ощупь, лиса гордо идет вперед при ясном свете дня» (2007: 109).
13 «Проститутка хочет иметь с мужчины сто долларов за то, что сделает ему приятно, а приличная женщина хочет иметь все его бабки за то, что высосет из него всю его кровь» (ibid., 15).
14 «...бродить по terra incognita современной сексуальности, исследовать ее пограничные области» (ibid., 267–268).

women. Such beings are able to know things at more than a thousand miles distance; they can poison men by sorcery, or possess and bewilder them, so that they lose their memory and knowledge; and when a fox is a thousand years old, it ascends to heaven and becomes a celestial fox." (ibid., 17)

All these characteristics are directly relevant to Pelevin's heroine. Even the fact that A Huli is already two thousand years old can be understood as a justification for the finale of the novel, when A Huli departs for the Rainbow Stream, becoming a celestial fox. Finally, many stories in Pu Songling's famous book *Strange Tales from a Chinese Studio* (*Laozhai zhiyi*, 17th century) are about a fox forsaking those men who turn out to be unworthy of her love—precisely this plot is reproduced in the relationship between A Huli and Seryi.

While reproducing and amplifying some of the qualities attributed to foxes in Chinese folklore, Pelevin consciously diminishes others. For example, he maximally downplays the associations of foxes with the world of the dead. His heroine assigns the opposite—sexual—meaning to the "vulpine odor," which is traditionally associated with sickness and death, openly challenging Chinese sources: "It's just the excess sexual energy transfuses us with the immortal nature of the primordial Yang principle and our bodies clean themselves through the corresponding influx of Yin. The faint odor that our skin gives off is actually extremely pleasant and reminiscent of Essenza di Zegna eau de cologne, except that it is lighter and more lucid." (ibid., 19)[15] A Huli explains incidents of foxes living in tombs by the fact that ancient Chinese tombs were often dry and comfortable living arrangements. The lethal outcome of relations between man and fox is imparted by her sister, I Huli, and motivated by her vengeance meted out to English aristocrats for their fox hunting. And in the only scene where A Huli causes death, when her client "slips off the tail," death comes not as a result of the foxtail-induced hallucination but as an effect of the truth the man sees once the delusion subsides; he is faced with a world which he is not able to endure.

---

15 «Просто избыток сексуальной энергии пропитывает нас бессмертной природой изначальной основы... А легкий запах, который оно источает, чрезвычайно приятен и напоминает одеколон Essenza di Zegna...» (ibid., 29).

These transformations are caused by the fact that, unlike werewolves, Pelevin's werefox, in a literal sense, feeds on the energy of Eros rather than Thanatos. According to tradition, as A Huli herself maintains, werefoxes may only be prostitutes.[16] However, with the help of her magic tail, Pelevin's werefox merely induces sexual hallucinations and then absorbs the sexual energy discharged by her "clients." Although she appears to be an underage girl, the werefox is a sexual veteran, and the energy of Eros is the source of her life force and eternal youth. In assigning these characteristics to A Huli, Pelevin follows ancient Chinese folklore tradition, although traditionally the sexual magic of a fox seems far more dangerous: "Using the art of metamorphoses and magic, the fox often engages in spiritual possession of people. As several Tang stories show foxes created illusionary visions for those they possessed, and the victims would go mad, talk nonsense, and laugh and wail uncontrollably." (Kang, 18) "Foxes bring upon those whom they bewitch sickness whereof they die; that's why they are so much feared," writes Pu Songling (30).

However, Pelevin's werefox, unlike her folkloric prototype, works with "clients" according to the principle of "the bride returns the earring" (Pelevin 2008: 24)[17]; i.e., she does not take all their life force: "In ancient times many foxes were killed purely because of their greed. But then we realized we had to share! Heaven does not frown so darkly when we show compassion and return part of the life force." (ibid., 24)[18] Pelevin obviously strives to cleanse his heroine from thanatological associations. But in doing so, he possibly also uses a motif from Pu Songling's novella *The Fox Maiden Lien Shiang*, in which a fox says: "'There are, of course, foxes,' (said Lien-shiang) 'who suck the vitality out of men; but I am not of that kind. There are foxes who are not harmful to men; but there are no ghosts who are harmless, because in them the dark element of nature predominates'" (35–6).

---

16   "For the Tang literati class, fox women represented a familiar category: courtesans who lived outside of their family circle but provided them sensual and emotional pleasures" (Kang, 26).
17   «невеста возвращает серьгу» (2007:34).
18   «В древние времена множество лис было убито исключительно из-за жадности. Тогда мы поняли—надо делиться! Небо не так хмурится, когда мы проявляем сострадание и отдаем часть жизненной силы назад» (ibid., 34-5). If desires, one can see in this were-fox commandment a paraphrase of Putin's famous phrase "one has to share!" («Надо делиться!») which was addressed towards the oligarchs during the YUKOS affair.

## CHAPTER SEVEN

Despite the mythological contexts surrounding the protagonists of *SKO*, it is not myth that flows from Pelevin's pen but a philosophical *fairytale* centered on an emphatically fantastic situation (the love of the two shape-shifters), which unfolds as the story of mutual attraction between two heroes who represent different types of "politico-cultural magic." But then again, even this plot resounds with the echo of ancient Chinese tradition:

> In medieval times, *hu* (fox) and *hu* (barbarian) were homophones that shared the same rhyme, the same tone, the same combination of syllabic transcriptions. [...] The concept of 'barbarian'... had manifold meanings for the late Tang literati. It represented a liminal entity linking a set of cultural dichotomies: Chinese and non-Chinese, the inside and the outside worlds, and the Confucian and non-Confucian... The correspondence between foxes and barbarian religions also explains why in many tales foxes appear as Buddhas, bodhisattvas, or foreign Buddhist monks, even though they are condemned as fake by both Daoists and Chinese Buddhists. (Kang, 27, 28, 31)

Pelevin not only transforms the homonym of fox and barbarian in the figures of werefox and werewolf, simultaneously preserving and radically reinterpreting the concept of the Other, but he also distinctly modernizes their magic. It is not exaggerated, I think, to define "fox magic" as postmodernist and liberal and "wolf magic" as pre-modern and neo-conservative. The love affair between the bearers of these two kinds of trickery thus cannot help but acquire political meaning.

### A FAIRYTALE ABOUT SHAPE-SHIFTERS

It is readily apparent that *SKO* is Pelevin's most intertextually saturated novel. This distinctive feature of the text is motivated by the erudition and longevity of its heroine-narrator, in whose consciousness Nabokov and ancient Chinese mythology, Dostoevsky and postmodernist theories, Stephen Hawking and Borges easily converse with one another. But it is the tongue-in-cheek recycling of *fairytale* plots and personages that plays the main role in the novel. In all these cases, the well-known fairytale motif provides the background against which we clearly see a shift in classical oppositions.

1. First of all, these are fairytale plots from children's tales about Fox and Wolf, as well as Little Red Riding Hood. Against this background of narratives about the simpleton and the trickster—roles which in Russian folk tales are traditionally assigned to a Wolf and Fox, respectively—it is particularly noticeable how complex and unpragmatic the relationship between Pelevin's heroes is. After falling in love with the wolf, A Huli not only refrains from subjugating the "shape-shifter in shoulder-boards" to her power, but eventually gives up all her power over others as a result of the relationship. Analogically, the overly simple opposition between villain (wolf) and his victim (Red Riding Hood) is undermined by jokes about a *blushing* wolf as well as the commentary of the protagonist's sister, I Huli, who considers A Huli to have subconsciously seduced the werewolf from the FSB.

2. The numerous allusions to the "Scarlet Flower" ("Alen'kii tsvetochek", 1858, a famous variation by Sergei Aksakov on the archetypal plot of the beauty and the beast) trigger an entire "firework" of improvisations. At first A Huli shocks the general Seryi, presenting a pseudo-Freudian interpretation of the subject, in which the scarlet floret stands as a symbol of defloration, the father embodies the theme of incest, and the heroine "discovers the essentially bestial nature of man and becomes aware of her own power over the beast." (2008: 103)[19] However, in the novel this fairytale is not simply projected onto the sexual relations of A Huli with Seryi: although the discussion of the "Scarlet Flower" does preface the appropriate scene, this is just a feint. More important is that in the English tradition this same fairytale is called *Beauty and the Beast*. The FSB general's transformation into a wolf during the sexual act with A Huli literalizes this fairytale metaphor, but with an important semantic displacement which breaks up the fairytale opposition: Pelevin's beauty is also a beast. What is more, the werewolf is only the second being in A Huli's long life on whom her fox magic does not work.

As we know by the end of the novel, before Seryim, only one other man, the Yellow Master—a Buddhist monk with a flute who met A Huli

---

19 «открывает звериную суть мужчины и осознает свою власть над этим зверем» (2007: 123).

one thousand and two hundred years ago—did not succumb to her magic. But it is from him that A Huli learned the formula for entering the Rainbow Stream, and in her love for the werewolf she found the key to this formula ("You must find the key" (ibid., 308)[20]—the monk says at the end). Meanwhile, the motif of the key is already accentuated, albeit differently, in the first conversation about the Scarlet Flower, in which A Huli establishes: "Who is such a key-holder [Pelageya, who supposedly told S. T. Aksakov this fairytale—M. L.]? The woman, who clenches the key in her hands... Not simply the key even, but the ring on which rides the key. Should I explain?" (2007: 123)[21]

Another important shift in the plot of *Beauty and the Beast* is linked to the scene of the kiss. In the fairytale, as we know, the kiss of the maiden changes the beast into a man. Pelevin drastically shifts this motif: A Huli's kiss changes Sasha Seryi from a werewolf into the hound Pizdets. It is no accident that this transformation is followed by a second dialogue about the Scarlet Flower:

> 'Sasha,' I called softly.
> He looked at me and asked: 'Do you remember the story about the Little Scarlet Flower?'
> 'Yes,' I said.
> 'I've only just realized what it really means.'
> 'What?'
> 'Love doesn't transform. It simply tears away the masks. I thought I was a prince. But it turns out... This is what my soul is like. [...] It's like hatching out from the egg,' he said sadly. 'You can't hatch back into it.' ( ibid., 245-6)[22]

---

20   «Тебе надо найти ключ» (ibid., 353).
21   «Кто такая ключница? Женщина, сжимающая в руках ключ... Даже не просто ключ, а кольцо, на котором висит ключ. Надо ли объяснять?»
22   «—Помнишь сказку про Аленький цветочек?
—Помню—сказала я.
—Я только сейчас понял, в чем ее смысл.
—В чем?
—Любовь не преображает. Она просто срывает маски. Я думал, что я принц. А оказалось... Вот она, моя душа.
Я почувствовала, как на моих глазах выступают слезы. [...]
—Как вылупиться из яйца—сказал он грустно.—Назад не влупишься» (ibid., 283).

After "hatching out from the egg," the new Seryi appears to be even further removed from the human form than the "enchanted" beast; he is opposed to life itself, materializing the energy of Thanatos in its purest form: this is why, immediately after transforming from werehound into a man, he sets off for the airport in order to fly to the North, where the dog Pizdets wakes up—where Garm must live. It is in the transformation of Seryi into the dog Pizdets that Eros transforms into Thanatos. This is also the point where love fails to unite the Fox and the Wolf, separating them forever. Yet it is also the recycling of the fairytale (or iteration, to use Derrida's term) that leads to this absolutely paramount plot twist.

3. Another explosive plot point—the episode where oil is summoned from the skull of the brindled cow by lupine howling—has its origin in the fairytale of Little-Khavroshechka (Kroshechka-Khavroshechka). Even those critics who are extremely hostile towards *SKO* have been left impressed by the "animal power" of this scene.[23] The brindled cow in the fairytale about Khavroshechka is actually an important symbol that dates back to the time of ancestor veneration and Mother Moist Earth worship. The meaning of Pelevin's cow is defined by Seryi: "You are everyone who lived here before us." (ibid., 219)[24] At the same time, the very word "howl" has a double meaning: in Russian howling is not the sole province of wolves; mourners also howl (wail) over the deceased. The brindled cow is of course, Russia—or rather, her totem.[25] The scene of the "summoning of oil" is paradoxical not only because one of those who causes the suffering of today's Khavroshechkas must move the brindled cow to pity, but because the role of the shaman, who "brings" oil to this world, is played by the spirit of death, namely the

---

23 "The scene where the werewolf milks the cow-Russia, milking, of course, oil, is of the animal strength. In order to give milk, the cow must burst into tears. Pelevin sees this animal-sentimental, humble and unreasoning soul of the homeland in all its detail, and here he for the first time in the entire novel is as great, even though the rhetoric of the episode is more Sorokin than Pelevin" (Bykov, 54). "The scene of pleading for oil before the skull of the Brindled Cow, it might be said, is among the powerful insights of modern Russian literature" (Kuz'minskii).
24 «Ты—это все, кто жил здесь до нас» (2007: 252).
25 Pelevin's image of the brindled cow reminds of a collaborative work, made long before the creation of Pelevin's novel, by Oleg Kulik and Vladimir Sorokin. See: Kulik Oleg and Vladimir Sorokin, *V glub' Rossii*. Moscow, 1995. It is characteristic that, in discussing in a conversation with Dmitrii Bavil'skii about the conception of this project, Kulik also pointed to the fairytale about Kroshechka-Khavroshechka (see Bavil'skii; the dialog was published in 2002, i. e., also before the publication of Pelevin's novel).

future hound Pizdets.

Furthermore, A Huli is drawn into the ritual. When Seryi compels the brindled cow's skull to cry, A Huli fills his howling with her own words:

> You can only give oil to ignominious wolves, so that kukis-yukis-yupsi-poops can shell out to its lawyer and the lawyer can give the head of security a kick-back, the head of security can grease his hairdresser's palm, the hairdresser can grease the cook's, the cook can grease the driver's, and the driver can hire your Little Khavroshechka for an hour for a hundred and fifty bucks ... And when your Little Khavroshechka sleeps off the anal sex and pays off all her cops and bandits, maybe she'll have enough left over for the apple that you wanted so much to become for her, brindled cow... (ibid., 219)[26]

In this scene, A Huli appears not only as the "interpreter" of Seryi's howl into the verbal language—by default inadequate to render the full meaning of the wolf's magic incantations—but also while listening to his howl, she begins to cry herself—along with the brindled cow. At the same time, her cry blends with the wolf's howling: "'How you howled!'—said Alexander.—'We were simply spellbound.'" (ibid., 220)[27] What is more, after the ceremony A Huli figures out that her sweetheart "showed [her] to the skull as Little Khavroshechka." (ibid., 221)[28]

The scene of the incantation is presented as a moment of *empathy*: for the first time in her life, the fox completely *accepts* the other, uniting in herself, it seems, incompatible roles, transforming simultaneously into the wolf, the cow, and Khavroshechka. Only after the fact does it occur to her that the wolf turned out to be a greater trickster than

---

26 «Ты можешь дать этим позорным волкам нефти, чтобы кукис-юкис-юкси-пукс отстегнул своему лоеру, лоер откинул шефу охраны, шеф охраны откатил парикмахеру, парикмахер повару, повар шоферу, а шофер нанял твою Хаврошечку на час за полтораста баксов... И когда твоя Хаврошечка отоспится после анального секса и отгонит всем своим мусорам и бандитам, вот тогда, может быть, у нее хватит на яблоко, которым ты так хотела для нее стать» (2007: 253).
27 «Как ты выла!—сказал Александр.—Мы просто заслушались» (ibid., 253).
28 «Знаешь, у меня такое чувство, что ты показывал меня черепу в качестве Хаврошечки.» (ibid., 255).

she herself: "Suddenly, I could no longer tell which of us really was the cynical manipulator of other minds." (ibid., 221–2)[29] At the same time, the force of tricksters' magic lies not only in their ability to shape-shift and create around themselves a field of liminality, but also in their abilities to establish relations with the sacred through these liminal reincarnations. Thus the wolf's magic trick functions as a form of art—in full accordance with the semantics of the trickster trope. "So you think art should be the truth?" (ibid., 221)[30] Seryi grins at his answer to A Huli's reproach that she is no Khavroshechka and the brindled cow has once again fallen victim to deception.

As we can see, all these fairytale plots are marked by the *effect of cynical transgression*. The fairytale oppositions are deliberately and consistently eroded and inverted, and it is the protagonist, A Huli herself, who features as the main agent of transgression (which, of course, is underlined by her "obscene" name). Indeed, A Huli lives up to her reputation as a trickster.

In the same way as it recycles fairytale motifs, the novel assimilates other literary and cultural intertexts. An openly displayed layer of motifs from Nabokov's *Lolita* is deconstructed by the fact that A Huli—as the author of the text, she remains behind after her disappearance—plays the role of Humbert, while her profession suggests that she is deliberately reenacting Humbert's victim, Lolita: "It's my own patented brand of provocation—brazenness and innocence in the same armor-piercing package: it zaps straight through the client and then ricochets back to get him again." (ibid., 106)[31] The deliberate staging of episodes from *Lolita* is detectable in the comparison of A Huli's mind with a tennis racquet and in her post-coital complaints to Seryi: "Don't call me darling, you beast,' I sobbed. 'You filthy depraved male. Nobody's done that to me in the past...' [...] 'I'm so tender and delicate down there,' I said in a pitiful voice. 'And you've torn everything with your

---

29 «Я вдруг перестала понимать, кто из нас циничный манипулятор чужим сознанием» (ibid.).
30 «А, по-твоему, искусство должно быть правдой?» (ibid.)
31 «Моя фирменная провокация, бесстыдство с невинностью в одном бронебойном флаконе, который прошивает клиента насквозь и потом еще добивает рикошетом...» (ibid., 126).

huge prick. I'll probably die now." (ibid., 110–111)³² A Huli's act is a deliberate parody of Lolita since she, unlike her "prototype," is much older and wiser than her seducer and therefore hardly fits the role of underage victim.

References to Dostoevsky's *Crime and Punishment* are overturned in exactly the same way: both A Huli and Sonechka combine prostitution with innocence, but it is the manipulation of the "client's" perception, via the "foxtail technology" described in detail by A Huli, that makes this combination possible. Furthermore, she comments directly on the Dostoevsky intertext, and in this commentary she shamelessly downplays the cultural authority to the level of the "lower body stratum"—thus acting as a classical trickster:

> 'Oh fuck your Dostoevsky,' I exploded. 'And I have.'
> He looked at me with interest.
> 'Well, how was it?'
> 'Nothing special.'
> We both laughed. I don't know what he was laughing at, but I had a good reason. I won't include it in these pages, out of respect for Russian literature, but let me just say that the red spider in *The Possessed* once crawled across the hem of my sarafan..." (ibid., 285)³³

The reference to Matresha—the victim of "Stavrogin's sin," a twelve-year-old girl raped and driven to suicide in *Besy* (*The Possessed*, 1871)—is even more ironic than references to Lolita, since if Matresha is A Huli there can be no talk of either rape (Pelevin's fox, as we remember, only puts her "clients" into a sexual trance) or a victim.

---

32  «Не называй меня милой, волчара,—всхлипнула я.—Грязный развратный самец... У меня там все такое нежное, хрупкое... А ты мне все разорвал своим огромным членом. Теперь я, наверно, умру...» (ibid., 131-2).
33  «—Д а е... я твоего Достоевского,—не выдержала я.
Он поглядел на меня с интересом.
—Ну, и как?
—Ничего особенного.
Мы оба засмеялись. Не знаю, чему он смеялся, а у меня причина была. Из уважения к русской литературе я не стану приводить ее на этих страницах, скажу только, что красный паучок из «Бесов» полз в свое время по подолу моего сарафана...» (2007: 327).

## THE TRICKSTER'S MAGIC/POLITICS: THE POINT OF BIFURCATION

Obviously, Pelevin's A Huli manifests many aspects of the trickster myth, and her character becomes a powerful embodiment of the trickster trope as a meeting point between different languages, or rather, between discourses of contemporary Russian "society of shape-shifters" and ancient Chinese mythology, masterfully enriched by references to Russian folklore as well as literary intertexts. Pelevin's heroine even calls herself Alisa Li, adding to her genealogy the fox Alisa from Aleksei Tolstoy's fairytale *Zolotoi kliuchik* (see chapter 4.) Pelevin transforms the magical nine tails that ancient Chinese tradition attributes to the werefox into the single powerful "lens" of mostly sexual hallucinations and illusions. In reality, A Huli's tricks by far do not always lead to a harmless sexual act between a client and nothing, which is evident from the manipulation of policemen she tricks into copulating with each other, and the bloody flogging of the "consultant-columnist" Pavel Ivanovich by a virtual lash.

Pelevin consistently accentuates A Huli's acts of mediation—between bestial and human (the scene with the theft of the chicken), between old age and youth, between innocence and temptation, between idealism and cynicism, etc. Even the kinship of A Huli with E Huli and I Huli underlines the heroine's role as a mediator: one sister lives in the West, in England, the other in the East, in Thailand, one mingles among aristocrats (selecting her next victim from among them), and the other suffers alongside other "proletarians of sexual labor." A Huli's aptitude for mediation also explains her transformation into the super-shape-shifter: she combines "vulpine" and "lupine" methods of magical suggestion and as a result rises to the state of superior being.

Pelevin's trickster figure is mainly characterized by a *combination of transgression with mediation*. It is the role of the mediator that distinguishes A Huli from Seryi, who habitually substitutes physical elimination of the opponent for mediation. This difference clearly has political rather than just mytho-poetic meaning. It is important to note that all the anti-liberal witticisms in *SKO*, which the critics so admired, belong to Sasha Seryi without exception, and A Huli naturally defines his position as "lupine views" («волчьи взгляды»). The general's proposition "to take an aspen stake and stuff it [contemporary discourse] back up the cocaine-amphetamine polluted backside that produced it" (ibid., 104)[34] is a particularly clear example of these views. As for A Huli, she just as easily engages in this same contemporary discourse, elegantly and convincingly refuting the perception of its founders as an "international gang of gypsy-horsethiefs, who at any opportunity with relish will steal in the darkness the last vestiges of simplicity and sound meaning"[35] (Pelevin 2003: 70), which is expressed by the narrator in another of Pelevin's works. And, although the "discourse" (implicitly assuming the epithet of "postmodernist") stands alongside "glamour" as one of the disciplines that nourishes the cynical power of the vampires in *Empire 'V'* (2006, the novel that follows *SKO*), the logic expounded by A Huli is that of the contemporary liberal postmodernist consciousness—liberal in the Western sense of course, not the Russian understanding of this term. "After all, we shape-shifters are natural liberals, in pretty much the same way as the soul is a natural Christian" (ibid., 233; changed translation)[36] —contends A Huli, forgetting, however, that the werewolf is in no way a liberal nor resembles one.

A Huli explains the difference between the Russian and Western interpretations of liberalism in the following terms:

> It's a classical inter-linguistic homonym. For instance it [in the West the word 'liberal'] means someone who is in favor of firearms control, single-sex marriage and abortion and feels more sympathy for the poor than the rich. But here in Russia...
>
> 'Here in Russia,' Alexander interrupted, 'it means an unscrupulous weasel who hopes someone will give him a little money if he makes big round eyes and keeps repeating that twenty greasy parasites should carry on squeezing Russia by the balls, simply because at the beginning of so-called privatization, they happened to be barbecuing grills

---

34   «... забить осиновым колом назад в ту кокаиново-амфетаминовую задницу, которая его породила» (ibid., 124).
35   «...международная банда цыган-конокрадов, которые при любой возможности с гиканьем угоняют в темноту последние остатки простоты и здравого смысла.»
36   «Ведь мы, оборотни—природные либералы, примерно как душа—природная христианка» (ibid., 269).

with pissed Yeltsin's daughter. (ibid., 174)³⁷

It seems that this is the sole case where A Huli and Seryi are in harmony over ideological questions. However, the fox is critical with respect to hypocrites in post-Soviet politics posing as liberals (according to many criteria, standing nearer to the ideology of America's republicans than its democrats, and even further from liberals); additionally, her irritation is directed at those public politicians who have compromised the liberal idea during their rise to power in the 1990s.

Under no circumstances does Pelevin idealize the liberal point of view. This is why he presents A Huli's liberalism as motivated by the mobility of her werefox mind, in which up to five internal voices coexist: "A fox's mind is simply a tennis racket you can use to keep bouncing the conversation from one subject to another for as long as you like. We give people back the ideas and opinion that we have borrowed from them—reflecting them from another angle, giving them a different spin, sending them into a vertical climb." (ibid., 136)³⁸ However, it is still clear which views—vulpine or lupine—are closer to Pelevin's own.³⁹ (For good reason Lev Danilkin sees the heroine of *SKO* as a metaphor for the contemporary Russian writer.⁴⁰)

If Pelevin transforms the werefox into a trope of some sort of "ur-postmodernist," then the werewolf is the contemporary Russian "Ur-Fascist," the direct manifestation of an extreme version of "negative

---

37    «…Это классический кросс-языковой омоним. Скажем, в Америке оно [слово "либерал"] обозначает человека, который выступает за контроль над оружием, за однополые браки, за аборты и больше сочувствует бедным, чем богатым. А у нас… —А у нас,—перебил Александр,—оно означает бессовестного хорька, который надеется, что ему дадут немного денег, если он будет делать круглые глаза и повторять, что двадцать лопающихся от жира паразитов должны и дальше держать Россию за яйца из-за того, что в начале так называемой приватизации они торговали цветами в нужном месте!» (ibid., 202).

38    «Лисий ум—просто теннисная ракетка, позволяющая сколь угодно долго отбивать мячик разговора на любую тему. Мы возвращаем людям взятые у них напрокат суждения—отражая их под другим углом, подкручивая, пуская свечой вверх» (ibid., 160).

39    It is not obvious, however, that the Fox is closer to the reader's consciousness. A very illustrative fact: on the cover of the 2007 edition of the novel (publisher "Éksmo"), the rendered image is not a fox but a wolf!

40    "And thanks, as it is, to Pelevin for a hundred new jests, and for the fact that he did not hesitate to get himself into the skin of a fox-prostitute, in order to communication via such a figure the name of the game: *A Khuli*—the Russian Writer" (Danilkin, 153).

identification" (Gudkov) in its neo-traditionalist guise. According to Umberto Eco, Ur-Facism is a generalized transnational type of cultural and political consciousness that is characterized by such features as the cult of tradition, rejection of modernism as a "degenerative culture," distrust of the intellectual world, xenophobia and nationalism, as well as the cult of heroes supported by the cult of death: "[T]he Ur-Fascist hero craves heroic death, advertised as the best reward for a heroic life. The Ur-Fascist hero is impatient to die. In his impatience, he more frequently sends other people to death" (Eco). Among other characteristics of Ur-Fascism Eco lists the insatiable quest for an enemy ("the enemies are at the same time too strong and too weak"); populism ("the sense of mass elitism"); and anti-individualism alongside the glorification of the masses usually represented by a charismatic leader. Eco remarks that fundamentally, "it is enough that one of them [characteristics] be present to allow fascism to coagulate around it." In this respect, Seryi perfectly fits this model: his half-bandit/half-official status, his Russian-Orthodox self-righteousness in conjunction with his readiness to kill, his machismo and homophobia—all these features portray him as a radical Other, in relation to postmodern liberalism.

Yet it is A Huli's love for *this* Other that challenges both postmodern liberalism and "vulpine" strategies alike. Thus, the fairytale of fox and wolf reappears in *SKO* as a new production of the classic Russian plot (developed predominantly in Turgenev's novels) of the "liberal at a rendezvous." It is worth noting that in his previous works Pelevin seemed not particularly interested in either sexuality in general or in the philosophy of love. As several critics observed, even the love between Peter Pustota and Anna in the novel *Chapaev i Pustota* was important only as a projection and catalyst of the relations between the protagonist, Pyotr, and his spiritual guru—Buddha-Chapaev. But Pelevin does not dissemble when he calls *SKO* a novel about love. As Irina Kaspe justly remarks,

> [T]he plot of Pelevin's novel centers on the impossibility of love. With unfamiliar and thus often elephantine poignancy the author of *SKO* prompts the heroes to make diverse attempts at being together. Their unstable identity undergoes catastrophic and irreversible transformations in the process and the figure of the other is never clearly

delineated... In carefully considering the problem of reality—and it is pointless to argue about its reality—the heroes of *SKO* above all consider the problem of coexistence with the 'others.' (Kaspe, 384)

Pelevin not only politicizes the figure of the trickster in the contemporary cultural-philosophical context but also shows the workings of two opposed trickster strategies in contemporary Russian (and more broadly postmodern, post-Cold War) culture. In doing so, he employs the metaphorical equation of politics and magic, which he worked out a long time ago, beginning with his early short story "Zombification" ("Zombifikatsiia," 1989). In *SKO* the opposition between the Putinesque "ur-Fascist" and the postmodern liberal is described as the difference between the emanation of the respective tails of werewolf and werefox.

The fox causes a *transformation of perception*: the heroine manipulates the impressions of her client, either by projecting his wishes or by inducing a trance. A Huli stipulates that "the transformation of perception is the basis not only of foxes' witchcraft, but also of many marketing techniques" (ibid., 227)[41]—however the distinction between the fox and, for example, the spin doctor and advertising magnate Vavilen Tatarsky who is transferred to *SKO* from the novel *Generation 'P'* is the fact that "foxes continue to see the initial reality just as, according to Berkeley, God sees it." (ibid.)[42] How a fox is successful at this only Pelevin knows, but in any case, the means of their magic is persuasively demonstrated in the scenes of "quasi-sexual services" extended to people by A Huli.

The lupine magic is based on opposite principles:

> Unlike us, werewolves use *perception of transformation*. They created an illusion, not for others, but for themselves. And they believe in it so strongly that the illusion ceases to be an illusion. [...] Their transformation is a kind of alchemical chain reaction. [...] And the emerging tail, which in wolves is the same kind of hypnotic organ as

---

41 «...трансформация восприятия является основой не только лисьего колдовства, но и множества рыночных технологий» (ibid., 261).

42 «... лисы продолжают видеть исходную реальность такой, какой ее, по мысли Беркли, видит Бог» (ibid., 262).

it is in foxes, exerts a hypnotic influence on the wolf's own consciousness, convincing him that he really is undergoing transformation and so on until he is completely transformed into a beast. (ibid., 228)[43]

Ur-fascism, unlike werefoxes' manipulations of others' perception, is always founded on faith, conviction, and dedication to an ideal. However, the violence inherent in the "lupine method" is that small bridge that helps to change one's own transformation into that of the Other.

Undoubtedly, while the "vulpine" method displays postmodern strategies of power and subjectivity, the "lupine" method falls back on the good old Soviet (and in general totalitarian) principles of modernization, where ideology acquires religious meaning and drives the homogenization and mobilization of society. However, the modernizing component in the politics of the general-werewolf is aimed only at increasing his own power—in all other respects, he at best strives to maintain the status quo.

But how independent are these strategies from each other? How non-violent is cynicism, and did doctrinaires and fanatics ever manage to get by without cynical manipulations? The experience of the 20th century clearly attests to the practical indivisibility of these two kinds of "magic." And besides, Pelevin himself, commenting on the novel, places the equal sign between "shape-shifters in shoulder-boards" and the spin doctor Tatarsky[44]—and the latter, as we have seen, is not far removed from the fox A Huli.

---

43  «Волки-оборотни в отличие от нас используют *восприятие трансформации*. Они создают иллюзию не для других, а для себя. И верят в нее до такой степени, что иллюзия перестает быть иллюзией. Кажется, в Библии есть отрывок на эту тему—"будь у вас веры с горчичное зерно..." У волков она есть. Их превращение—своего рода цепная алхимическая реакция... Ту энергию, которые лисы направляли на людей, волки замыкали сами на себе, вызывая трансформацию не в чужом восприятии, а в собственном, а уж потом, как следствие—в чужом» (2007: 262-3; italics belongs to the author).

44  "I am writing about the shape-shifters in uniform. But the hired political consultant like Tatarskii—is also a shape-shifter, only in civilian clothes. Such a, you know, liberal conservative is in a position of permanent bifurcation. A five-legged hound with an unprintable name—this is the natural conclusion to the evolution of the shape-shifter in uniform. And the night-time visit of such a hound [to Tatarsky] serves as the natural conclusion to the political consultant's road" (Kochetkova, 15).

## CYNIC VERSUS KYNIC

Pelevin long ago demonstrated the creative forces of cynicism—in fact, the whole novel *Generation 'P'* is about this. But evidently, only in *SKO*, having subjugated the narrative to the cynical reason of the werefox, has he accomplished the fission of (post)modernist cynicism into its thanatological and erotic constituents, into Seryi and A Huli. Naturally, one should not regard these characters as poles of a binary opposition, but as complementary. The wolf reveals the underlying cynical foundation of both negative identification and the "neo-traditionalist" politics of the Putin period. The fox embodies the invigorating and restorative component of cynicism (which is similar to artwork)—which, following Sloderdijk, can be more adequately defined as *kynicism*. In other words, *SKO* testifies to the fact that in post-Soviet culture the trickster remains the central symbol of modernization, and the rethinking of that trope reflects the revision of the intelligentsia's position towards liberal modernization, which dominated politics in the early 1990s and which, many think today, suffered defeat in the new millennium.

As mentioned earlier, kynicism, according to Sloterdijk, returns the sense of authenticity to love, sexuality, irony and laughter, whereas cynicism diminishes the value of everything without exception. Pelevin seems to agree with Sloterdijk in the belief that the kynic (unlike the dogmatic or the idealist) is the only one who is able to deconstruct from within the cynical picture of the world, inherent to the society of shape-shifters. The strategies of transgression, which is kynical at the root and seems characteristic of the fox's postmodern subjectivity, are not opposed to the profoundly cynical post-Soviet society but share its nature. Nevertheless, the author does not forget to emphasize that the wolf is *at home* in a cynical world, while the kynic A Huli is *always a stranger*. A telling conversation between A Huli and Seryi takes place after the wolf has turned into the apocalyptic hound:

> 'Well, who's going to decide what's just and what isn't?'
> 'People.'
> 'And who's going to decide what the people should decide?'
> 'We'll think of something,' he said and glanced at a fly soaring past. The bluebottle dropped to the floor.
> 'What are you doing, you brute? Do you want to be like

them?'
I nodded in the direction of the city.
'I am like them,' he said.
'Like who?'
'The nation [*narod*].'
'The nation?' I echoed incredulously. (ibid., 284)[45]

Pelevin problematizes the opposition between "one's own" and "the other": after all, this is a novel on the *love* of two tricksters—a cynic and a kynic. True to herself, A Huli remains the mediator in this relationship: she finds ways of connecting physical with intellectual through shared fantasies: the fox and the wolf watch a film together, their magical tails entwined, and plunge into a joint hallucination. She enters into a relationship with Seryi, which is simultaneously physical and non-physical—in spite of the fact that their tastes "didn't just differ, they belonged to different universes." (ibid., 232)[46] Owing to the unification of their two kinds of magic, the fantasy of each of the heroes assumes physical reality for both of them (this is where the love games between the wolf and the fox differ from A Huli's manipulation of the consciousness's of her "clients"). Thus, Pelevin's portrayal of the trickster resonates with kynical *embodiment of the intellectual and the intellectualism of the physical*, or in Sloterdijk's words: "The embodied is that which wants to live" (118).

Most importantly, A Huli expresses her love for the wolf neither by subjugating him nor by subjecting her own worldview to his. Paradoxically, she attempts to love him without diminishing, or assimilating to, his "otherness": "I could see all the sinister sides of his

---

45   —...А кто будет решать, что справедливо, а что нет?
—Люди.
—А кто будет решать, что решат люди?
—Придумаем,—сказал он и посмотрел на летевшую мимо него муху. Муха упала на пол.
—Ты чего, озверел?—спросила я.—Хочешь быть, как они?—И я кивнула головой в сторону города.
—А я и есть как они,—сказал он.
—Кто они?
—Народ.
—Народ?—переспросила я недоверчиво (ibid., 326).
46   «Наши вкусы не то что различались, они относились к различным вселенным» (ibid., 267).

character but, strangely enough, those things only added to his charm in my eyes. My reason even came to terms with his barbarous political views and began to discover a certain harsh northern originality in them. Love was absolutely devoid of any meaning. But it gave meaning to everything else." (ibid., 239)[47]

The meaning of love as realized by the philosophical—postmodern and liberal—position of the heroine is most accurately conveyed by the succession of intratextual leitmotifs, as a rule deliberately cynical, for example: the mention of a blowjob and the motif of a prostitute going down on a truck driver, and the description of the method of masturbation with the Nabokovian name "Ultima Thule," as well as the discussion of the vagina dentata. But especially important, and without any parallel in the folklore and literature about "foxes' witchcraft," is the motif of the tail as the organ of shame for A Huli. It indirectly correlates with the sensitivity of folkloric werefoxes to injustice and human baseness. But the shame which A Huli feels when she tugs her tail is directed at herself, putting her in touch with a physically piercing emotional reaction to the pain which she has caused to others. This feeling, or even deliberate meditation, which is linked to her fits of shame, generates a chain of bizarre variations on this motif.

Thus shame, experienced by the fox, is mockingly mirrored by the sweet masochism of the "right-wing liberal" Pavel Ivanovich, who, having assumed personal responsibility for all the woes of the motherland, soothes his soul by "a flogging once or twice a week from a *Young Russia*, which he had condemned to poverty by forcing it to earn a living by flogging old perverts instead of studying in university" (ibid., 44)—yet another textual uroboros. Knowing that A Huli induces fantasies with the help of her tail and that she deliberately pulls her own tail for the purpose of spiritual cleansing, one cannot fail to notice the association between the motif of the organ of shame and the model of the world, which A Huli expounds to the taxi driver, who angers her with his hypocritical sympathy:

---

47  «Я видела все его жуткие стороны, но они, как ни странно, лишь прибавляли ему очарования в моих глазах. Мой рассудок примирился даже с его дикими политическими взглядами и стал находить в них какую-то суровую северную самобытность. В любви начисто отсутствовал смысл. Но зато она придавала смысл всему остальному.» (ibid., 275).

## CHAPTER SEVEN

'Do you know the story of Baron Munchhausen, who pulled himself out of a bog by his own hair?'
'I do,' said the driver, 'I've even seen the film.'
'The foundations underlying the reality of this world are very similar. Only you have to imagine Munchhausen suspended in a total void, squeezing his own balls as hard as he can and screaming in unbearable pain. Look at it in one way and you feel kind of sorry for him. But look at it a different way, and he only has to let go of his own balls and he'll immediately disappear, because by his very nature he is simply a vessel of pain with a grey ponytail, and if the pain disappears, then he'll disappear as well. [...]'
'Maybe it would be better if he did? Who the hell needs a life like that?'
'A good point. And that's precisely why the social contract exists [...] Munchhausen can let go of himself, as you so correctly observed. But the more someone hurts him, the more he hurts the two that he's holding on to. And so on for six billion times. Do you understand?' (ibid., 33-34)[48]

This picture of the world is more serious than it may seem at first glance. Along with the reference to the classic trickster Munchhausen, it also mockingly alludes to the famous dream of Pierre Bezukhov about

---

48 «—Вы знаете историю про барона Мюнхгаузена, который смог поднять себя за волосы из болота?
—Знаю,—сказал шофер.—В кино даже видел.
—Реальность этого мира имеет под собой похожие основания. Только надо представить себе, что Мюнхгаузен висит в полной пустоте, изо всех сил сжимая себя за яйца, и кричит от невыносимой боли. С одной стороны, его вроде бы жалко. С другой, пикантность его положения в том, что стоит ему отпустить свои яйца, и он сразу же исчезнет, ибо по своей природе он есть просто сосуд боли с седой косичкой, и если исчезнет боль, исчезнет он сам. [...]
—Так, может, лучше ему исчезнуть? На фиг ему нужна такая жизнь?
—Верное замечание. Именно поэтому и существует общественный договор [...] Каждый отдельный Мюнхгаузен может решиться отпустить свои яйца, но... [...] Но когда шесть миллиардов Мюнхгаузенов крест-накрест держат за яйца друг друга, миру ничего не угрожает.
—Почему?
—Да очень просто. Сам себя Мюнхгаузен может и отпустить, как вы правильно заметили. Но чем больнее ему сделает кто-то другой, тем больнее он сделает тем двум, кого держит сам. И так шесть миллиардов раз. Понимаете?» (ibid., 41-2).

the planet-like sphere constituted of interconnected droplets, each of which is a human being. This picture also recalls the philosophic model of "algodicy" (a metaphysical justification of pain), which, according to Sloterdijk, replaces all other values in the cynical modernity: "Every polemical subjectivity arises in the final analysis from the struggles of denial of egos against pain, which they inevitably encounter as living beings. They carry on 'reconstruction,' armament, wall building, fencing in, demarcation, and self-hardening in order to protect themselves. However, *within them*, the fermentation goes on unceasingly. Those who build up and arm will one day 'build down' and let loose." (Sloterdijk, 468)

This thesis is especially important in relation to the werefox: the heroine of Pelevin's novel, following the kynical principle of embodiment, *physically embodies* the paradox of pain as the sole proof of reality in a world woven from illusions. A Huli's tail appears as both the source of trance and as the organ of a pain that is caused by shame. The feeling of shame which she experiences not only correlates her with others, but also obviates the unfeigned *authenticity* of her existence (the imitation of pain by Pavel Ivanovich is evidence of the reverse). Yet, A Huli completes her lecture about Munchhausen with an almost mocking—tricksterish—reversal:

> 'It's an extremely male picture of the universe. I'd even call it chauvinistic. There is no place in it for a woman at all.'
> 'Why?'
> 'Because women don't have any balls.' (2008: 34)[49]

There is also a third situation wherein the motif of the tail is accentuated, arousing in A Huli an acute sense of shame—this is the sexual scene:

> Alexander hadn't deliberately pulled my tail. He was just holding it, quite gently in fact. But the blows of his

---

49 «...Это предельно мужская картина мироздания. Я бы даже сказала, шовинистическая. Женщине просто нет в ней места.
—Почему?
—Потому что у женщины нет яиц» (ibid., 43).

hips pushed my body forward, and the result was as if he was trying to rip my tail out of my body. I tensed all my muscles, but I just wasn't strong enough. With every jerk of my soul was inundated by waves of unbearable shame. But the most terrible thing was that the shame didn't simply sear my heart, it also mingled into a single whole with the pleasure I was getting from what was going on.

It was something quite unimaginable—truly beyond good and evil. It was then that I finally understood the fatal abysses trodden by De Sade and Sacher-Masoch, who I had always thought absurdly pompous. No, they weren't absurd at all—they simply hadn't been able to find the right words to convey the true nature of their nightmare. And I knew why—there were no such words in any human language. [...] I couldn't hold back any longer and I started crying. But they were tears of pleasure, a monstrous, shameful pleasure that was too enthralling to be abandoned voluntarily. I soon lost any idea of what was happening—perhaps I even lost consciousness too. (ibid., 151)[50]

This scene, in essence, reveals itself as the high point of A Huli's kynicism and the apotheosis of mediation: bestial pleasure and human shame merge into the energy of Eros, being drawn beyond the verbal, granting the heroine freedom not *from* the Other, but *for* and *alongside* the Other—yet not in an abstract manner or place, but in an utterly

---

50 «Александр не дергал меня за хвост специально. Он просто держал его, причем довольно нежно. Но удары его бедер толкали мое тело вперед, и результат был таким же, как если бы он пытался выдрать хвост у меня из спины. Я напрягла все мышцы, но сил не хватало. С каждым рывком мою душу заливали волны непереносимого стыда. Но самым ужасным было то, что стыд не просто жег мне сердце, а смешивался в одно целое с удовольствием, которое я получала от происходящего.

Это было нечто невообразимое—поистине по ту сторону добра и зла. Только теперь я поняла, в каких роковых безднах блуждал де Сад, всегда казавшийся мне смешным и напыщенным. Нет, он вовсе не был нелеп—просто он не мог найти верных слов, чтобы передать природу своего кошмара. И я знала, почему—таких слов в человеческом языке не было. [...] Я больше не могла сдерживаться и зарыдала. Но это были слезы наслаждения, чудовищного, стыдного—и слишком захватывающего, чтобы от него можно было отказаться добровольно. Вскоре я потеряла представление о происходящем—возможно, и сознание тоже» (ibid., 175-6).

concrete and physical way. Here transgression (directly, evoking associations with the novels of the Marquis de Sade) and mediation are combined, forming the living and physical experience of an explosive aporia of freedom and painful pleasure. To me, this scene seems to be the most important philosophical metaphor of the entire novel; its erotic intensity paradoxically reinforces its intellectual persuasiveness (in a kynical sense).

It is significant that the physical experience described by Pelevin is inseparable from the womanly and "vulpine" anatomy of A Huli. It reveals a graphic departure from the picture of the world as represented by the Munchhausens who "hold each other up by the balls." From the quoted scene it becomes clear that reality arising from pain—i.e., the desire for death—can just as well arise from love—i.e., the desire for the Other, entailing shame before the Other, as well as pleasure in that very shame.

The intensification of the Other's otherness, however, expresses itself in Seryi's transformation into the dog Pizdets: under the influence of A Huli's love, he also evolves, although not in the direction of Eros as represented by A Huli but in the direction of Thanatos. This is why he forsakes her, not waiting to learn her way to the freedom and power of the super-shape-shifter. The cause of Seryi's transformation lies in A Huli's capacity not to suppress, but to *reveal* the ultimate potential of the werewolf as an Other. It is thanks to A Huli's love that Seryi attains his "internal maximum," although this "maximum" is frightening and deadly.

The alternative to vulpine kynicism is the cynical lupine version of the "super-shape-shifter," which boils down to the refusal of mediation, and consequently, of love—hence, Seryi's metamorphosis. His route is the absolutization of one's own power, which does not tolerate any competition or anyone else's superiority. The logical end of this route is the transformation of Seryi into the personification of Thanatos—in the larger perspective, into an apocalyptic beast. Thus, the plot of the novel leads to A Huli's defeat: a kynical trickster fails to ennoble a cynical shape-shifter. Furthermore, her failure logically follows from her highest achievement—her love for Seryi. In a way, this defeat is the flipside of her victory.

The version of kynicism performed by A Huli is based on love, understood as the *refusal of power over the Other*, despite having both the capacity and the right to wield that power. This refusal follows from kynical logic: "... taking leave of the spirit of long-term goals, insight into the original purposelessness of life, limiting the wish for power and power of wishing... the knowledge—decried as nihilism—that we must snub the grand goals." (Sloterdijk, 194) However, in the post-Soviet cynical society of shape-shifters, where power is the sole universally accepted value, A Huli's gesture is completely eccentric. It is just as eccentric in the context of the history of the Soviet trickster, who—as has been shown in other chapters—always embodies *alternative power*. Pelevin's trickster achieves the status of the super-shape-shifter (or ultimate trickster) by refusing *any* strategy of power, including alternative power, in favor of freedom. And this decision emerges as a paradoxical epilogue to Soviet tricksterdom. The trickster in post-Soviet conditions can either become a functionary-cynic, and thus transform into an agent of death and destruction, or remain a free kynic—but only at the cost of waiving any claims to power.

It is interesting that in her representation of a radical trickster-kynic, A Huli goes beyond patriarchal scenarios of femininity. One might even say that Pelevin's heroine operates in accordance with the ideas of Hélène Cixous, who confronts power over the Other with "women's power," understood as *"power over oneself* [...] a relation not based on mastery but on availability [disponibilité]" (cit. by Moi, 125). The wolf cannot and does not want to relinquish power precisely because his "exaggerated masculine" "I" breaks up into a set of symbols of power and status, forming, in its sum, a complete lack—a negative identity, expressed by the deadly magic of Pizdets.

A Huli's refusal of power, despite the possibility of gaining it through magical means, represents the maximal version of trickster's transgression in a world where transgression is normalized and pain serves as a substitute for theodicy. In this respect, Pelevin's A Huli appears as a character comparable to Antigone in Lacan's portrayal (Lacan, 345-63) or to Žižek's later projection of this description onto De Sade's *Justine* and Gudrun Ensslin, the famous terrorist and founder of the Red Army Faction. (1989: 114-7) All these characters strive to transcend every thinkable border and reach the impossible, the Greek *Até*, in the realization of their dominant principle—desire for death in Antigone, desire for pleasure in Justine, desire for revolutionary destruction in Ensslin. A Huli's desire for freedom and the rejection of power as a value is such a principle, for the fulfillment of which she impels herself beyond the symbolic horizon of post-Soviet society.

However, A Huli's kynical response to the central question about the relationship between freedom and power (even super-power) does not in any way suggest the disappearance of self as evidence of freedom. Instead, the kynical trickster's self is *embodied* in *SKO* as visibly resisting cynical negativity. But unfortunately, in the finale, Pelevin forces the heroine into the path of *self-erasure*. Possibly this finale is prompted by the inertia of Pelevin's previous novels: A Huli's escape from the world of illusions to the Rainbow Stream of pure emptiness and absolute freedom is no different from Pyotr Pustota's leap into the river U. R. A. L., which carries its waves—unseen to the world—to the shores of "Inner Mongolia." Yet, in *SKO*, Pelevin has added to the previously known "formula of freedom" another unknown value—love:

> When a werefox comprehends what love is, she can leave this dimension behind. [...] Then the werefox must breathe in and out several times, engender in her heart love of the greatest possible power and, shouting out her own name in a loud voice, direct the love as deeply as possible into her own tail. [...] If the love engendered was genuine, then following the shout, the tail will cease creating this world for a second. This second is the moment of freedom, which is more than enough to leave this realm of suffering behind forever. (2008: 331, 332-3)[51]

The abstractness of this formula cannot help but raise eyebrows when compared with the dramatic love between A Huli and Seryi. It is as though Pelevin does not fully trust his heroine, and at the finale of the novel interferes in her logic with his own pre-prepared recipe for salvation. In any case, it is clear that he does not trust her *femininity*. This is why he is adamant—without any viable reason—that A Huli

---

51  «Когда оборотень постигнет, что такое любовь, он может покинуть это измерение... надо сделать несколько глубоких вдохов и выдохов, зародив в своем сердце истинную любовь максимальной силы, и, громко выкрикнув свое имя, направить ее в хвост так далеко, как возможно. [...] Если зарожденная в сердце любовь была истинной, то после крика хвост на секунду перестанет создавать этот мир. Эта секунда и есть мгновение свободы, которого более чем достаточно, чтобы навсегда покинуть пространство страдания» (ibid., 378-9).

only has a simulacrum vagina, "a rudimentary cavity under our tails, an elastic bag of skin that's not connected with any other organs," "a 'prick-catcher.'" (ibid., 112) This narrative operation recalls the castration of women or the *castration of the feminine* as described by Luce Irigaray: "To castrate a woman is to then inscribe her into the law of the same desire, the desire of the same" (64)—which signifies the portrayal of woman as a "small man." "The desire of the same," in the context of Pelevin's novel, corresponds to the desire of power which is realized through the subjugation (and in the extreme—the liquidation) of the Other.[52] And Pelevin indeed realizes this desire—which belongs in the wolf's repertoire as opposed to the fox's—with respect to the female kynical trickster-postmodernist.

Although the final disappearance of A Huli was promised in the mock preface to the novel, (and, for its part, is ironically tinted by a hidden reference to John Ray's preface to *Confessions of a White Widowed Male*) it is impossible to avoid the impression that A Huli's escape to the Rainbow Stream stems from the author's desire to escape from the consciousness of an Other which in this case is not only a trickster, but also female. Pelevin can only do so by enforcing his tried and tested, and invariably masculine, version of transcendental freedom. The author's unconscious distrust towards A Huli's strategy of yielding power to the Other is evident here. As if the trickster's freedom has exceeded the limits acceptable even to her creator—a paradox which adds to the forced finale of *SKO*—a new and unexpected meaning arises; apparently, the trickster trope remains such a powerful weapon that even the writer, who has seemingly entrusted such a vast investment into its development, in the end staggers back, terrified by the trickster's transgression of all possible borders.

---

52   It is interesting that a similar symbolic castration of the woman-mediator with certain characteristics of a trickster (sexuality, shape-shifting) occurs in the film by Aleksandr Rogozhkin *The Cuckoo* (2002), where the symbolic power of Sami Anni is tamed by the stereotypes of colonial representation of "savages." See a detailed analysis of this film in my article "In the Cuckoo's Nest: From a Postcolonial Wondertale to a Post-Authoritarian Parable" (Lipovetsky 2008).

# CONCLUSION

The trickster lacks a stable identity, but is able to reproduce any identity as an artistically imitated role: s/he slips betwixt and between the antinomies of the social, political, and cultural order, and is constantly ambivalent and elusive, destructive and constructive, malevolent and benevolent; as such, this character appears to be the classic example of the floating (or empty) signifier—a signifier with "a zero symbolic value." (Lévi-Strauss, 64) While explaining the meaning of *mana* (magic energy, force) in the ethnographic theory of Marcel Mauss, Claude Lévi-Strauss emphasized the two major semiotic functions of floating signifiers: 1) they are necessary to overcome "a fundamental opposition, in the history of human mind, between symbolism, which is characteristically discontinuous, and knowledge characterized by continuity"(60);
2) "always and everywhere, those types of notions, somewhat like algebraic symbols, occur to represent an indeterminate value of signification, in itself devoid of meaning and thus susceptible of receiving any meaning at all; their sole function is to fill a gap between the signifier and the signified, or, more exactly, to signal the fact that in such a circumstance, on such an occasion, or in such a one of their manifestations, a relationship of non-equivalence becomes established between signifier and signified, to the detriment of the prior complementary relationship" (55-56).

What do these functions of a floating signifier mean when applied to Soviet tricksters? First of all, as floating signifiers, Soviet tricksters embody the chasm and unrecoverable contradictions between the symbolic languages through which Soviet society modeled and described itself, on the one hand, and social practices that developed in a relative independence from these languages, on the other. Soviet double-speak and double-thought are only a few examples of these practices; rather, our examination of tricksters permits us to detect the co-existence of two parallel and mutually contradictory realms in Soviet society and its culture—the symbolic and the practical. These realities are certainly aware of each other's existence, they constantly overlap and collide in the space of the individual subjectivity; however, they lack channels of mutual communication—and this very *lack* can be defined as crucial to the "closed" character of the Soviet society.

Our study demonstrates that tricksters provided symbolic justifications for the broad array of "shadow" social practices, unacknowledged by or repressed by the symbolic languages—the intellectual freedom (Khulio), the "second economy" (Ostap Bender) and underground art (Venichka), the intelligentsia's conformism (Buratino, Stierlitz), and its modest rebellions against universal cynicism (Detochkin, Buzykin, Munchhausen). Furthermore, books and films about Soviet tricksters taken together provide the most extensive image of the *universe of Soviet cynicism*—with its bricolage language and schizophrenic social psychology as revealed in Il'f and Petrov's diptych, its art and the philosophy of the artist as a free marionette, exemplified by Tolstoy's *Zolotoi kliuchik*, with its metaphysics based on the betrayal of the individual voice by the Logos as investigated by Erofeev in *Moskva-Petushki* and its politics of a double game for the sake of an impeccable alibi in any situation as vividly presented (albeit through a historical "transfer" to the image of the enemy, the other) in *Semnadtsat' mgnovenii vesny* by Tatiana Lioznova. The trickster texts created in the post-Soviet period—as exemplified by Pelevin—testify to the fact that the cynical universe did not disappear with the collapse of the Soviet regime; conversely, it solidified and expanded, producing its own political structure (the society of shape-shifters) and mythology. Apparently, tricksters serve as the living *connection* between the Soviet and post-Soviet societies.

At the same time, as floating signifiers, Soviet tricksters paradoxically *overcome* these chasms and contradictions by transforming the communicative gap into a space of "freeplay"—to use Derrida's term—between signifiers of the symbolic language and their multiple (mutually contradictory) signifieds in social practice, and vice versa. Thus the trickster demonstrates the totally linguistic (and playful) nature of both the symbolic and the practical levels of Soviet subjectivity, and restores its unity and coherence—albeit in a performative dimension. The Soviet trickster grants to the Soviet cynical universe "the affirmation of a world of signs without fault, without truth, and without origin which is offered to an active interpretation. *This affirmation then determines the non-center otherwise than as loss of the center. And it plays without security."* (Derrida, 518) The mechanism of "freeplay" also serves as the leverage with which the Soviet trickster elevates cynical practices to the level of a kynical performance, and most importantly, manifests the kynical *embodiment,*—the faculty that, according to Sloterdijk, is opposed to the cynical splitting of consciousness and subjectivity immanent for the cynical aspect of modernity (see Sloterdijk, 120–124).

In all the texts that we discussed above, the trickster simultaneously symbolically justifies the discourses and practices of soviet cynicism and confronts them, in both cases using kynicism as a performative weapon. In this respect, the trickster as a floating signifier appears as the empty center (non-center, according to Derrida) of Soviet cynicism. Without it, the Soviet social machine as well as Soviet subjectivity could not have functioned for so long. Simultaneously, Soviet tricksters also continuously generated and embodied the critical impulse that eventually undermined the Soviet civilization from the inside, leading to its demise. Granted, all of the practices that required the trickster's symbolic justification stemmed from the "closed" nature of the Soviet society—from the ban on the market economy and non-existent freedom of expression to the ideological monopoly and political xenophobia. Yet, our analysis permits us to maintain that the "place" of the trickster in Soviet culture is defined by the contradictions between the classical model of the "closed" society and Soviet social practices: the trickster flourishes where the Soviet "closedness" undermines itself and, for the sake of survival, generates the "shadow" mechanism of social, economic, cultural and political mobility and flexibility that sustained it for more than seventy years.

At the same time, the trickster represents the hero whose superiority over his/her opponents is grounded in its intellect, imagination and talent—and never on violence and terror. In other words, this character serves as the manifestation of the intelligentsia's dream about a victory of wit over a power based on violence, about non-violent power, or even more so, about the non-violent strategies of modernization. This theme becomes especially noticeable in post-Soviet culture—not only in Pelevin's *Sviashchennaia kniga oborotnia,* but also, and most explicitly, in Lev Gurskii (Roman Arbitman)'s "mockumentary" novel *Roman Arbitman: Biografiia vtorogo prezidenta Rossii (Roman Arbitman: The*

*Biography of the Second President of Russia*, 2008). The novel's second president in question is not a KGB officer, but a former philologist, who succeeds Yeltsin in power. This president, Roman Il'ich Arbitman, is directly compared with Ostap Bender—one of the political analysts "cited" in Gurskii's book writes about the "second president": "If the place of Lenin and Stalin would be taken by someone like Il'f and Petrov's Ostap Bender, probably, Russia would have reached capitalism not by such a long, curved and painful path." (Gurskii, 141) At the same time, this trickster is quite "cleansed," much like the tricksters from the Soviet films of the late 1960s through the early 1980s—symptomatically, all of the destructive aspects of the trickster are given to the prime-minister Boris Berezovskii (whom Arbitman gets rid of very promptly). One of the Russian critics reasonably called this book a "liberal utopia" (Fishman), although it should be necessary to add that this is an ironic utopia of the trickster in power. This tongue-in-cheek biography of "the second president" accompanied by a long list of fictitious sources and with well-known political figurants (although with different patronymics) as its characters, is written along the lines of recent post-Soviet history and is intended to be read in direct comparison with it. The main difference concerns those moments in post-Soviet history that are marked by either violence or by political cynicism. Yet, when the actual authorities employed violence or cynical manipulations, the book's protagonist, Roman Arbitman, uses witty tricks—intellectual and cultural, rather than political—thus peacefully resolving such painful issues as the war in Chechnya, army hazing, corruption, relations with the West, the Khodorkovskii affair, etc. Arbitman substitutes for the tank assault on Grozny a competition between Yeltsin and Johar Dudaev in the composition of Japanese *tanka* (which Yeltsin intentionally loses, thus avoiding a military conflict); he resolves the tension between the oligarchs through a football game; he launches numerous TV shows seeking people with extra-sensory abilities all across Russia, only to appoint these X-men to strategic positions in the government: he invites the famous magicians David Copperfield and Uri Geller to lead the FSB and MVD; and he passes presidential power—by the means of free elections of course—to a popular comedian... In the end, it is even hinted that Arbitman is related to Superman, at least by a connection to Krypton. The result of these tricks appears to be quite opposite to the well-known reality: by the end of his 8-year tenure in office "the second president of Russia" leaves to his successor a liberal and peaceful country, respected by its neighbors and fully integrated into the world community. Arbitman's "recipes" for the liberalization of Russia are obviously ironic and humorous (although they quite seriously point at the political significance of the cultural tools of power); however, they manifest a very important aspect of all Soviet and post-Soviet tricksters—they represent the non-violent and non-repressive strategies for modernization. This function of the trickster appears to be equally relevant to the Soviet and post-Soviet societies.

However, the collapse of the Soviet "closed society," despite expectations, did not lead to the triumph of "openness," liberalism, and democracy, precisely because the *alternative* to the Soviet social and cultural order lay in "cynical reason," which served as the *necessary condition* for the effective functioning of the Soviet societal organism. In fact, there is no exaggeration in saying that the collapse of late Soviet culture can be interpreted as the result of a quiet cynical revolution, during which "cynical reason" infiltrated all spheres and institutions of social life and eroded them from the inside to the point of their collapse. In this perspective, the post-Soviet society should be interpreted as the triumph of the former Soviet "cynical reason," which acquires the functions of the official mainstream in cultural, social, ideological, and economic spheres.

Notably, in the post-Soviet period, the trickster starts to directly influence "real" politics and public culture, literally moving into the sphere of power—while in the past the bond between the trickster and the power was mainly located in the sphere of the cultural imagination. The aforementioned link between Stierlitz and Putin is just one such example; one may also recollect such fantastic political tricksters of the 1990s as Dmitrii Iakubovskii ("General Dima"); Boris Berezovskii; as well as the veteran of the post-Soviet politics, member of the Russian Duma since its formation in 1989, and the head of the Liberal-Democratic quasi-party, Vladimir Zhirinovskii. A pure trickster, Kseniia Sobchak—a daughter of the late liberal of the Yeltsin era, Anatolii Sobchak—became the main symbol of the post-Soviet glamorous culture. Quite telling in this respect—not as a fact, but as a possibility—is the rumor that the postmodernist "gangsta fiction" novel, *Okolonolia (Around Zero)* published in 2009 under the pseudonym Natan Dubovitskii, was purportedly written by Vladislav Surkov, the main Kremlin ideologist and the creator of such aggressively conservative movements as "Nashi," "Molodaia gvardiia," etc. (see L'vovskii 2009).

Yet, "cynical reason" does not support the "open society," as Sloterdijk has demonstrated; rather, it represents the "enlightened false consciousness" (6) and cultivates tendencies potentially leading to totalitarian "reductionism." Aside from being an inseparable part of the Soviet societal organism, the discourse and the practices of "cynical reason" inevitably bear the imprints of the symbolic order to which they served as the alternative. This interconnection between cynical reason and the Soviet symbolic order transforms the former into the hostage of the latter—which becomes especially obvious in the 2000s.

While "cynical reason" was triumphantly moving away from the "shadow" and into the spotlight, the trickster's function could not help but change, too. First, from the 1970s onwards, cynicism needs less and less cultural legitimation—hence, the kynical aspects of the trickster's representation either fade away (as in Detochkin and Buzykin) or take a clearly non-conformist turn, as in Pelevin's *A Huli*, or in the works of such artists-tricksters as Oleg Kulik, Vladislav Mamyshev-Monro, and the "Blue Noses" group (Aleksandr Shaburov and Viachelsav Mizin). But, simultaneously, the very position of the trickster undergoes something comparable with the "automatization of the device," to use Victor Shklovsky's term. A symptomatic illustration to this process may be found in numerous TV, film and theatre productions based on classic Soviet texts about tricksters—such as, for instance, the TV mini-series *Master i Margarita* by Vladimir Bortko and *Zolotoi telenok* (2006) by Uliana Shilkova; as well as the musicals based on *Dvenadtsat' stuliev*—by Tigran Keosaian and Aleksandr Tsekalo (2003) and by Maksim Papernik (2004). All these productions either transform the tricksters into lifeless monuments to themselves (as in the cases of Bortko's and Shilkova's mini-series) or represent them as vulgar thugs, thus trivializing the character (as in the musicals).

In other words, the appreciation of the trickster's role in post-Soviet culture is accompanied by a distancing from this cultural function as far too accessible, too widely used and abused, as a stereotype that does not produce any new meanings due to its automatization.

Tellingly, the 2009 cluster on artists-tricksters in the Moscow-based magazine *Art-Khronika* opens with an article by the St. Petersburg critic Dmitrii Ozerkov, who states quite emphatically that "it is easy to become a trickster today. It is much harder not to become it" (60).

Thus, with the triumphant expansion of "cynical reason," post-Soviet culture demonstrates very ambivalent attitudes to tricksters. Instead of referring to the inner contradictions of the hidden mechanisms of the Soviet "closed society," the trickster as the floating signifier starts to refer to "cynical reason" itself, and in this capacity becomes the object of cultural critique. This approach is applicable not only to Pelevin's novel discussed above, but also to the Presniakov brothers' play and Kirill Serebrennikov's film *Izobrazhaia zhertvu* (*Performing Victim*, 2006) or to numerous radically innovative theatrical productions based on Gogol—such as, for example, *Revizor* (*Inspector General*, 2005) in Kolyada-Theatre in Ekaterinburg or Aleksandr Pantykin's opera *Mertvye dushi* (*Dead Souls*, 2009). Furthermore, the post-Soviet culture presents enough examples of the demonization of the trickster as in Aleksandr Zel'dovich' and Vladimir Sorokin's film *Moskva* (*Moscow*, 2002) and Vasily Sigarev's *Volchok* (*The Wolfy*, 2009), as well as in Dmitrii Bykov's novel *ZhD* (2006) and Pelevin's *Empire V* (2007).

At the same time, the presence and the significance of tricksters in contemporary Russian literature and film is noticeably lower than in previous periods, and especially lower than in, for instance, contemporary American culture, which was literally flooded by aesthetically sound and socially meaningful tricksters in the 2000s. One may recall Sacha Baron Cohen (*Borat*, 2006, and *Bruno*, 2009), such influential political analysts/tricksters as Jon Stewart and Stephen Colbert, such film tricksters as the fierce Tyler Durden (Brad Pitt) from *Fight Club* (the 2004 movie by David Fincher based on Chuck Palahniuk's novel), the almost-tragic Joker (Heath Ledger in Christopher Nolan's *The Dark Knight*, 2008), the lighthearted Frank Abagnale, Jr. (Leonardo Di Caprio in Steven Spielberg's *Catch Me If You Can*, 2002), the maliciously and hedonistically conniving Cartman from Trey Parker and Matt Stone's animated series *South Park*, a whole bunch of magicians as tricksters-by-trade (*The Prestige* [2006] by Christopher Nolan, *The Illusionist* [2006] by Neil Burger, *Scoop* [2006] by Woody Allen), and many others. Russian society under Putin was hardly less cynical than its American counterpart, yet it did not generate a comparable amount of aesthetically powerful images of tricksters.

In this respect, the high or low activity of the trickster in contemporary culture may be interpreted as a *symptom*. One may conclude that *tricksters flourish in culture when society is over-saturated by cynicism and is aware of this; in these images the excess of cynicism is channeled and turned against its own sources.* Tricksters serve as cultural "leukocytes," whose commotion stands in direct proportion to social "infections'"—cynical and potentially proto-fascist, as well as proto-totalitarian. But if the "illness" is quite obvious, yet the organism's reaction remains passive, then the society is either not aware of its own cynicism (or does not perceive it as a problem), or its cultural "immunity" is weakened and cannot resist the "infection." It looks like both of these scenarios are unfolding in Russian culture today—otherwise, it would be flooded by the trickster novels and films.

However, it would be too early to declare that the history of the trickster in Russian culture is over. The trickster as a floating signifier possesses at least one more cultural referent, the exploration of which is only beginning in Russian culture. The trickster's representation of the social world as a space for language games paradoxically points at the trauma which their strategies inadvertently reflect and evade. In a certain way, the trickster is the cultural embodiment of the cynical *jouissance*, which, according to Lacan and Žižek, is necessarily associated with trauma—the trauma(s) of modernity, in the trickster's case: "Pain generates surplus-enjoyment via the magic reversal-into-itself by means of which the very material texture of our expression of pain... gives rise to enjoyment [...] *Jouissance*... emerges when *the very symbolic articulation of the Loss gives rise to a pleasure of its own.*" (Žižek 1997: 47, italics are the author's). The trauma, in turn, leads to the Lacanian Real—the unconscious zone of existence and experience which cannot be inscribed into the language practices. In the article "Why Do Empty Signifiers Matter in Politics?" Ernesto Laclau maintains that empty (floating) signifiers "are trying to signify the limits of signification—the real, if you want, in the Lacanian sense—and there is no direct way of doing so except through the subversion of the process of signification itself." (Laclau, 407) The trickster's encounter with the Real, and his/her immersion in historical traumas, may be interpreted as the ultimate goal of this character's quest for an anti-hierarchical and anti-systemic sacred—a kynical freedom in a cynical world. *Moskva-Petushki* by Venedikt Erofeev and especially its tragic finale may serve as the best illustration to this meaning of the trickster as a floating signifier. Glimpses of this meaning are also detectable in Khurenito's suicide, the final chapters of *Zolotoi telenok*, Detochkin's transformation into Hamlet and back into a prisoner and Buzykin's endless marathon along the streets of Leningrad, and the scene where oil is summoned by howling at the skull of the sacred cow in *Sviashchennaia kniga oborotnia*... The direction this quest must take is marked by the tricksters alone, and its elucidation has barely begun, let alone been accomplished, though its vital necessity for contemporary Russian culture is obvious.

# WORKS CITED

Abrahamian, Levon. "Lenin as a Trickster," *Anthropology and Archeology of Eurasia*, 38:2 (1999): 7–26.
Agamben, Giorgio. *Homo Sacer: Sovereign Power and Bare Life*. Transl. by Daniel Heller-Roazen. Stanford: Stanford UP, 1998.
Al'tshuller, Mark. "Moskva-Petushki" Venedikta Erofeeva i traditsiia klassicheskoi poemy, *Novyi zhurnal* 146 (1982): 75–85.
Andrew, Christopher and Vasili Mitrokhin. *The Mitrokhin Archive: The KGB in Europe and the West*. New York and London: Penguin, 2000.

Babcock-Abrahams, Barbara. "A Tolerated Margin of Mess": The Trickster and His Tales Reconsidered," *Journal of the Folklore Institute*, 11:3 (1975): 161–5.
Bakhtin, Mikhail 1981. *The Dialogic Imagination: Four Essays*. Ed. by Michael Holquist. Transl. by Caryl Emerson and Michael Holquist. Austin: University of Texas Press.
Bakhtin, Mikhail 1984. *Problems of Dostoevsky's Poetics*. Ed. and transl. by Caryl Emerson. Introduction by Wayne C. Booth. Minneapolis: University of Minnesota Press.
Baraban, Elena. "Figvam utilitarista," *Veselye chelovechki: Kul'turnye geroi sovetskogo detstva*. Ed. by Ilya Kukulin, Mark Lipovetsky, and Maria Maiofis. Moscow: NLO, 2008.
Barth Roland. *Mythologies*. Selected and transl. from the French by Anette Lavers. New York: Hill and Wang, 1972.
Bascom, William. *Ifa Divination: Communication between Gods and Men in West Africa*. Bloomington: Indiana University Press, 1991.
Basso, Ellen B. *In Favor of Deceit: A Study of Tricksters in an Amazonian Society*. Tucson: University of Arizona Press, 1987.
Bataille, Georges 1988. *The Accursed Share: An Essay in General Economy*. Vol. 1. Transl. by Robert Hurley. New York: Zone Books.
Bataille, Georges 1985. *Visions of Excess: Selected Writings, 1927–1939*. Ed. and with an Introduction by Alan Stoekl. Minneapolis: University of Minnesota Press.
Belousov, A.F 1987. *Gorodskoi fol'klor*. Tallinn.
Belousov, A.F. 1996. "Vovochka," *Anti-mir russkoi kul'tury: Iazyk. Fol'klor. Literatura*. Ed. by Nikolai Bogomolov. Moscow: Ladomir: 165–87.
Benito-Vessels, Carmen and Michael Zappala, eds. *The Picaresque: A Symposium on the Rogue's Tale*. Newark: London; Cranberry, NJ : University of Delaware Press; Associated University Presses, 1994.
Beraha, Laura. "Out of and Into the Void: Picaresque Absence and Annihilation," *Venedikt Erofeev's: Moscow-Petushki: Critical Perspectives*. Ed. by Karen Ryan-Hayes. New York, Washington, D.C./Baltimore, Bern, Frankfurt am Main, Berlin, Vienna, Paris: Peter Lang, 1997: 19–52.
Berar, Eva (Berard Ewa). *Burnaia zhizn' Il'i Erenburga*. Introduction by Efim Etkind. Transl. from French by Olga Panova. Moscow: NLO, 2009 (originally published in 1991: Bérard

Ewa. *La Vie Tumultueuse D'Ilya Ehrenbourg, Juif, Russe et Sovetique.* Paris: Ramsay, 1991).
Beriia, Sergo. *Moi otets – Lavrerntii Beriia.* Moscow: Sovremennik, 1994.
Bethea, David. *The Shape of Apocalypse in Modern Russian Fiction.* Princeton: Princeton University Press, 1989.
Beumers, Birgit. "Masiania," *Veselye chelovechki: Kul'turnye geroi sovetskogo detstva.* Ed. by Ilya Kukulin, Mark Lipovetsky, and Maria Maiofis. Moscow: NLO, 2008: 507–524.
Blackburn, Alexander. *The Myth of the Picaro: Continuity and Transformation of the Picaresque Novel, 1554–1954.* Chapel Hill: University of North Carolina Press, 1979.
Boas, Franz. "Introduction," *Traditions of the Thompson River Indians of British Columbia by James Teit. Memoirs of the American Folk-Lore Society.* Vol. 6. Houghton Mufflin, 1898: 1–18.
Bogdanov, Konstantin A. *Vox Populi: Fol'klornye zhanry sovetskoi kul'tury.* Moscow: NLO, 2009.
Borev, Yurii 1964. *Vvedenie v éstetiku.* Moscow: Sovetskii khudozhnik.
Borev, Yurii 2003. *Staliniada.* Moscow: Olimp.
Brook-Shepherd, Gordon. *Iron Maze. The Western Secret Services and the Bolsheviks.* London: Macmillan, 1998.
Brown, Norman O. *Hermes the Thief.* Madison: University of Wisconsin Press, 1947.
Bulgakov, Mikhail 1996. *The Master and Margarita.* Transl. by Diana Burgin and Katherine Tiernan O'Connor. Annotations and Afterword by Ellendea Proffer. New York: Vintage Books.
Bulgakov, Mikhail 1999. *Sochineniia.* Moscow: Knizhnaia palata.

Carroll, Michael. "The Trickster as Selfish-Buffoon and Culture Hero," *Ethos* 12:2 (Summer 1984): 105–131.
Chernysheva, M.A. "Utverzhdaia igru... (Iz tvorcheskoi istorii *Zolotogo kliuchika* A.N.Tolstogo)," *A.N.Tolstoy: Novye materially i issledovaniia.* Moscow: Nasledie, 1995: 111–25.
Chudakova, Marietta."Voland i Starik Khottabych," Chudakova Marietta, *Novye raboty: 2003–2006.* Moscow: Vremia, 2007: 469–480.
Costello, John and Oleg Tsarev. *Deadly Illusions: The KGB Orlov Dossier Reveals Stalin's Master Spy.* New York: Crown Publishing, 1993.

Danilkin, Lev. "Pora mezh volkom i sobakoi," *Afisha*, November 22, 2004: 153.
Darfi, Ol'ga. "Trezvyi PR-1," *Documental'nyi teatr.* Ed. by Elena Gremina and Mikhail Ugarov. Moscow: Tri kvadrata, 2004: 26–49.
Day, C.B. *Chinese Peasant Cults: A Study of Chinese Paper Gods.* Taipei: Ch'eng Wen Publ., 1974.
Debord, Guy. *Comments on the Society of Spectacle.* Trans. by Malcolm Imrie. London: Verso, 1998.
Derrida Jacques. "Structure, Sign, and Play in the Discourse of the Human Science," *Postmodernism: Critical Concepts.* Ed. by Victor E. Taylor and Charles E. Winquist. Vol.1. London and New York: Routledge, 1997: 504–520.
Dionysius the Areopagite. *The Divine Names and The Mystical Theology.* Transl. by C.E. Rolt. London: SPCK, 1940.
Dobrenko, Evgeny 2007. *Political Economy of Socialist Realism.* Transl. by Jesse M. Savage. London, New Haven: Yale UP.

# WORKS CITED

Dobrenko, Evgeny 2009. *Stalinist Cinema and the Production of History: Museum of the Revolution*. London, New Haven, Yale University Press.

Doty, William G. and William J. Hynes. "Historical Overview of Theoretical Issues: The Problem of the Trickster," *Mythical Trickster Figures: Contours, Contexts, and Criticisms*. Ed. by William J.Hynes. Tuscaloosa and London: Univ. of Alabama Press, 1993: 13-32.

Doueuhi, Anne. "Inhabiting the Space Between Discourse and Story in Trickster Narratives," *Mythical Trickster Figures: Contours, Contexts, and Criticisms*. Ed. by William J. Hynes. Tuscaloosa and London: Univ. of Alabama Press, 1993: 193-201.

Dubin, Boris 2001. *Slovo-pis'mo-literatura: Ocherki po sotsiologii sovremennoi kul'tury*. Moscow: NLO.

Dubin, Boris 2004. *Intellektual'nye gruppy i simvolicheskie formy: Ocherki sotsiologii kul'tury*. Moscow: Novoe izdatel'stvo.

E. M. [Eleazar Meletinskii], "Fenrir," *Mify narodov mira*, vol. 2. Moscow: Sovetskaia entsiklopediia, 1982. 561.

Eco, Umberto. "Ur-Fascism," *The New York Review of Books*. Transl. by Stephen Sartarelli. June 22, 1995. http://www.nybooks.com/articles/1856 Accessed November 8, 2009.

Erenburg, Ilya. *Khulio Khurenito*. Berlin: Petropolis, no year [1920s].

Erenburg, Ilya 2004. *"Dai oglianut'sia": Pis'ma 1908-1930*. Ed. by Boris Frezinskii. Moscow: Agraf.

Ehrenburg, Ilya 1963. *Julio Jurenito*, Transl. by Anna Bostock in collaboration with Yvonne Kapp. Philadelphia: Dufour Eds.

Emerson, Caryl. *The Cambridge Introduction to Russian Literature*. Cambridge, New York: Cambridge UP, 2008.

Epshtein, Mikhail. *Postmodern v Rossii: Literatura i teoriia*. Moscow: Izd. Ruslana Elinina, 2000.

Erofeev, Venedikt 1990. *Moskva-Petushki*. Moscow: Izd-vo SP "Interbuk."

Erofeev, Venedikt 1997. *Moscow to the End of the Line*. Transl. by H. William Tjalsma. Evanston: Northwestern UP.

Etkind, Aleksandr. *Eros nevozmozhnogo: Razvitie psikhoanaliza v Rossii*. Moscow: Gnosis-Progress, 1994.

Fishman, Leonid. "Dobryi liberal'nyi fei," *Znamia* 11 (2008), http://magazines.russ.ru/znamia/2008/11/fi23.html Accessed November 8, 2009.

Fisher, Anne O'Brien. *I. Il'f and E. Petrov's Ostap Bender novels: The (re)production of anti-Soviet Soviet classics*. Ph.D. dissertation, University of Michigan, 2005; AAT 3192634.

Fitzpatrick, Sheila 1999. *Everyday Stalinism. Ordinary Life in Extraordinary Times: Soviet Russia in the 1930s*. New York: Oxford University Press.

Fitzpatrick, Sheila 2000. "*Blat* in Stalinist Culture," *Bribery and* Blat *in Russia*. Ed. by Stephen Lovell, Alena Ledeneva, and Andrei Rogachevskii. London: McMillan: 166-82.

Fitzpatrick, Sheila 2000a, ed. *Stalinism: New Directions*. London and New York: Routledge.

Fitzpatrick, Sheila 2005. *Tear Off the Masks! Identity and Imposture in Twentieth-Century Russia*. Princeton and Oxford: Princeton UP.

Fomenko, Igor' V., ed. *Analiz odnogo proizvedeniia: "Moskva-Petushki" Ven. Erofeeva*. Tver', 2001.

Foucault, Michel. *Aesthetics, Method, and Epistemology*. Ed. by James D. Faubion. Transl. By Robert Hurley and others. New York: The New Press, 1998.

Gaidar, Yegor. *State and Evolution: Russia's Search for a Free Market.* Transl. by Jane Ann Miller. Seattle and London: University of Washington Press, 2003.

Garros, Veronique, Natalia Korenevskaya, and Thomas Lahusen, eds. *Intimacy and Terror: Soviet Diaries of the 1930's.* Transl. by Carol A. Flath. New York: New Press, 1995.

Gates, Henry Louis, Jr. *The Signifying Monkey.* New York: Oxford University Press, 1988.

Geisser-Schnittmann, Svetlana. *Venedikt Erofeev* Moskva-Petushki, *ili «The Rest is Silence»* Bern: Peter Lang, 1989.

Genis, Aleksandr. *Ivan Petrovich umer: Stat'i i rassledovaniia.* Moscow: NLO, 1999.

Gerlach, Christian and Nicolas Werth. "State Violence – Violent Societies," *Beyond Totalitarianism: Stalinism and Nazism Compared.* Ed. by Michael Geyer and Sheila Fitzpatrick. Cambridge, New York: Canbridge University Press, 2009: 153–179.

Girard, René. *The Scapegoat.* Transl. by Yvonne Freccero. Baltimore and London: The John Hopkins UP, 1989.

Golynko-Vol'fson, Dmitrii. "Kartiny mira est' kartina mira," *Novoe literaturnoe obozrenie* 57 (2002): 319–22.

Graham, Seth 2003. "The Wages of Syncretism: Folkloristic New Russians and Post-Soviet Popular Culture," *The Russian Review* 62: 33–53.

Graham, Seth 2008. *Resonant Dissonance: The Russian Joke in Cultural Context.* Evanston: Northwestern University Press.

Grekov, V., ed. "Letters of Aleksei N.Tolstoy to N.V.Krandievskaia," *Minuvshee. Istoricheskii al'manakh.* Moscow: Progress, 1991. Vol 3: 283–340.

Gremina, Elena and Mikhail Ugarov, eds. *Documental'nyi teatr.* Moscow: Tri kvadrata, 2004.

Gudkov, Lev 2004. *Negativnaia identichnost': Stat'i 1997–2002.* Moscow: NLO.

Gudkov, Lev 2005. "'Pamiat'' o voine i massovaia identichnost' rossiian," *Neprikosnovennyi zapas.* 40–41: 46–57.

Guillén, Claudio. *The Anatomies of Roguery: A Comparative Study in the Origins and the Nature of Picaresque Literature.* New York: Garland Publ., 1987.

Gurskii, Lev (Roman Arbitman). *Roman Arbitman: Biografiia vtorogo prezidenta Rossii.* Volgograd: Print-Terra, 2008.

Gutiérrez, Ellen Turner. *The Reception of the Picaresque in the French, English, and German Traditions.* New York: P. Lang, 1995.


Halfin, Igal. *Terror in My Soul: Communist Autobiographies on Trial.* Cambridge, MA; London: Harvard University Press, 2003.

Hawley, John Stratton. *Krishna, the Butter Thief.* Princeton: Princeton University Press, 1983.

Hellbeck, Jochen. *Revolution on My Mind: Writing a Diary Under Stalin.* Cambridge, MA; London: Harvard University Press, 2006.

Hesse, Petra. "K funktsii 'probela' v neofitsial'noi literature 60-kh godov: *Moskva-Petushki* Venedikta Erofeeva," *Russian Literature* 42 (1998): 221–43.

Hyde, Lewis. *Trickster Makes This World: Mischief, Myth, and Art.* New York: North Point Press, 1998.

Hynes, William J. 1993, ed. *Mythical Trickster Figures: Contours, Contexts, and Criticisms.* Ed. by William J. Hynes. Tuscaloosa and London: Univ. of Alabama Press, 1993.

Hynes, William J. 1993a. "Inconclusive Conclusions: Tricksters – Metaplayers and Revealers," *Mythical Trickster Figures: Contours, Contexts, and Criticisms.* Ed. by William

J.Hynes. Tuscaloosa and London: Univ. of Alabama Press: 202-18.

Hynes, William J. 1993b. "Mapping Mythic Tricksters," *Mythical Trickster Figures: Contours, Contexts, and Criticisms.* Ed. by William J.Hynes. Tuscaloosa and London: Univ. of Alabama Press: 33-46.

Ianovskaia, Lidiia. *Pochemu vy pishete smeshno? Ob I.Il'fe i E.Petrove.* Moscow: Nauka, 1969.

Il'f, Il'ia and Petrov Evgenii 1933. "Nash tretii roman," *Komsomol'skaia pravda,* August 24.

Il'f, Il'ia and Petrov Evgenii 1992. *The Twelve Chairs.* Transl. from the Russian by John H.G. Richardson. Evanston, IL: Northwestern University Press.

Il'f, Il'ia and Petrov Evgenii 1995a. *Dvenadtsat' stuliev.* With the commentary by Yurii Shcheglov. Moscow: Panorama.

Il'f, Il'ia and Petrov Evgenii 1995b. *Zolotoi telenok.* With the commentary by Yurii Shcheglov. Moscow: Panorama.

Il'f, Il'ia and Petrov Evgenii 1997. *Dvenadtsat' stuliev: Pervyi polnyi variant.* Moscow: Vagrius.

Il'f Il'ia and Petrov Evegenii 2000. *Zolotoi telenok. Pervyi polnyi variant romana.* Moscow: Vagrius.

Ilf Ilya and Petrov Evgeny 2009. *The Little Golden Calf.* Transl. by Anne O. Fishcer. Montpelier, VT; Russian Life Books.

Irigaray, Luce. *This Sex Which is Not One.* Transl. by C. Porter and C. Burke. Ithaca: Cornell University Press, 1985.

Ivanov, Boris. "Viktor Krivulin – poet rossiiskogo Renessansa," *Novoe Literaturnoe Obozrenie* 68 (2004), http://magazines.russ.ru/nlo/2004/68/iv23-pr.html Accessed November 8, 2009.

Jung, C.G. "On the Psychology of the Trickster Figure," Radin Paul. *The Trickster: A Study in American Indian Mythology.* With commentaries by Karl Kerényi and C.G.Yung. New York: Schocken Books, 1972. 195-211.

Jurich, Marilyn. *Scheherazade's Sisters: Trickster Heroines and Their Stories in World Literature.* Westport, Conn.: Greenwood Press, 1998.

Kaganskaia, Maiia and Bar-Sella Zeev. *Master Gambs i Margarita.* Tel Aviv, 1984.

Kang, Xiaofei. *The Cult of the Fox: Power, Gender and Popular Religion in Late Imperial and Modern China.* New York: Columbia UP, 2005.

Kantor, Vladimir. "Metafizika evreiskogo 'net' v romane Il'i Erenburga *Khulio Khurenito,*" *Slovo/Word,* 53 (2006), http://magazines.russ.ru/slovo/2006/53/ka16.html Accessed November 8, 2009.

Kardin, V. "Vremena ne vybiraiut: Zametki o Iurie Trifonove," *Novyi mir* 7 (1987): 236-57.

Kashintsev, A. [Review of *Dvenadtsat' stuliev*], *Zvezda* 10 (1929): 204-205.

Kaspe, Irina. "Nizkii obman, ili vysokaia real'nost," *Novoe Literaturnoe Obozrenie* 71 (2005): 384-5.

Kerényi, Karl. "The Trickster in Relation to Greek Mythology," Radin P. *The Trickster: A Study in American Indian Mythology,* with commentaries by Karl Kerényi and C.G.Jung. N.Y.: Schocken Books, 1972. 173-91.

Kharkhordin, Oleg. *The Collective and the Individual in Russia: A Study of Practices.* Berkeley, Los Angeles, London: University of California Press, 1999.

Kheteni, Zhuzha (Hetényi Zsuzsa). "Éntsiklopediia otritsaniia: *Khulio Khurenito* Il'I Erenburga," *Studia Slavica Hungaricae* 45 (2000): 317-23.
Kiaer, Christina and Eric Naiman, eds. *Everyday Life in Early Soviet Russia: Taking the Revolution Inside.* Bloomington and Indianapolis: Indiana University Press, 2006.
Kichin, Valerii. "Milliardy mgnovenii vesny: Serial pro Shtirlitsa i cherez tridtsat' let ostaetsia liubim zriteliami," *Rossiiskaia gazeta,* 11 August 2003: 5.
Kliamkin, Igor' and Timofeev Lev. *Tenevaia Rossiia: Ekonomiko-sotsiologicheskoe issledovanie.* Moscow: RGGU, 2000.
Kliuchkin, Konstantin. "Zavetnyi mul'tfil'm: Prichiny populiarnosti *Cheburashki,*" *Veselye chelovechki: Kul'turnye geroi sovetskogo detstva.* Ed. by Ilya Kukulin, Mark Lipovetsky, and Maria Maiofis. Moscow: NLO, 2008: 354-77.
Kochetkova, N. "Viktor Pelevin: '...Inogda mne kazalos', chto ia pechataiu lis'imi lapami,'": *Izvestia.* 2004. November 16 (213): 15.
Komandir Mochalkin. *Narod i Von Shtirliz.* Moscow, 1990. http://lib.ru/ANEKDOTY/vonstir.txt
Kotkin, Steven. *Magnetic Mountain: Stalinism as a Civilization.* Berkeley: University of California Press, 1995.
Kozlova, Natalia. *Sovetskie liudi: Stseny iz istorii.* Moscow: Evropa, 2005.
Kukulin, Ilya 2008a. "Igra v satiru, ili Neveroiatnye prikliucheniia berzrabotnykh meksikantsev na Lune," *Veselye chelovechki: Kul'turnye geroi sovetskogo detstva.* Ed. by Ilya Kukulin, Mark Lipovetsky, and Maria Maiofis. Moscow: NLO, 2008: 204-222.
Kukulin, Ilya, Mark Lipovetsky, and Maria Maiofis, eds. *Veselye chelovechki: Kul'turnye geroi sovetskogo detstva.* Moscow: NLO, 2008.
Kukulin, Ilya 2008b. "Chetvertyi zakon robototekhniki: Fil'm *Prikliucheniia Elektronika* i formirovanie 'pokoleniia devianostykh'," *Veselye chelovechki: Kul'turnye geroi sovetskogo detstva.* Ed. by Ilya Kukulin, Mark Lipovetsky, and Maria Maiofis. Moscow: NLO, 2008: 458-506.
Kulik, Oleg and Vladimir Sorokin, *V glub' Rossii.* Moscow, 1995.
Kurdiumov, A. [Lur'e Iakov]. *V kraiiu nepugannykh idiotov.* Paris, 1983.
Kuritsyn Viacheslav. "My poedem s toboiu na 'A' i na 'Iu'," *Novoe Literaturnoe Obozrenie* 1 (1992): 296-304.
Kuz'minskii, Boris. "Trek no.9," *Russkii zhurnal,* November 18, 2004 http://old.russ.ru/culture/literature/20041118.html Accessed November 8, 2009.
Kuznetsov, Sergei. "Zoo, ili Fil'my ne o liubvi," *Veselye chelovechki: Kul'turnye geroi sovetskogo detstva.* Ed. by Ilya Kukulin, Mark Lipovetsky, and Maria Maiofis. Moscow: NLO, 2008: 354-59.

Laclau, Ernesto. "Why Do Empty Signifiers Matter in Politics?" *Deconstruction: A Reader.* Ed. by Martin McQuillan. New York: Routledge, 2001: 405-413.
Lakan, Zhak (Lacan Jacques). *Seminary: Etika psikhoanaliza (1959-1960).* Ed. by Jacque-Allan Miller, transl. by A. Chernoglazov. Moscow: Gnosis, Logos, 2006.
Lakshin, Vladimir. "Bezzakonnyi meteor," *Znamia* 7 (1989): 225-7.
Landay, Lori. *Madcaps, Screwballs, and Con Women: The Female Trickster in American Culture.* Philadelphia: University of Pennsylvania Press, 1998.
Lebedev, V. *Beriia: Samyi effektivnyi menedzher XX veka.* Moscow: Eksmo, 2008.
Ledeneva, Alena V. 2000. "Continuity and Change of *Blat* Practices in Soviet and Post-Soviet Russia," *Bribery and* Blat *in Russia,* Ed. by Stephen Lovell, Alena Ledeneva, and Andrei

Rogachevskii. London: McMillan, 2000: 183–205.
Ledeneva, Alena V. 1998. *Russia's Economy of Favours:* Blat, *Networking and Informal Exchange.* Cambridge and London: Cambridge UP.
Ledeneva, Alena V. 2002. *How Russia Really Works: The Informal Practices That Shaped Post-Soviet Politics and Business.* Ithaca and London: Cornell UP.
Levin, Yurii. *Kommentarii k poeme "Moskva-Petushki" Venedikta Erofeeva.* Graz, 1996.
Leving, Yurii. "'Kto-to tam vse-taki est'...' Vinni-Pukh i novaia animatsionnaia estetika," *Veselye chelovechki: Kul'turnye geroi sovetskogo detstva.* Ed. by Ilya Kukulin, Mark Lipovetsky, and Maria Maiofis. Moscow: NLO, 2008: 315–53.
L'vovskii, S. 2003. "Bol'shoi zhiraf, miatyi zhiraf," *Russkii zhurnal,* July 31, http://old.russ.ru/krug/20030731_sl.html Accessed November 8, 2009.
L'vovskii, S. 2009. "Postaviat krestik, napishut nolik," *OpenSpace,* August 26, http://www.openspace.ru/literature/events/details/11942/ Accessed November 8, 2009.
Lévi-Strauss, Claude. *Introduction to the Works of Marcel Mauss.* Transl. by Felicity Baker. London: Routledge and Paul Kegan, 1987.
Lewis, R. W. B. *The Picaresque Saint; Representative Figures in Contemporary Fiction.* Philadelphia: Lippincott, 1959.
Likhachev, Dmitrii. "Literaturnyi 'ded' Ostapa Bendera," Likhachev D.S. *Literatura—Real'nost'—Literatura.* Leningrad: Sovetskii pisatel', 1981: 180–89.
Likhachev, Dmitrii, Panchenko Aleksandr, and Ponyrko Natalia. *Smekh v Drevnei Rusi.* Leningrad: Nauka, 1984.
Lindow, John 1999. *Norse Mythology: A Guide to the Gods, Heroes, Rituals, and Beliefs.* Oxford: Oxford University Press.
Lindow, John 2001. *Handbook of Norse Mythology.* Santa-Barbara: ABC-CLIO.
Lipovetsky, M. 2000. "Vladimir Sorokin's Theater of Cruelty," *Endquote: Russian and Soviet Grand Style.* Ed.by Marina Balina, Yevgeny Dobrenko, and Nancy Condee. Evanston: Northwestern University Press, 2000: 167–92.
Lipovetsky, M. 2000a. "Prezident Schtierlits," *Iskusstvo kino* 11 (2000): 73–6.
Lipovetsky, M. 2003. "New Russians as a Cultural Myth," *Russian Review* 62 (January): 54–71.
Lipovetsky, M. 2008. *Paralogii: Transformatsii (post)modernistskogo diskursa v russkoi kul'ture 1920–2000-kh godov.* Moscow: NLO.
Lipovetsky, M. 2008a. "In the Cuckoo's Nest: From a Postcolonial Wondertale to a Post-Authoritarian Parable," *Russia and Its Other(s) on Film: Screening Intercultural Dialogue.* Ed. by Stephen Hutchings. London: Palgrave: 62–76.
Lock, Helen. "Transformations of the Trickster," *South Cross Review* 18 (2002), http://www.southerncrossreview.org/18/trickster.htm Accessed April 22, 2010.
Lotman, Yuri M. *Universe of Mind: A Semiotic Theory of Culture.* Transl. by Ann Shukman. Introduction by Umberto Eco. Bloomington and Indianapolis: Indiana University Press, 1990.
Lovell, Stephen, Alena Ledeneva, and Andrey Rogachevskii, eds. *Bribery and* Blat *in Russia: Negotiating Reciprocity from the Middle Ages to the 1990s.* London: McMillan, 2000.
Lowie, Robert H. "The Trickster-Hero Discussion," *Journal of American Folklore* 22 (1909): 431–33.
Lukšić, Irena. "Kalendar' russkoi literatury," *Russian Literature* 42 (1998): 259–70.
Lunts, Lev. *Obeziany idut: Proza, dramaturgiia, publitsistika, perepiska.* St. Petersburg: Inapress, 2003.
Lunacharsky, Anatolii. "Introduction," Ilf Ilya and Petrov Eugene. *The Little Golden Calf: A*

*Satiric Novel.* Authorized translation from the Russian by Charles Malamuth, with an Introduction by Anatole Lunacharsky. New York: Farrar and Reneheart, 1932: xi–xix.

Lur'e, Iakov. *Rossiia drevniaia i Rossiia novaia.* St. Petersburg, 1997.

Lur'e, Lev. *Prestuplenie v stile modern.* St. Petersburg: Amfora, 2005.

Maimonides, Moses. *The Guide for the Perplexed.* Transl. from the Arabic by M. Friedlander. N.Y.: Dover Publ., 1956.

Maiofis, Maria. "Milyi, milyi trikster: Karlson i sovetskaia utopia o nastoiashchem detstve," *Veselye chelovechki: Kul'turnye geroi sovetskogo detstva.* Ed. by Ilya Kukulin, Mark Lipovetsky, and Maria Maiofis. Moscow: NLO, 2008: 241–275.

Maiorino, Giancarlo, ed. *The Picaresque: Tradition and Displacement.* Minneapolis: University of Minnesota Press, 1996.

Makarius, Laura. "The Myth of Trickster: The Necessary Breaker of Taboos," *Mythical Trickster Figures: Contours, Contexts, and Criticisms.* Ed. by William J. Hynes. Tuscaloosa and London: Univ. of Alabama Press, 1993: 66–86.

McClintock, Anne. *Imperial Leather: Race, Gender, and Sexuality in the Colonial Contest.* London: Routledge, 1995.

Meletinskii, Eleazar 1973. "Typological Analysis of the Paleo-Asiatic Raven Myth," *Acta Etnographica,* Budapest, 22: 107–155.

Meletinskii, Eleazar 1998. *The Poetics of Myth.* Transl. from Russian by Guy Lanoue and Alexander Sadetsky. New York and London: Garland Publ.

Meletinskii Eleazar, Nekliudov Sergei, Novik Elena, Segal Dmitrii. *Struktura volshebnoi skazki.* Moscow: RGGU, 2001.

Mills, Margaret A. "The Gender of the Trick: Female Tricksters and Male Narrators." *Asian Folklore Studies* 60.2 (2001): 237–58.

Moi, Toril. *Sexual/Textual Politics: Feminist Literary Theory.* London and New York, Methuen, 1985.

Mokienko, V.M, Nikitina T.G. *Bol'shoi slovar' russkogo zhargona.* St. Petersburg, 2000.

Monteser, Frederick. *The Picaresque Element in Western Literature.* University of Alabama Press, 1975.

Monroe, Alexei. *Interrogation Machine: Laibach and NSK.* Cambridge, MA: The MIT Press, 2005.

Moss, Kevin. "A Russian Munchausen: Aesopian Translation," *Inside Soviet Film Satire: Laughter with a Lash.* Ed. by Andrew Horton. Cambridge and London: Cambridge University Press, 1993: 20–35.

Munblit, Georgii and Aleksandr Raskin. *Vospominania ob Il'fe i Petrove.* Moscow: Sovetskii pisatel', 1963.

Murav, Harriet. *Holy Foolishness: Dostoevsky's Novels and the Poetics of Cultural Critique.* Stanford: Stanford University Press, 1992.

Murav'ev, Vladimir. [No title], in: "Neskol'ko monologov o Venedikte Erofeeve," *Teatr* 9 (1991): 92–4.

Nepomnyashchy, Catharine Theimer. "The Blockbuster Miniseries on Soviet TV: Isaev-Shtirlits, the Ambiguous Hero of *Seventeen Moments in Spring,*" http://arts.monash.edu.au/lcl/research/projects/pcpapers/pc-paper-nepomnyashchy.pdf Accessed November 8, 2009.

Nikolaev, D.D. "Voland protiv Khulio Khurenito, " *Vestnik Moskovskogo universiteta*, Philology, 2006:3: 81-90.
No author, "Semnadtsat' mgnovenii vesny": Segodnia – tsvetnaia versiia!," *VestiRu*, May 4, 2009, http://www.vesti.ru/doc.html?id=282491
Novikova, Liza, "Knigi nedeli," *Kommersant*, November 11, 2004: 12.

Odesskii, Mikhail. "Bor'ba magov: neobychainye pokhozhdeniia Gurdzhieva v romane Erenburga," *Literaturnoe obozrenie* 2 (1998): 3-8.
Odesskii, Mikhail and David Feldman. "Legenda o velikom kombinatore (v trekh chastiakh, s prologom i epilogom)," in: Il'f Il'ia and Petrov Evgenii. *Zolotoi telenok. Pervyi polnyi variant romana*. Moscow: Vagrius, 2000: 5-66.
Otto, Beatrice K. *Fools are Everywhere: The Court Jesters Around the World*. Chicago and London: The University of Chicago Press, 2001.
Oushakine, S. *The Patriotism of Despair: Nation, War, and Loss in Russia*. Ithaca and London: Cornell UP, 2009.
Ozerkov, Dmitrii. [No title], *Art-Khronika* 5 (2009): 57-61.

Panchenko, Alexander. "The Cult of Lenin and 'Soviet Folklore'," *Folklorica* 10:1 (Spring 2005): 18-38.
Paperno, Irina and Boris Gasparov. "Vstan' i idi," *Slavica Hierosolymitana* 5-6 (1981): 389-400.
Paramonov, Boris. "Portret evreia," *Konets stilia*. Moscow: Agraf, St. Petersburg: Aleteia, 1997: 402-449.
Pelevin, Viktor 2003. *Dialektika perekhodnogo perioda: Iz Niotkuda v Nikuda*. Moscow: Eksmo.
Pelevin, Viktor 2005. *Relic: Rannee i neizdannoe*. Moscow: Eksmo.
Pelevin, Viktor 2007. *Sviashchennaia kniga oborotnia*. Moscow: Eksmo.
Pelevin, Viktor 2008. *The Sacred Book of the Werewolf*. Transl. by Andrew Bromfield. New York: Viking.
Pelton, Robert. *The Trickster in West Africa*. Berkeley: University of California Press, 1980.
Petrov, Evgenii. "Moi drug Il'f," publication and commentaries by Alexandra Il'f. *Voprosy literatury* 2001 (1), http://magazines.russ.ru/voplit/2001/1/petrov.html
Petrovskii, Miron. *Knigi nashego detstva*. Moscow: Kniga, 1986.
Pomerants, Grigorii 1995. "Ten' Venichki Erofeeva: Moda na vopli otchaiannia – gibel'naia moda," *Literaturnaia gazeta* February 22 (1995): 5.
Pomerants Grogorii 1995a. "Na puti iz Petushkov v Moskvu, " *Novoe vremia* 28 (1995): 40-42.
Popova, Iuliia. "*Semnadtsat' mgnovenii vesny* (1973): Luchshii otechestvennyi fil'm o chuvstve formy," *Veshch'* 4(68), 29 May 2006, http://www.expert.ru/printissues/thing/2006/04/shtirlic/ Accessed November 8, 2009.
Prigov, Dmitrii A. and Shapoval Sergei. *Portretnaia galereia D.A.P.* Moscow: NLO, 2003.
Prokhorov G.S. "Bibleiskii prototekst v poeme Ven. Erofeeva 'Moskva-Petushki'," *Analiz odnogo proizvedeniia: Moskva-Petushki Venedikta Erofeeva*, Ed. by Igor' Fomenko, Tver', 2001: 6-19
Prokhorov, Aleksandr 2003. "Cinema of Attractions versus Narrative Cinema: Leonid Gaidai's Comedies and El'dar Riazanov's Satires of the 1960s," *Slavic Review* 62 (Fall 2003): 455-72.
Prokhorov, Aleksandr 2007. *Unasledovannyi diskurs: Paradigmy stalinskoi kul'tury v literature i*

*kinematografe "ottepeli."* St.Petersburg: Akademicheskii proekt, 2007.

Prokhorov, Aleksandr 2008. "Tri Buratino: Évoliutsiia sovetskogo kinogeroia," *Veselye chelovechki: Kul'turnye geroi sovetskogo detstva.* Ed. by Ilya Kukulin, Mark Lipovetsky, and Maria Maiofis. Moscow: NLO, 2008: 153–180.

Prokhorova, Elena. "The Post-Utopian Body Politics – Masculinity and the Crisis of National Identity in Brezhnev-Era TV Miniseries," *Gender and National Identity in Twentieth-Century Russian Culture.* Ed. by Helena Goscilo and Andrea Lanoux, DeKalb: Northern Illinois UP, 2006: 131–138.

Propp, Vladimir. *Fol'klor i deistvitel'nost'.* Moscow: Nauka, 1976.

Pu, Songling. *Chinese Ghost and Love Stories.* With the Introduction by Martin Buber. New York: Pantheon, 1946.

Reingol'd, Sergei. "Russkaia literatura i postmodernism," *Znamia* 9 (1998), http://magazines.russ.ru/znamia/1998/9/reing.html Accessed November 8, 2009.

Rubenstein, Joshua. *Tangled Loyalties: The Life and Times of Ilya Ehrenburg.* New York: BasicBooks, 1996.

Rudnev, Vadim. *Entsiklopedicheskii slovar' kul'tury 20 veka.* Moscow: Agraf, 2001.

Ryan-Hayes, K., ed. *Venedikt Erofeev's* Moscow-Petushki: *Critical Perspectives.* (Middlebury Studies in Russian Language and Literature. Vol. 14) N.Y.: Peter Lang Publ., 1997.

Sappak, V. "Ne nado ovatsii," *Voprosy teatra: Sbornik statei i materialov.* Moscow: VTO, 1965: 102–124.

Selivanovskii, A. "Smekh Il'fa i Petrova," *Literaturnaia gazeta,* August 23, 1932: 3.

Shaginian, Marietta. *Literaturnyi dnevnik: Stat'i 1921–1923 gg.* Moscow: Krug, 1923.

Shcheglov, Yurii K. *Romany I.Il'fa i E.Petrova: Sputnik chitatelia.* Vol.1. Wien: Wiener Slawistischer Almanach Sonderband 26/1, 1990.

Shklovsky, Viktor 1934. "*Zolotoi telenok* i starinnyi plutovskoi roman," *Literaturnaia gazeta,* April 30.

Shklovsky, Viktor 1933. "Iugo-Zapad," *Literaturnaia gazeta,* January 5.

Shmeleva, E. and Shmelev A. *Russkii anekdot: tekst i rechevoi zhanr.* Moscow: Iazyki slavianskoi kul'tury, 2002.

Sinyavsky, Andrey. *Ivan the Fool: Russian Folk Belief. A Cultural History.* Transl. by Joanne Turnbull and Nikolai Formozov. Moscow: Glas, 2007.

Sitkov, I. [Review of *Dvenadtsat' stuliev*], *Kniga i revoliutsiia,* 8 (1929): 38.

Slezkine, Yuri. *The Jewish Century.* Princeton and Oxford: Princeton UP, 2004.

Sloterdijk, Peter. *Critique of Cynical Reason.* Transl. by Michael Eldred. Foreword by Andreas Huyssen. Minneapolis: University of Minnesota Press, 1987.

Smirnova, O.A. "Khristianskie reministsentsii v posmodernistskom kontekste (*Moskva-Petushki* Venedikta Erofeeva)," http://www.moskva-petushki.ru/articles/3mkttgu/xristianskie_reministsentsii_v_postmodernisticheskom_kontekste_moskva-petushki_ven_erofeeva/ Accessed November 8, 2009.

Smyers, Karen A. *The Fox and the Jewel: A Study of Shared and Private Meanings in Japanese Inari Worship.* Honolulu: University of Hawaii Press, 1999.

Spence, Richard B. *Trust No One: The Secret World of Sidney Reilly,* Los Angeles: Feral House, 2003.

Stepanov, Andrei. "Mifologicheskie i religioznye cherty tvorchestva Aronzona," http://

alestep.narod.ru/critique/aronson4.htm#mythos Accessed November 8, 2009.
Stepanov, Yurii. "Buratino," Stepanov Yu. *Konstanty: slovar' russkoi kul'tury*. Moscow: Akademicheskii proekt, 2001: 11–25.
Strukov, Vlad. "Masiania, or Reimagining the Self in the Cyberspace of Rusnet, " *Slavic and East European Journal*, 48:3 (2004): 438–61.
Struve, Gleb. *Russian Literature under Lenin and Stalin, 1917–1953*. Norman, OK: University of Oklahoma Press, 1971.
Surya, Michel. *Georges Bataille: An Intellectual Biography*. Transl. by Krysztof Fijalkowski and Michael Richardson. London: Verso, 2002.


Tarasenkov, A. "Kniga, o kotoroi ne pishut," *Literaturnaia gazeta*, June 17, 1929.
Tiupa, Valerii and E. Liakhova. "Esteticheskaia modal'nost' prozaicheskoi poemy Erofeeva," *Analiz odnogo proizvedeniia:* Moskva-Petushki *Venedikta Erofeeva*, ed. by Igor' Fomenko, Tver', 2001: 34–44.
Tolstaia, Elena D. "Buratino i podteksty Alekseia Tolstogo," *Izvestiia Akademii Nauk. Seriia literatury i iazyka*. 56 (1997): 2: 28–39.
Tolstoy Aleksey N. *Sobr. soch. V 10-ti tt*. Moscow: GIKhL, 1960.
Tolstoy's archive I. [Notebook], Archive of the Institute of the World Literature (Moscow) F. 43:1:141.
Tolstoy's archive II. [Manuscript of the Play *Zolotoi Kliuchik*], Archive of the Institute of the World Literature (Moscow). F. 43:1: 359.
Tolstoy's archive III. [Notebook], Archive of the Institute of the World Literature (Moscow). F. 43: 1: 471.
Troshchenko, E. "Poslednie prikliucheniia anarkhicheskogo individuuma," *Krasnaia nov'* 9 (1933): 169–76.
Tumanov, Vladimir. "The End in V. Erofeev's *Moskva-Petushki*," *Russian Literature*. 39 (1996): 95–114.
Turner, Victor. *The Ritual Process: Structure and Anti-Structure*. Chicago: Aldine Publ., 1969.
Tynianov, Yurii N. *Istoriia literatury. Kritika*. St. Petersburg: Azbuka-klassika, 2001.


Vail', Petr and Aleksandr Genis. *Rodnaia rech'. Sovetskoe barokko. 60-e: Mir sovetskogo cheloveka*. Vol.1. Ekaterinburg: U-Faktoriia, 2003.
Vattimo, Gianni. *The Transparent Society*. Translated by David Webb. Baltimore: John Hopkins UP, 1992.
Verkhovsteva-Drubek, Nataliia. "*Moskva-Petushki* kak parodia sacra," *Solo* 2 (1991): 85–95.
Vlasov, Eduard. *Bessmertnaia poema Ven.Erofeeva* Moskva-Petushki: *Sputnik pisatelia*. Sapporo: Slavic Research Center, 1998. (No. 57.)
Volkov, Solomon. *The Magical Chorus: A History of Russian Culture from Tolstoy to Solzhenitsyn*. Transl. from the Russian by Antonina W. Bouis. New York: Alfred A. Knopf, 2008.
Vulis, Abram 1960. *I.Il'f, E.Petrov: Ocherk tvorchestva*. Moscow: GIKhL.
Vulis, Abram 1990. "Poétika Mastera," *Zvezda Vostoka* 11: 109–125.
Vyleta, Daniel Mark. "City of Devil: Bulgakovian Moscow and the Search for the Stalinist Subject," *Rethinking History*, 4:1 (2000): 37–53.


Welsford, Enid. *The Fool: His Social and Literary History*. London, 1935.

Whitbourn, Christine J., ed. *Knaves and Swindlers: Essays on the Picaresque Novel in Europe.* London, New York: University of Hull by Oxford University Press, 1974.

Wicks, Ulrich. *Picaresque Narrative, Picaresque Fictions: A Theory and Research Guide.* New York: Greenwood Press, 1989.

Willeford, William. *The Fool and His Specter: A Study of Clowns and Jesters and Their Audience.* Evanston: Northwestern UP, 1969.

Yurchak, Alexei 1997. "The Cynical Reason of Late Socialism: Power, Pretense, and the *Anekdot*," *Public Culture* 9: 161–188.

Yurchak, Alexei 2006. *Everything Was Forever Until It Was No More: The Last Soviet Generation.* Princeton and Oxford: Princeton University Press.

Zagitdullina Marina, "Vremia kolokol'chikov, ili *Revizor v Neznaike*," *Veselye chelovechki: Kul'turnye geroi sovetskogo detstva.* Ed. by Ilya Kukulin, Mark Lipovetsky, and Maria Maiofis. Moscow: NLO, 2008: 223–240.

Zholkovsky, Alexander. *Bluzhdaiushchie sny: Iz istorii russkogo modernizma.* Moscow: Sovremennyi pisatel', 1992.

Žižek, Slavoj 1989. *The Sublime Object of Ideology.* London, New York: Verso.

Žižek, Slavoj 1991. *For They Know What They Do: Enjoyment as a Political Factor.* London, New York: Verso.

Žižek, Slavoj 1997. *The Plague of Fantasies.* London, New York: Verso.

Žižek, Slavoj 2001. *Did Somebody Say Totalitarianism? Five Interventions in the (Mis)Use of a Notion.* London, New York: Verso.

Zorich, A. "Kholostoi zalp: Zametki chitatelia," *Prozhektor,* 7–8 (1933): 23-4.

Zorkaia, Neiia and Zorkii A. "*Osennii marafon,* fil'm Georgiia Daneliia," http://www.russkoekino.ru/books/danelya/danelya-0006.shtml Accessed November 8, 2009.

# INDEX

Abdulov, Aleksandr, 207
Abrahamian, Levon, 40, 277
Agamben, Giorgio, 191, 277
Akhmatova, Anna, 161
Akimov, Nikolai, 212
Aksakov, S.T., 245, 246
Aksenov, Vasilii, 42
Altshuller, Mark, 156, 277
Aleinikov, Petr, 13, 37, 199
Aleksandrov, Grigorii, 198
Allen, Woody, 273
Alov, Aleksandr, 14, 220
Andrew, Christopher, 100, 277
Andropov, Yurii, 210
Arbitman, Roman (Lev Gurskii), 269-71, 280
Arendt, Hannah, 87
Aronson, Leonid, 169
Aroseva, Olga, 202

Babcock-Abrahams, Barbara, 27, 30, 277
Babel, Isaac, 95
Babichenko, Dmitrii, 129
Bai Juyi, 241
Bakhtin, Mikhail, 20, 28, 29, 31, 32, 51, 110, 155, 277, 283
Balina, Marina, 9
Balzac, Honoré de, 16
Banionis, Donatas, 211
Baraban, Elena, 9, 15, 131, 277
Barnet, Boris, 211
Bar-Sella, Zeev, 95, 122, 281
Barth, Roland, 218, 229, 277
Bascom, William, 11, 277
Basilashvili, Oleg, 201

Basov, Vladimir, 211
Basso, Ellen B., 277
Bataille, Georges, 34, 35, 36, 37, 54, 170, 277, 287
Bavil'skii, Dmitrii, 247
Beaumarchais, Pierre de, 11, 16
Beauvoir, Simone de, 171
Belousov, A.F., 15, 277
Belov, Vasilii, 198
Bely, Andrei, 127, 143
Benito-Vessels, Carmen, 16, 277
Beraha, Laura, 155, 277
Berar, Eva (Berard Ewa), 64, 278
Beriia, Lavrentii, 42, 283
Beriia, Sergo, 42, 278
Berezovskii, Boris, 270, 271
Bethea, David, 175, 278
Beumers, Birgit, 278
Blackburn, Alexander, 16, 18, 19, 278
Blok, Aleksandr, 143, 144, 165, 66
Boas, Franz, 11, 27, 278
Bogdanov, Konstantin A., 9, 41, 278
Bogomolov, Nikolai, 277
Bondarchuk, Sergei, 216
Borev, Yurii, 102, 278
Borges, Jorge Luis, 244
Bormann, Martin, 218, 229, 221
Bortko, Vladimir, 272
Bourdieu, Pierre, 57
Braginskii, Emil', 200
Brezhnev, Leonid, 286
Brinton Daniel, 27
Briusov, Valerii, 143
Brodsky, Joseph (Iosif), 169
Bromberg, Konstantin, 15
Bronevoi, Leonid, 207, 221, 223
Brook-Shepherd, Gordon, 100, 278

## INDEX

Brown, Norman O., 11, 278
Bubnov, A.S., 92
Budberg, Maria, 128
Bukharin, Nikolai, 64, 92
Bukhlev, V.B., 23
Bulgakov, Mikhail, 13, 14, 34, 38, 39, 51-53, 95, 102, 132, 190, 219, 278
Bulgarin, Faddei, 16
Bullitt, William Christian Jr., 39
Burger, Neil, 273
Butler, Judith, 57
Bykov, Dmitrii, 247, 273

Caine, Michael, 12
Camus, Albert, 19
Carroll, Michael, 11, 278
Casteneda, Carlos, 170, 238, 239
Cavani, Liliana, 219
Cervantes, Miguel de, 11, 16
Chaplin, Charlie, 12, 75, 95
Charkin, D.S., 23
Chernysheva, M.A., 141, 278
Chudakova, Marietta, 14, 278
Chukhrai, Grigorii, 212
Chulkov, Mikhail, 16
Churikova, Inna, 207
Cixous, Hélène, 264
Claudel, Paul, 64
Cohen, Sacha Baron, 12, 273
Colbert, Stephen, 77, 273
Collodi, Carlo, 127, 129, 131, 141
Copperfield, David, 270
Costello, John, 100, 278
Coster, Charles de, 14

Dal', Oleg, 211
Dali, Salvador, 12
Daneliia, Georgii, 7, 37, 203-209
Danilkin, Lev, 253, 278
Darfi, Ol'ga, 229, 278
Daudet, Alphonse, 14
Day, C.B., 239, 240, 241

Debord, Guy, 119, 278
Defoe, Daniel, 16
Demianenko, Aleksandr, 197, 198
Derrida, Jacques, 57, 71, 247, 268, 269, 278
Di Caprio, Leonardo, 291
Dionysius the Areopagite, 172-3, 278
Dobrenko, Evgeny, 9, 39, 45, 46, 279, 283
Dobzhanskaia, Elizaveta, 201
Dolinskii, Vladimir, 207
Dostoevsky, Fedor, 11, 16, 20, 64, 71, 78, 189, 244, 250, 277, 284
Doty, William G., 27, 28, 279
Doueuhi, Anne, 21, 279
Dubin, Boris, 225, 279
Duchamp, Marcel, 12
Dudaev, Johar, 270
Dulles, Allen, 222
Dunaevskii, Maksim, 124
Durov, Lev, 218

Eco, Umberto, 254, 279, 283
Efremov, Oleg, 201
Eisenstein, Sergei, 40
El'sberg, Iakov, 102
Emerson, Caryl, 9, 17, 277, 279
Engels, Friedrich, 175
Ensslin, Gudrun, 264
Eremin, Mikhail, 169
Erenburg (Ehrenburg), Ilya, 13, 18, 60, 63-88, 95, 278, 279, 281, 282, 285
Erofeev, Venedikt, 13, 15, 18, 20, 30, 56, 60, 153-92, 208, 209, 268, 274, 277-79, 280, 283, 284, 285, 286, 287
Etkind, Aleksandr, 9, 39, 278, 279
Etush, Vladimir, 199
Evstigneev, Evgenii, 217
Ezekiel, 177-82, 186, 187

# INDEX

Faintsimmer, Aleksandr, 212
Feldman, David, 91, 98, 285
Fincher, David, 273
Fisher, Anne O'Brien, 97, 111, 124, 279
Fishman, Leonid, 270, 279
Fitzpatrick, Sheila, 42-4, 46, 117, 279, 280
Fomenko, Igor' V., 153, 280, 287
Foucault, Michel, 34, 35, 280
Fowler Jr., Gene, 234

Gaidai, Leonid, 18, 60, 124, 197-200, 209-212, 220, 286
Gaidar, Arkadii, 130
Gaidar, Yegor, 195, 280
Gandhi, 30
Garros, Veronique, 280
Gasparov, Boris, 157, 169, 285
Gates, Henry Louis, Jr., 11, 280
Gavrilova, Tatiana, 202
Geisser-Schnittmann, Svetlana, 153, 155, 165, 169, 280
Geller, Uri, 270
Genis, Aleksandr, 170, 196, 280, 287
George, Roy Hill, 12
Georgiev, V., 211
Gerlach, Christian, 86, 280
Geyer, Michael, 280
Girard, René, 41, 189, 280
Gogol, Nikolai, 11, 16, 95, 165, 200, 273
Goldoni, Carlo, 16
Golynko-Vol'fson, Dmitrii, 169, 280
Gorin, Grigorii, 14, 33, 37, 56, 206-208, 209, 218
Göring, Hermann, 218
Gorodetsky, Sergei, 127
Goscilo, Helena, 9, 286
Gradova, Ekaterina, 225
Graham, Seth, 15, 280
Grekov, V., 129, 280
Gremina, Elena, 229, 278, 280

Gritsenko, Nikolai, 218
Gudkov, Lev, 211, 254, 280
Guillén, Claudio, 16, 280
Gumilev, Nikolai, 127
Gundareva, Natal'ia, 203
Guo Pu, 241
Gurskii, Lev (Roman Arbitman), 269
Gutiérrez, Ellen Turner, 16, 280

Halfin, Igal, 46, 280
Hašek, Jaroslav, 12, 14
Hawking, Stephen, 244
Hawley, John Stratton, 11, 280
Headly Glenne, 12
Hellbeck, Jochen, 46, 280
Herzen, Aleksandr, 164, 165
Hesse, Petra, 158, 280
Himmler, Heinrich, 218, 219, 222
Horkheimer, Max, 12, 97
Huizinga, Johan, 140
Hyde, Lewis, 11, 21, 22, 30, 34, 51, 280
Hynes, William J., 21, 27, 28, 29, 31, 279, 281, 284

Iakubovskii, Dmitrii, 271
Iankovskii, Oleg, 206, 207
Ianovskaia, Genrietta, 130
Ianovskaia, Lidiia, 94, 281
Iasulovich, Igor', 197
Il'f, Ilya, 13, 18, 33, 60, 91-124 197, 200, 268, 270, 279, 281, 284, 285, 286, 287
Ilic, Dragan, 61
Irigaray, Luce, 266, 281
Isaiah, 177, 179, 180, 187
Iskander, Fazil', 13
Iurskii, Sergei, 197
Ivanov, Boris, 169, 281
Ivanov-Vano, Ivan, 129
Ivchenko, Viktor, 216

## INDEX

Ji Yun, 240
Jung, Carl Gustav, 27, 28, 281, 282
Jurich, Marilyn, 32, 381

Kachanov, Roman, 32, 15
Kadochnikov, Pavel, 211
Kaganskaia, Maiia, 95, 122, 281
Kalinin, Ilya, 9
Kanevsky, A., 128, 136
Kang, Xiaofei, 239, 240, 241, 243, 244, 281
Kantor, Vladimir, 70, 281
Kardin, V., 205, 281
Kashintsev, A., 95, 281
Kaspe, Irina, 254-5, 281
Kataev, Valentin, 91, 197, 205
Katin-Iartsev, Yurii, 218
Keosaian, Tigran, 124, 272
Kerényi, Karl, 28, 281-2
Kerouac, Jack, 168
Kesey, Ken, 168
Kharkhordin, Oleg, 56-7, 196, 282
Kheifets, Iosif, 198
Kheteni, Zhuzha (Hetényi Zsuzsa), 69, 282
Khitruk, Fedor, 15
Khodorkovskii, Mikhail, 270
Khrushchev, Nikita, 165
Kiaer, Christina, 46, 282
Kichin, Valerii, 212, 282
Kim, Anatolii, 205
Kireev, Ruslan, 205
Klee, Paul, 79
Kliamkin, Igor', 44, 282
Kliuchkin, Konstantin, 15, 282
Kochetkova, N., 234, 256, 282
Kokshenov, Mikhail, 197
Komandir Mochalkin, 227, 282
Konic, Andrzej, 211
Koreneva, Elena, 208
Korenevskaya, Natalia, 280
Korovko, Konstantin, 117

Kostiukovskii, Iakov, 197
Kotkin, Steven, 46, 282
Kovalev, Evgeny, 9
Kozhevnikov, Vadim, 211
Kozintsev, Grigorii, 13, 39, 199
Kozlova, Natalia, 46, 282
Kramskoi, Ivan, 167
Krandievskaia, Natalia, 128, 280
Krivulin, Viktor, 169
Kryzhanovskii, N., 24
Kuchinke, Norbert, 204
Kukryniksy, 93, 94
Kukulin, Ilya, 9, 15, 277, 278, 282, 283, 284, 286, 288
Kulik, Oleg, 247, 272, 282
Kulish, Savva, 211
Kuravlev, Leonid, 220, 197
Kurbanov, Eldeniz, 24
Kuritsyn, Viacheslav, 282, 154
Kuvaev, Oleg, 15
Kuz'minskii, Boris, 247, 282
Kuznetsov, V., 159
Kuznetsov, Sergei, 15, 282
Kvasha, Igor, 207

L'vovskii, Stanislav, 234, 272, 283
Lacan Jacques [Lakan, Zhak], 59, 110, 264, 274, 282
Laclau, Ernesto, 274, 282
Lagin, Lazar, 14, 36
Lahusen, Thomas, 280
Lakshin, Vladimir, 156, 282
Landay, Lori, 32, 282
Landis, John, 234
Lanoux, Andrea, 286
Lanovoi, Vasilii, 220, 221, 230
Lavrenev, Boris, 212
Lebedev, V., 42, 283
Ledeneva, Alena V., 43-44, 46, 195-5, 279, 283
Leiderman, Daniil, 9
Leiderman, Naum, 5, 9
Lenin, Vladimir, 40-41, 64, 70-71, 165,

166, 175, 184, 270, 277, 285, 287
Leonov, Evgenii, 204
Lesage, Alain-René, 11, 16, 38
Levada, Yurii, 226
Levin, Yurii, 153, 165, 283
Leving,Yurii, 15, 283
Lévi-Strauss, Claude, 28, 138, 267, 283
Lewis, R. W. B., 16, 283
Liakhova, E., 174, 175, 287
Liampe, Grigorii, 219
Likhachev, Dmitrii, 95, 283
Lindgren, Astrid, 14
Lindow, John, 238, 283
Lioznova, Tatiana, 14, 18, 20, 210-30, 268
Lipovetsky, Mark, 15, 22, 159, 228, 229, 266, 277, 278, 282, 283, 284, 286, 288
Liubshin, Stanislav, 211
Lock, Helen, 32, 283
Lotman, Yurii M., 19-20, 283
Lovell, Stephen, 44, 279, 283
Lowie, Robert H., 27, 283
Lucian, 63
Lukov, Leonid, 13
Lukšić, Irene, 159, 284
Lunacharsky, Anatolii, 93, 284
Lunts, Lev, 63-4, 284
Lur'e, Iakov (A. Kurdiumov), 95, 282, 284
Lur'e, Lev, 117

Maimonides, Moses, 181, 284
Maiofis, Maria, 277, 278, 282, 283, 284, 286, 288
Maiorino, Giancarlo, 16, 284
Makanin, Vladimir, 205
Makarius, Laura, 34, 37, 284
Mamyshev-Monro, Vladislav, 272
Mandel'shtam, Osip, 127
Mantselev, S., 159
Martin, Steve, 12

Marx, Karl, 48, 175
Mauss, Marcel, 36, 267, 283
Mayakovsky, Vladimir, 161
McClintock, Anne, 224, 284
Medvedkin, Aleksandr, 47
Meletinskii (Meletinsky), Eleazar, 11, 137-9, 238, 279, 284
Men'shikov, Aleksandr, 40
Meterlink, Moris, 143
Meyerhold, Vsevolod, 143
Mikhailova, Tatiana, 9
Mikulski, Stanislaw, 211
Milliar, Aleksei, 32
Milton, Emilia, 214, 228
Mironov, Andrei, 202
Mirosenko, Liubov', 52
Mit'ki (the group), 58, 77, 154, 161, 169
Mitrokhin, Vasili, 100, 277
Mizha, Stefan, 183, 184
Mizin, Viacheslav, 272
Moi, Toril, 264, 284
Mokienko, V.M., 182, 284
Monroe, Alexei, 77, 284
Morgunov, Evgenii, 198, 199
Moss, Kevin, 207, 284
Munblit, Georgii, 93, 284
Murav, Harriet, 18, 19, 284
Murav'ev, Vladimir, 190, 284

Nabokov, Vladimir, 159, 244, 249, 259
Naiman, Eric, 46, 282
Naumov, Vladimir, 14, 220
Nechaev, Leonid, 129
Neelova, Marina, 203
Nekliudov, Sergei, 137-9, 284
Nemirovsky, Igor, 9
Nepomnyashchy, Catharine Theimer, 227, 229, 285
Newman, Paul, 12
Nietzsche, Friedrich, 64,190
Nikitina, T.G., 270
Nikolaev, D.D., 67, 285

Nikulin, Yurii, 198, 199
Nolan, Christopher, 273
Nosov, Nikolai, 15
Novik, Elena, 137, 284
Novikova, Liza, 234, 285

O'Henry, 200
Odesskii, Mikhail, 71, 91, 98, 285,
Okudzhava, Bulat, 129
Olesha, Yurii, 13, 139
Osterman, Laura, 9
Otto, Beatrice K., 18, 285
Oushakine, Serguei, 285
Owens, Sean, 9
Ozerkov, Dmitrii, 272, 285

Palahniuk, Chuck, 273
Panchenko, Aleksandr [Sr.], 18, 283
Panchenko, Alexander [Jr.], 285, 40
Pantykin, Aleksandr, 273
Papanov, Anatolii, 202
Papernik, Maksim, 124
Paperno, Irina, 157, 169, 285
Paramonov, Boris, 70, 285
Parfenov, Leonid, 210, 213, 224
Parker, Trey, 273
Pasternak, Boris, 161
Pelevin, Viktor, 18, 33, 60, 170, 231-66, 273, 282, 285
Pelton, Robert, 11, 285
Peter the Great, 40, 128
Petronius, 63
Petrov Evgenii   13, 18, 33, 60, 91-124 197, 200, 268, 270, 279, 281, 284, 285, 286, 287
Petrov, Vladimir, 40
Petrovskaia, Nina, 127
Petrovskii, Miron, 127, 129, 131, 143-4, 285
Piaf, Édith, 214
Pichul, Vasilii, 124
Pitt, Brad, 273

Pliatt, Rostislav, 217
Podlubnyi, Stepan, 46
Pomerants, Grigorii, 156, 285
Ponyrko, Nataliia, 283
Popov, Vladimir, 15
Popova, Iuliia, 219, 285
Presniakov Brothers (Oleg and Vladimir), 273
Prigov, Dmitrii A., 77, 154, 161, 184, 185, 285
Prokhorov, Alexander (Aleksandr), 129, 149, 199, 200, 201, 202, 286
Prokhorov, G.S., 169, 285
Prokhorova, Elena, 225, 286
Prokhorova, Irina, 9
Prokopovich, Nikolai, 219
Propp, Vladimir, 147, 286
Protazanov, Iakov, 14
Ptushko, Aleksandr, 32, 127, 129, 149
Pu, Songling, 242-3, 286
Pushkin, Aleksandr, 161, 165, 185, 187
Putin, Vladimir, 228-9, 235, 243, 255, 257, 271, 273
Pyriev, Ivan, 13

Rabelais, François, 11, 28, 63, 110
Radin, Paul, 27, 281
Raskin, Aleksandr, 93, 284
Raspe, Rudolph Erich, 206, 14, 20, 37
Redford, Robert, 12
Reingol'd, Sergei, 168, 286
Riazanov, El'dar, 18, 286, 200-203, 209, 286
Rogachevskii, Andrey, 44, 279, 283
Rogozhkin, Aleksandr, 266
Romanov, Artemi, 9
Romm, Mikhail, 41
Roosevelt, Franklin Delano, 222
Rostotskii, Stanislav, 216
Rubenstein, Joshua, 64, 286
Rudnev, Vadim, 214, 215, 286
Ryan-Hayes, Karen, 220

## INDEX

Sade, Marquis de, 262-3, 264
Salys, Rimgaila, 9
Sandomirskaya, Irina, 9
Sappak, Vladimir, 94, 286
Sartre, Jean-Paul, 171
Schellenberg, Walter, 219, 220, 221, 222, 226
Segal, Dmitrii 284
Selezneva, Natalia, 198
Selivanovskii, Aleksandr, 92, 286
Semenov, Yulian, 210, 212
Semina, Tamara, 197
Serebrennikov, Kirill, 273
Shaburov, Aleksandr, 272
Shaginian, Marietta, 63, 64, 286
Shapiro, Adol'f, 130
Shaporin, Yurii, 128
Shapoval, Sergei, 285
Shashkova, Ekaterina, 225
Shcheglov, Yurii K., 94-6, 106, 112, 122, 281, 286
Shilkova, Ul'iana, 124, 272
Shklovsky, Viktor, 32, 286
Shmelev A., 15, 286
Shmeleva, E., 15, 286
Sholokhov, Mikhail, 40
Shostakovich, Dmitrii, 47
Shukshin, Vasilii, 198
Shvarts, Elena, 169
Shveitser, Mikhail, 124, 196
Sigarev, Vasilii, 273
Sinyavsky, Andrey, 197, 286
Sitkov, I., 92, 286
Skradol, Natalia, 9
Skuratov, Maliuta, 40, 54
Slezkine, Yuri, 12-13, 286
Slobodskii, Moris, 197
Sloterdijk, Peter, 114, 121, 164, 189, 191, 257, 258, 261, 264, 269, 272, 286
Smirnova, O.A., 169, 286
Smoktunovskii, Innokentii, 200-201

Smyers, Karen A., 239, 286
Sobchak, Kseniia, 271
Solomin, Yurii, 211
Soloviev, Leonid, 14
Solzhenitsyn, Aleksandr, 198, 237, 287
Sophocles, 174, 208
Sorokin, Vladimir, 228, 247, 273, 282, 283
Soshnikova, Ol'ga, 225
Spence, Richard B., 100, 286
Spengler, Oswald, 64
Spielberg, Steven, 273
Stalin, Iosif (Joseph), 225, 270, 278, 279, 280, 282, 286
Stepanov, Andrei, 169, 287
Stepanov, Yurii, 130, 287
Stewart, Jon, 273
Stone, Matt, 273
Strizhenov, Oleg, 212
Strukov, Vlad, 287
Struve, Gleb, 65, 287
Surkov, Vladislav, 271
Surya, Michel, 34, 287
Svetlichnaia, Svetlana, 220

Tabakov, Oleg, 219, 220
Tarasenkov, Anatolii, 92, 297
Tarkovsky, Andrei, 169
Tashkov, Evgenii, 211
Tikhonov, Viacheslav, 210, 212, 213, 215, 216, 225, 226
Timofeev, Lev, 44
Tiupa, Valerii, 174, 175, 287
Tolstaia, Elena D., 129, 140, 142, 143, 287
Tolstoy, Aleksei N., 14, 18, 30, 32, 33, 40, 60, 127, 125-50, 287
Trafton, Math, 9
Trauberg, Leonid, 13, 39, 199
Trifonov, Yurii, 205, 281
Troshchenko, E., 92, 287
Trotsky, Lev, 92

## INDEX

Tsarev, Oleg, 278
Tsekalo, Aleksandr, 124
Tsilinkis, Gunar, 211
Tsvigun, Semen, 210
Tumanov, Vladimir, 175, 287
Turner, Victor, 30, 287
Tvardovskii, Aleksandr, 13, 40, 198, 199
Twain, Mark, 12, 37, 95
Tynianov, Yurii N., 64, 287

Ugarov, Mikhail, 229
Ul'ianova, Irina, 225
Ursuliak, Sergei, 229
Uspenskii, Eduard, 15

Vail', Petr, 196, 287
Vattimo, Gianni, 168, 287
Verkhovtseva-Drubek, Nataliia, 169, 287
Veltistov, Evgenii, 15
Vitsin, Georgii, 198, 199
Vizbor, Yurii, 220, 221
Vladimirskii, L., 130, 145,
Vlasov, Eduard, 153, 165, 176, 177, 186, 287
Vogiazos, Antonis, 211
Volkov, Solomon, 162, 287
Voroshilov, Klim, 128, 129, 147
Voynich, Ethel Lilian, 212
Vulis, Abram, 287, 38, 93, 94
Vyleta, Daniel Mark, 51, 287
Vyshinskii, Andrei, 44

Waggner, George, 234
Walker, Stuart, 234
Warhol, Andy, 12, 77
Weller, Anthony, 234
Welsford, Enid, 18, 288
Werth, Nicolas, 86, 280
Whitbourn, Christine J., 16, 288

Wicks, Ulrich, 16, 288
Willeford, William, 18, 288
Wofson, Boris, 9

Yurchak, Alexei, 57-8, 76-7, 161, 196, 220, 288

Zagitdullina, Marina, 288
Zakharov, Mark, 14, 33, 37, 56, 206-208, 209, 218
Zakhoder, Boris, 15
Zamiatin, Evgenii, 64
Zappala, Michael, 16, 277
Zarkhi, Aleksandr, 198
Zel'dovich, Aleksandr, 273
Zharov, Mikhail, 40
Zhirinovskii, Vladimir, 271
Zholkovsky, Alexander, 94, 96, 105, 116, 118, 288
Zhukov, Georgii, 224
Zhzhenov, Georgii, 201
Zitzewitz, Josephine von, 9
Žižek, Slavoj, 47, 59, 76-7, 80, 209, 264, 274, 288
Zorich, A., 92, 288
Zorkaia, Neiia, 204-205, 288
Zorkii A., 204-205, 288
Zybkov, I., 124

Also from Academic Studies Press

**50 Writers: An Anthology of 20th Century Russian Short Stories**
Edited, selected, and introduced by Mark Lipovetsky and Valentina Brougher
Translated and annotated by Valentina Brougher and Frank Miller, with Mark Lipovetsky

Cloth 978-1-936235-14-8; Paper 978-1-936235-22-3
792 pp.

The largest, most comprehensive anthology of its kind, this volume brings together significant, representative stories from every decade of the 20th century. It includes the prose of officially recognized writers and dissidents, both well-known and neglected or forgotten, plus new authors from the end of the 20th century. The selections reflect the various literary trends and approaches to depicting reality in the 20th century: traditional realism, modernism, socialist realism, and post-modernism. Taken as a whole, the stories capture every major aspect of Russian life, history and culture in the 20th century. The rich array of themes and styles will be of tremendous interest to students and readers who want to learn about Russia through the engaging genre of the short story.

"This selection of mainly newly translated stories from the 20th century includes both well-known writers and new voices. It eschews traditional selections from the former category and presents startling writings from the latter. As the editors- translators put it themselves in their lucid Introduction, these stories together form a 'mega-novel' about Russia of the previous century from its first revolutions to post-perestroika times."
—*Irene Masing-Delic, Ohio State University*

"I've seen many English-language anthologies of Russian literature, but this is the first one that I want to give to all my non-specialist friends, so that they can finally understand what is so wonderful about modern Russian literature."
—*Eliot Borenstein, New York University*

Editors and Translators:

**Valentina Brougher** is Professor Emerita of Russian Language and Literature in the Department of Slavic Languages at Georgetown University. Her articles on 20th century Russian literature have been published in major academic journals in the USA and abroad, and her translations of 20th century fiction have appeared in several anthologies. She is co-translator of a collection of Vsevolod Ivanov's prose, *Fertility and Other Stories*, and translator of a novel by Aleksandr Kondratiev, *On the Banks of the Yaryn*.

**Mark Lipovetsky** is Associate Professor of Russian Studies in the Department of Germanic and Slavic Languages and Literatures at the University of Colorado at Boulder. He is the author of eight monographs and numerous articles in major American and Russian journals. His publications include: *Russian Postmodernist Fiction: Dialogue with Chaos*; *Paralogii: Transformatsii (post)modernistskogo diskursa v russkoi kul'ture 1920-2000-kh godov*; *Performing Violence: Literary and Theatrical Experiments of New Russian Drama* (with Birgit Beumers).

**Frank Miller** is Professor of Slavic Languages in the Department of Slavic Languages at Columbia University and coordinator of the Columbia-Barnard College Russian language program. He is the author of *Folklore for Stalin; A Handbook of Russian Verbs; A Handbook of Russian Prepositions*; and co-translator of Vsevolod Ivanov's *Fertility and Other Stories*. He is a co-author of the widely used textbook for intermediate Russian, *V puti*, as well as the recently published *Beginner's Russian with Interactive Online Workbook*.

**"I am to be read not from left to right, but in Jewish: from right to left"**
*The Poetics of Boris Slutsky*
Marat Grinberg
486 pp.
Cloth 978-1-934843-73-4

Boris Slutsky (1919-1986) is a major original figure of Russian poetry of the second half of the twentieth century whose oeuvre has remained unexplored and unstudied. The first scholarly study of the poet, Marat Grinberg's book substantially fills this critical lacuna in the current comprehension of Russian and Soviet literatures. Grinberg argues that Slutsky's body of work amounts to a Holy Writ of his times, which daringly fuses biblical prooftexts and stylistics with the language of late Russian Modernism and Soviet newspeak. The book is directed toward readers of Russian poetry and pan-Jewish poetic traditions, scholars of Soviet culture and history and the burgeoning field of Russian Jewish studies. Finally, it contributes to the general field of poetics and Modernism.

"Boris Slutsky, according to this brilliant book, accomplished the seemingly impossible: a poet of Soviet times, he reforged the totality of Russian literary culture, from Church Slavonic to Pushkin to Khlebnikov and beyond, within the crucible of Jewish self-understanding. Marat Grinberg, author of this impressive study, has also accomplished the seemingly impossible. He demonstrates how this supremely Russian poet can and must be read in his totality: "from right to left," from beginning to end, and from his desk drawer to Red Square."
— David G. Roskies, Ben Gurion University of the Negev

"In this erudite and insightful book, Marat Grinberg rescues a great poet from a numbing set of mid-century clichés. No longer a 'war poet,' or 'Soviet diarist,' or sometime Jew, Boris Slutsky emerges as he was in fact—a sometimes playful, sometimes anguished heir to Russian modernism, who read Jewish catastrophe through Jewish texts."
— Alice Nakhimovsky, Colgate University

**Marat Grinberg** (PhD University of Chicago) is an assistant professor of Russian and Humanities at Reed College in Portland, Oregon. He is the author of numerous essays in English and Russian on literature and Jewish intellectual history and politics.

CPSIA information can be obtained at www.ICGtesting.com
Printed in the USA
LVOW070134040613

336782LV00002B/5/P